CASE STUDIES IN
CULTURAL ANTHROPOLOGY

GENERAL EDITORS
George and Louise Spindler
STANFORD UNIVERSITY

CHINA'S URBAN VILLAGERS

Life in a Beijing Commune

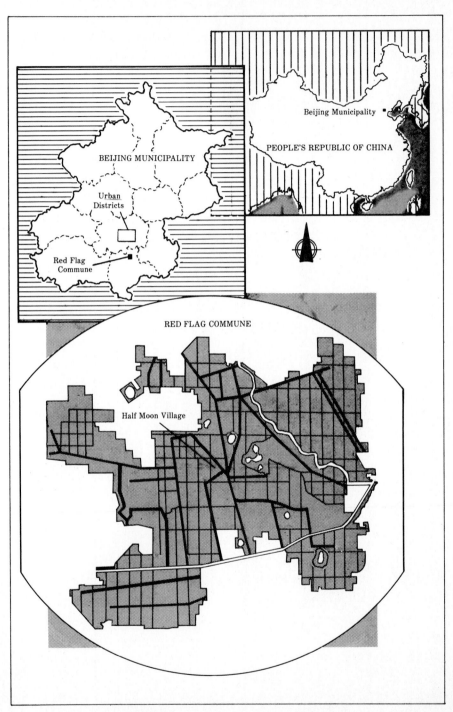

Red Flag Commune and Half Moon Village.

CHINA'S URBAN
VILLAGERS

Life in a Beijing Commune

By

NORMAN A. CHANCE

University of Connecticut

HOLT, RINEHART AND WINSTON

NEW YORK   CHICAGO   SAN FRANCISCO   PHILADELPHIA

MONTREAL   TORONTO   LONDON   SYDNEY   TOKYO

MEXICO CITY   RIO DE JANEIRO   MADRID

Cover photograph: A young peasant farmer from Half Moon Village.

Credit: Excerpt from "A Worker Reads History" in *Selected Poems*, copyright 1947 by Bertolt Brecht and H. R. Hays; renewed 1975 by Stefan S. Brecht and H. R. Hays. Reprinted by permission of Harcourt Brace Jovanovich, Inc.

Cataloging in Publication Data

Chance, Norman A. (Norman Allee), 1927–
  China's urban villagers.

  (Case studies in cultural anthropology)
  Bibliography: p. 159
  1. Peking (China)—Social life and customs.
2. China—Social life and customs—1949–
I. Title.   II. Series.
DS795.2.C48   1984   306'.0951'156   83–12849

ISBN 0-03-060329-3

Copyright © 1984 by CBS College Publishing
Address correspondence to:
383 Madison Avenue
New York, N.Y. 10017
All rights reserved
Printed in the United States of America
Published simultaneously in Canada
4 5 6 7   016   9 8 7 6 5 4 3 2 1

CBS COLLEGE PUBLISHING
Holt, Rinehart and Winston
The Dryden Press
Saunders College Publishing

To My Parents

Harold and Wanneta Chance

Foreword

ABOUT THE SERIES

These case studies in cultural anthropology are designed to bring to students, in beginning and intermediate courses in the social sciences, insights into the richness and complexity of human life as it is lived in different ways and in different places. They are written by men and women who have lived in the societies they write about and who are professionally trained as observers and interpreters of human behavior. The authors are also teachers, and in writing their books they have kept the students who will read them foremost in their minds. It is our belief that when when an understanding of ways of life very different from one's own is gained, abstractions and generalizations about social structure, cultural values, subsistence techniques, and other universal categories of human social behavior become meaningful.

ABOUT THE AUTHOR

Norman A. Chance is Professor of Anthropology at the University of Connecticut. He was born in Lynn, Massachusetts, and studied anthropology at the University of Pennsylvania before receiving his Ph.D. degree from Cornell University in 1957. He taught previously at the University of Oklahoma and at McGill University, where he also served as Director of the Programme in the Anthropology of Development until 1968, when he moved to Connecticut to head the newly formed Department of Anthropology. Prior to developing an interest in China, he undertook research in the southwest United States, Alaska, Canada, and Mexico. He is the author of an earlier case study in this series, *The Eskimo of North Alaska.*

ABOUT THE BOOK

This case study of Half Moon Village within Red Flag Commune near Beijing is largely based on two visits to the People's Republic of China. Periods of residence and participant observation in the village include time spent in agricultural field labor as well as sharing in the social and cultural life of the people. Fifty in-depth interviews were also conducted with a wide range of personnel including peasants, factory workers, students, local leaders, government officials, and intellectuals. Few field researchers have been able to learn enough about modern China and its complex history to write knowledgeably about more than one small aspect of it. That aspect, for Norman Chance, is a mid-sized village in a large commune in the shadow of China's capital city. Half Moon village is an understandable and relatively manageable unit for study from an anthropological, ethnographic point of view. That this case study is credible is attested to not only by Dr. Chance's professional status as an experienced anthropologist but also by extensive reviews by other students of modern China and by qualified individuals in the People's Republic who gave their assistance while the manuscript was taking shape.

The study is remarkable for its combination of two quite unlikely themes: One is the effort to analyze socialist political and economic processes aimed at developing viable solutions to the country's pressing problems. The other is a study of family and kin, the nature of sex roles and marriage, the events and contexts of socialization, and going to school. This combination makes the case study much more than it could have been were only one of these themes emphasized. Without the direct observation in the field and participant interaction with the people—two constant features of the anthropological approach—the latter theme would not have appeared.

The style of presentation in this case study contributes to readability and understanding. The author not only draws on his own direct observations in telling anecdotes that enliven the pages and evoke images—he also uses dialogue extensively, permitting the people themselves to tell about their lives and circumstances as closely to their own way as translation and the ethics of field research permit. The reader feels close to the concerns of everyday life as well as to the issues of socialism at the grass-roots level in modern China.

There is no country in the world today about which Americans are more curious than the People's Republic of China. And there is no country about which we have more misinformation, more hazy understandings, and gross misunderstandings. This case study is a step in the direction of improving our knowledge and understanding.

It is also a demonstration of the capabilities of anthropology as an approach to the study of complex societies. Though Half Moon is only one of many villages in China, knowing about it permits us to form some relevant perspective on the complex whole of which it is a part. If relations between the People's Republic and the United States improve, we may acquire enough comparative material from other village studies to make firmer judgments about the whole. For the present, we are fortunate to have this study of a village in the vicinity of a large urban center—one that is neither the poorest nor the richest, nor the most backward or most progressive of its kind.

GEORGE AND LOUISE SPINDLER
Editors
Calistoga, California

Preface

Fieldwork is a hallmark of anthropology. Living with the people, experiencing their work, social patterns, thought, and values is what often distinguishes our approach from that of other social sciences. Yet on-the-scene rural studies of China's mainland by Western anthropologists or other social analysts have been almost nonexistent since 1949.

Even within China itself, few government-sponsored ethnographic and sociological investigations are made available to the public. The actual teaching of cultural anthropology was abandoned in 1952 (Whyte and Pasternak 1980:148). The resulting loss of a generation of scholars trained in comparative investigation and social science methodology is only just now being realized as academic institutions seek to reestablish cultural anthropology, sociology, psychology, and similarly oriented disciplines into their curriculum.

From the early 1950s through the Cultural Revolution of the 1960s and 1970s, such fields of inquiry were perceived as reactionary and therefore unworthy of recognition in a revolutionary society committed to socialist transformation. Instead of making the more common Western distinction between the development of anthropological knowledge and the uses to which it could be put, Chinese leaders of the time placed the whole subject matter outside the bounds of political acceptability. They assumed that such intellectual activity challenged the views of Marx and Lenin, and opened the door to new forms of foreign colonialism.

The slowness with which cultural anthropology and related fields are now returning to the academic fold is only partly due to established priorities and the limited availability of trained teachers and researchers. Although the Chinese Academy of Social Sciences has recently emphasized the importance of these subjects in strengthening the country's drive toward modernization, some still express concern over the possible emergence of a scholarly elite committed to challenging the present direction of Chinese society in the name of objective social science— emphasizing that objectivity cannot be separated from politics and its impact on human beings. Such issues are not just academic, but reflect important problems in how best to build a modern socialist society.

Needless to say, questions of objectivity in the development and utilization of knowledge are raised in the United States and other countries too. A well-known American example is the heated debate carried on by members of various social (and physical) scientific societies on the role of their professions in the Vietnam War. Still, social research in the United States receives continuing recognition and support, whereas in China it is just now reemerging within universities and institutes. The fact that so little field research has been undertaken in rural China for the past thirty years—whether accomplished by Chinese social scientists or others—is one reason to encourage more in-depth village studies. Chinese peasants represent one-fifth of the world's population. It would certainly behoove the other four-fifths to learn more about them. Still, paucity of knowledge is not the only reason for studying rural China.

Beginning in the 1950s and continuing to the present, a dramatic increase has taken place in the comparative study of economic development. Many years ago, when I first began teaching a seminar on the topic, I kept coming across references to China's alternative "model" (see Frolic 1978). Why is it, I asked myself, that China—the most ancient of civilizations—has stimulated such great interest among Western social scientists and intellectuals of the increasingly independent Third World? Is it the case, as many sympathetic analysts proposed, that China has found a more humane way of developing, one that places a higher value on meeting social needs over rapid economic growth?

Can underdeveloped countries like China improve their standard of living without succumbing to the myriad problems of expanding urbanization, with its attendant dislocation and unemployment; heavy industrialization, with its heightened exploitation of the rural sector; increased economic dependence on outside capital, with the all-too-frequent inflationary spiral that accompanies it; and the subtler but powerful cultural blandishments of Western consumer-oriented society? Some knowledgeable economists, historians, and China specialists thought so (see Gurley 1971; Stavrianos 1975; Nee and Peck 1975). Others, such as Simon Leys, were far more critical of China's post-1949 development, calling the Mao-led efforts at socialist development "essentially totalitarian and feudal bureaucratic" (Leys 1977:xi).

Having become deeply concerned over the seeming inability of Western-based development programs to meet the needs of the people to whom they were directed, I wanted to learn more. I hoped that a first-hand visit to China would provide some enlightenment and perhaps even a few tentative answers. At least it was worth a try.

In 1971, following the advent of "ping-pong" diplomacy (in which the Chinese government invited an American table-tennis team to play in Beijing), the process of renewing formal ties between China and the United States was begun. I immediately applied to the Chinese Embassy in Ottawa to undertake a brief study of changing patterns of education resulting from the Cultural Revolution policies then being implemented. Having recently become head of an anthropology department, I was particularly interested in academic administration and felt that I could learn something from China's seemingly innovative efforts in this regard. Given the existing political climate, it was also clear that more in-depth field research by an American anthropologist was out of the question. At that time, even a one- or two-month field trip to China was uncommon (see Schell 1977).

The following spring, I learned from the embassy in Ottawa that my proposal had indeed been approved and that I was expected in Beijing in the next two weeks! Shortly thereafter, in April and May of 1972, together with Nancy F. Chance, also an anthropologist, I had the rather heady experience of traveling to five major cities and many towns and villages, visiting schools, colleges, research institutes, and universities, interviewing faculty, administrators, and students, and gathering initial data on the impact of the "Great Proletarian Cultural Revolution" on the social and educational life of the Chinese people.

As one of the first American anthropologists to visit China in over thirty years, I soon found myself being treated as "an honored guest"—an experience perhaps best described as "un-humbling"—complete with an overwhelming array of culinary delights, flashbulb lights, and breathtaking sights. Introduced to many of the country's scientific leaders in the Academy of Sciences and other key educational institutions, I was quickly presented with an overview of China's recent academic innovations. Almost impossible to achieve in the politically rarified atmosphere of the capital city, on the other hand, was an insight into the educational system from the perspective of students, teachers, administrators, and other participants not so imbued with the official policy.

However, I did have several lively discussions with faculty members of the Beijing Central Institute of Minorities, including the anthropologist Fei Xiaotong. Fei, an internationally known social scientist trained in England and the United States, had only recently reestablished ties with Westerners after having undergone a long period of intellectual isolation in China's countryside following his active criticism of the government (Fei et al. 1973; Fei 1980; and McGough 1979).

Invited to give a formal lecture on "Minority Life in America" to the student body of the Institute, I soon found myself engaged in a four-hour discussion that dramatically illustrated how limited East-West scholarly contact had been in the past two decades, and also, how different were our perspectives on the relationship between minority and majority cultures.

After leaving the capital for politically less intense areas of the country, I was able to undertake some preliminary research of the sort that had originally brought me to China—though, of course, not all that I had hoped. Still, this first trip helped me to appreciate the immense historical complexity of China that has led some in the past to describe it as "unfathomable," "unpredictable," or simply "unknowable."

However, on returning to the United States, I was soon asked to put aside the complexities in favor of simple generalizations. That is, as one of the few academic visitors to China at that time, I was immediately (and temptingly) called upon to draw large-scale conclusions based on a modicum of experience. Indeed, symptoms of "instant expertise" were showing up in many literary and scholarly circles at that time.

Actually, it was rather easy to report on the positive aspects of China's development effort, given the ease of access to those models and experiments deemed successful by the initiators and participants. Many people, including myself, were impressed with Mao Zedong's strategy of reducing economic inequalities through the immense collective effort of the people (Chance 1973). It was the failures—economic, political, and personal—which were barely glimpsed, if seen at all, that I found difficult to assess, and that knowledge was also necessary to any well-rounded picture of contemporary China. Unfortunately, all other requests to return to China for more in-depth anthropological investigation were either ignored or rejected. Obviously, I had to settle for what had already been accomplished. Looking back on these years, I now realize that my initial evaluation of China was based more on what I had hoped was occurring than on what was actually happening—hardly a scientific appraisal. As a result, my interpretations were often more illusory than real.

Six years later, I joined millions of other Americans in observing a major turn-around in China's internal government policies. External relations, too, were changing as the country decided to open the door wider to foreign visitors. In just a few years, over a quarter of a million tourists had savored the country's cultural fare. Government and scientific delegations began formal talks culminating in a proliferation of exchanges, including a few of an educational and scholarly nature. In August and September of 1978, I led a delegation of academic and professional people to Beijing and northeast China, focusing on education, population control, and related issues. Changes in the six years since my first trip were striking. The revolutionary fervor of the late 1960s and early 1970s had dissipated significantly as post-Mao China sought to quell old conflicts and instill a new sense of purpose directed toward realizing the "Four Modernizations" in agriculture, industry, science and technology, and defense. Talks with village leaders, agricultural special-ists, population planners, educators, and health professionals suggested that, at least for the moment, a new openness was in the air and that prospects for the kind of wide-ranging discussion and expression of varied opinion necessary to sound anthropological field research might well become possible in the not-too-distant future.

As changing international affairs continued to draw China and the United States closer together, culminating in the establishment of diplomatic relations, a proposal was submitted to China by Fred Engst and Nancy Chance: that an opportunity be provided for a small group of Americans of differing socioeconomic, occupational, and racial backgrounds to live and work with the Chinese people for several months in the fall of 1979. Approval was eventually given. The group then took up residence in a small village on one of the larger communes on the outskirts of Beijing City and within the municipality. Members lived in different households, eating and working with peasant families and spending at least some time each day as part of an agricultural work team, as well as conducting their own research on different aspects of village life. A month and a half later, the group spent several weeks working in a textile factory in adjacent Hebei Province, interspersed with travel to other cities, rural areas, and a brief stay in a banner village in Inner Mongolia.

The book draws extensively on research undertaken in this and nearby villages during the fall of 1979, including one additional month that Nancy Chance and I spent in China after the conclusion of the group trip. Between September and December of that year I taped and transcribed over fifty detailed interviews con-ducted with people from a wide range of backgrounds, including peasant leaders, factory workers, young, middle-aged, and older men and women, students, teachers, paraprofessional "barefoot doctors" and many others who I felt could help in putting together a picture of changing village life in a North China commune.[1]

This research data was then compared with earlier information accumulated on

---

[1] These and other interviews all required the use of a translator. However, in the chapters that follow, accounts of dialogues with villagers seldom make reference to this fact. This was done for literary convenience, so as not to distract the reader by having to introduce an interpreter at each instance. Obviously, Fred Engst and the others who helped me with translation were essential to the success of the study.

village and commune life during previous trips—including interviews with two members of the commune in Beijing Municipality dating back to the spring of 1972; data gathered on a short trip to the commune headquarters and outlying agricultural and industrial sectors in the late summer of 1978; and other information received from Chinese and Americans who had lived, worked, or visited the area during this time—including several Chinese exchange scholars to the United States who earlier had resided in nearby villages as "educated youth."

Finally, in the summer of 1979, just prior to leaving for China, I had the unique experience of traveling with several leaders and agricultural workers from that same commune while they were visiting rural farms in Pennsylvania studying the latest techniques of dairy mechanization. This opportunity enabled me to observe a little of how the Chinese respond to and gain from exposure to greater knowledge of the advanced agricultural practices followed by many American farmers. But what particularly stood out in my mind was not the technological transfer, as important as that was, but the open, generous, and helpful attitude that characterized the members of these rural Pennsylvania farm families as they offered to explain their means of livelihood. It was the same open and sharing attitude I had found among Chinese peasants halfway around the world.

N. A. C.

Acknowledgments

The fieldwork on which this book is based was conducted between the years 1972 and 1979; more specifically, in April and May of 1972, August and September of 1978, and September through December of 1979. The data is drawn from several different settings in North China, the most important of which is a well-known commune located approximately 25 miles from the capital city of Beijing.

It should be noted at the outset that the names of individual Chinese, as well as those associated with communes, villages, and other localities, are fictitious, so as to protect the privacy of the people involved. Their anonymity should not be construed to mean that their efforts were not appreciated.

Of the numerous people providing assistance, I am particularly grateful for the support of the director and staff of the commune where much of the research was undertaken, as well as that of the leaders of the several village brigades that were studied. All gave considerably more aid than was either required or expected.

I also wish to express my appreciation to the villagers themselves, who were so helpful in home, field, factory, and school: answering the continual questions, correcting mistakes, and responding to census forms and questionnaires. Students from the First Foreign Language Institute and several other educational institutions in Beijing were also of assistance, aiding in interviewing, translating, and gathering statistical data. In different ways, these individuals illustrate why it is that anthropologists so often speak positively about the experience of living with the people they wish to learn from and understand—that is, the sharing of one's life with others promotes a common cause.

Many people have stimulated my interest in and knowledge of China, including Professor Paul T. K. Lin, past director of the East Asian Studies Centre at McGill University; William Hinton, author of the classic ethnography *Fanshen* (1966), one of the early detailed studies of revolutionary change in a Chinese village; Sid Engst and Joan Hinton, who went to China in the late 1940s, and after a period of work with the United Nations Relief and Rehabilitation Administration, decided to remain; and their son, Fred Engst. Born and raised in China prior to his coming to the United States in 1975, Fred Engst was a co-leader of the 1979 "work-study" delegation of which I was a member. He was also a key translator for most of the in-depth interviews conducted in the commune. Given my inadequate knowledge of Chinese, his frequent assistance in translation was invaluable.

Also acknowledged should be Isabel and David Crook of the English Language Section of the Beijing Foreign Language Institute, authors of several volumes pertaining to the North China village Ten Mile Inn (1959, 1966, 1979), who helped in many ways both in the field and in the analysis and write-up phase of the research; Professor Clifford DuRand, Daniel Sipe, and other members of the 1979 delegation who assisted in gathering field data; and most of all, Professor Nancy F.

Chance, co-leader of the 1979 trip, co-worker with me for over thirty years, and the person who first introduced me to the intellectual adventure called anthropology.

Of the North American China scholars whose suggestions and criticisms of earlier chapters and drafts of this book have helped clarify my thinking, I particularly want to thank Robert Dewar, Norma Diamond, Christina Gilmartin, Frank Kehl, Julia Kwong, Vera Schwarcz, Mark Selden, and Peter Seybolt. In addition, I express my appreciation to Charles Cell for his statistical analysis of village census data; to Clifford DuRand for sharing his analysis of economic life; to Nancy Chance for sharing her research on education and women; and to Stephen C. Chance for his line drawings.

Similar acknowledgment is due to three young Chinese scholars from Beijing, who, while attending the University of Connecticut as graduate students, graciously shared their knowledge and experience with me. They are Jia Liling (political science), Yang Haipang, and Zang Junhong (anthropology).

Appreciated, also, is the aid of the Chinese People's Association for Friendship with Foreign Countries, whose invitation and arrangements for the 1972 and 1979 field trips were essential; of the China Travel Service; and of the University of Connecticut Research Foundation and Department of University Computer Systems for their generous financial support offered in the years 1972–1974 and 1979–1983.

Grateful acknowledgment is due as well to Harcourt Brace Jovanovich, Inc. for permission to use five lines from "A Worker Reads History," from *The Selected Poems of Bertolt Brecht*, translated by H. R. Hayes.

Finally, I want to thank George and Louise Spindler, editors of the Case Studies in Cultural Anthropology, for the many suggestions they offered while this book was being written. Their insightful blend of constructive criticism and continuing encouragement was always helpful and much appreciated.

Contents

Foreword   vii

Preface   ix

Introduction   1

The Rise of Revolution, 2
The Nature of Chinese Socialism, 4
Problems of Development, 6

1. The Meeting   13

A Brief Discussion, 13
The New Brigade Leader, 16
A Criticism Offered, 21

2. Half Moon Village   26

The Setting, 26
Local History, 33
Relations with the Commune, 39
The Party and the People, 40

3. Working   45

Household Economy, 45
Collective Enterprise, 46
From Field to Factory, 51
Resolving Conflicts, 55

4. Growing Up   60

Birth, 60
Infancy, 63
Childhood, 67

5. Schooling   74

A Visit from the Teacher, 74
Primary Education, 77

Middle School, 83
Portrait of an Educated Youth, 86

6. Becoming an Adult   95

   Relations between the Sexes, 95
   Selecting a Mate, 99
   Being Engaged, 103
   The Marriage Day, 105

7. Family Relations   112

   Kin Ties, 112
   The Changing Status of Women, 117
   Family Planning, 124
   The Later Years, 127

8. The Changing Political Economy   131

   Agricultural Modernization, 131
   Differences between Villages, 133
   Productivity, Ownership, and Distribution, 137
   The Problem of Bureaucracy, 141

9. The Face of the Future   148

   A Turning Point, 148
   The Individual, the Collective, and the State, 151

Postscript   156

Glossary   157

References Cited and Recommended Reading   159

Index   163

A Note on Romanization

For rendering Chinese characters into English, this book utilizes *pinyin* (literally: "combination of sounds"), the official Chinese system of spelling. A major advantage is that it assists people who are unfamiliar with the Chinese language to pronounce it more accurately than do other systems, which tend to confuse the unfamiliar reader. In the *pinyin* system, most letters are pronounced approximately the same as in those languages using the Latin alphabet, including English. There are a number of exceptions, such as *c*, which is pronounced *ts* (as in *its*); *x* is pronounced as *sh* (as in *show*), *zh* as *j* (as in *jump*), *e* as in *her*, and *q* as *ch* (as in *cheese*).

A few well-known names romanized from the Cantonese, such as Chiang Kai-shek, retain their more common spelling, as does the Kuomintang (Party) in order to preserve its familiar association with the acronym KMT.

CASE STUDIES IN
CULTURAL ANTHROPOLOGY

GENERAL EDITORS
George and Louise Spindler
STANFORD UNIVERSITY

CHINA'S URBAN VILLAGERS

Life in a Beijing Commune

Introduction

Who built the seven towers of Thebes?
The books are filled with the names of kings.
Was it the kings who hauled the craggy blocks
of stone? . . .
In the evening when the Chinese wall was finished.
Where did the masons go? . . .

Bertolt Brecht

A little over one billion people live in China—more than one-fourth of the world's population. Of that number, 80 percent are men and women who seek their subsistence largely from the soil in an agrarian pattern that has changed rather slowly for much of the past 2000 years, from the abolition of an ancient form of feudalism in the third century B.C. to the penetration of Western capital and culture in the nineteenth century.

Beginning in the 1920s and continuing through the 1950s and 1960s, the pace of change increased significantly as China's villagers became involved in a massive revolutionary transformation that produced a sufficiently impressive increase in their standard of living to eventually draw recognition from other Third World countries and even from the West. Still, China's development is very limited, as any visitor who has passed beyond the usual tourist sights can quickly attest. Just how limited is it? If we compare the level of agricultural productivity in China with that of the United States, the comparison is striking: whereas one American farmer feeds almost one hundred city dwellers, it takes the intensive labor of between three and four peasants to feed one urbanite in China. With little more than 11 percent of China's land arable, and needing to feed over four times the American population, it is no wonder that the country is studying how best to modernize its agricultural sector.

Note too, the different use of the words "farmer" and "peasant." The distinction is important. Farmers produce primarily for others—exchanging what they make for quite different goods and services, often at the national and even international level. Peasants, on the other hand, produce more for themselves—for their own use —and only secondarily for others through the medium of local and regional markets, rent, taxes, and the like. In China today, the agricultural work force is changing from peasant to farmer, producing both for their own use and for exchange. What part peasant and what part farmer? It varies greatly, not only between regions, but between communes and even villages. In the large majority of instances where grain

1

Women field workers at Half Moon Village, Red Flag Commune.

is the major agricultural crop, a rough indicator of the degree of transition from peasant to farmer is the amount of grain kept and the amount sold.[1]

Another significant measure of the difference between old and new China is seen in the increasing number of peasants now working in small village sideline enterprises and larger commune and state-owned industries and factories that are rapidly emerging in semirural areas surrounding China's big cities. Young men and women, peasants in upbringing and outlook, but occupationally workers with newly acquired technical skills, represent a potentially vibrant force in the development of China.

This dialectic of cyclical and developmental change, of persisting in old ways while at the same time being increasingly involved in the larger modern society is not limited to China's rural population. It sums up the dilemma of contemporary peasants the world over. One important difference in China, however, is the active role played by the peasantry in revolutionizing the countryside in order to better their own economic and social conditions.

THE RISE OF REVOLUTION

What social conditions led to the assumption of power by China's revolutionary leaders? While such a complex question cannot be addressed here (see Bianco 1971), two historical factors should be stressed since they continue to have an important bearing on the daily life of the peasants described in this book. One is the impact of foreign capital, technology, and occupation on China for a period of over 100 years. The other is the social turmoil occurring in the country during that time, generated in part by that contact.

---

[1] Of the 300 million tons of food grain produced each year by the peasantry, approximately 250 million tons are self-consumed (Vermeer 1982).

For many centuries, China was ruled by powerful dynasties. But in the mid-1850s, following defeat by the British Empire in the so-called Opium War, Qing dynasty officials were forced to open China's ports to foreign trade, including the importation of opium, to consent to a customs tariff fixed by treaty, to grant extraterritoriality (the right of foreign consular officers to try their own nationals in China), and to agree to other unequal treaties that dealt crippling blows to the country's sovereignty and economy.

The eventual collapse of the dynasty and the rise of a new Republic of China under Sun Yatsen and the Kuomingtang (KMT) Party in 1911 instilled hope for a stronger centralized government. However, its success was hampered by many factors.

Foreign capital severely disrupted the internal economy, promoting inflationary spirals, which then forced large rent increases. For peasants and others unable to pay, this meant land foreclosure. Taxes and surtaxes rose, not only dramatically but, from the villager's point of view, inequitably.[2] The introduction of Western technology into an expanding urban textile industry brought a sharp decline in the need for rural handicrafts, with a resulting further loss in peasant income. Problems of corruption in government and the military increased the unpredictability of rural life.

Large landowners began moving out of villages to the more attractive life of nearby towns and cities. This disrupted traditional economic relations between landlord and peasant, an arrangement once based on a clearly recognized pattern of reciprocity. Lawlessness increased. Finally, as perceived by Chiang Kai-shek, leader of the KMT government after the death of Sun in 1925, the most serious threat of all was the rapid rise of the Chinese Communist Party, first organized in 1921. However, to Chiang's constant frustration, numerous attempts by the KMT military to rid the country of these "bandits" were unsuccessful.

For China's villagers, on the other hand, increasing impoverishment and threat of famine led some to accept the proposal of the CCP that only by following their policies, summed up in the slogan "Land to the Tiller," could the lives of the vast majority be improved. Mostly illiterate and lacking contact with the outside world, these rural people knew little about socialism. But they did know that their existing world held few benefits for them. And so the Communist Party's rural ranks continued to grow.

Then, in the mid-1930s, after the Japanese occupied Manchuria, promoted the "autonomy of Inner Mongolia," and threatened much of China's Northern Plain, communist leaders changed their strategy, urging that past differences between the KMT and the CCP be put aside in favor of a "United Front" against Japan's military expansion. Under great difficulty, the alliance held until the defeat of

---

[2] Chesneaux reports that in Sichuan Province in 1933, peasants were forced to pay taxes in advance up to the year 1971. Actually, such taxes reflect a much deeper inequity pervading at least part of China's countryside at that time. For example, a study undertaken in Wuxi (near Nanjing) found that in 1929, poor peasants, comprising 69 percent of the population, owned less than 14 percent of the land; whereas landlords, representing 6 percent of the population, owned 47 percent (Chesneaux 1973:78–79). Other scholars have questioned the pervasiveness of such inequities within peasant villages (see Myers 1970).

Japan in 1945, when the question of who was to lead postwar China again re-turned to the fore. The result of that civil conflict is now well known. The KMT was simply unable to gain sufficient support from the people to achieve its goal. By the autumn of 1949, Mao's communist forces had achieved victory. It was a time of exhaustion. But it was also a time of dramatic opportunity.

THE NATURE OF CHINESE SOCIALISM

October 1 is celebrated in China as National Day. On this date in 1949, in front of a huge crowd of supporters at Tiananmen Square in Beijing, Mao Zedong, Chairman of the Chinese Communist Party, proclaimed the establishment of the People's Republic of China. Its first task was an all-out effort to remove the national ills that had led to the stigma of being called "The sick man of Asia." This was to be accomplished by a revolutionary transformation in the economic and social relations of the country, resolving long-festering internal problems caused by a combination of foreign intervention and social decay. Mao predicted that out of this massive upheaval would emerge a highly productive socialist society whose collective endeavor could enable the people to significantly raise their standard of living and whose political structure could provide them with the tools to more fully determine their own lives. This book is largely concerned with how villagers living in Red Flag Commune, located on the outskirts of Beijing, are responding to that challenge.

Among the rural issues first addressed by the CCP leaders following their assump-tion of power, the question of land reform was central. In those areas of the country not previously under their political control, the government immediately initiated a massive new program aimed at completely restructuring land ownership. Millions of needy peasants, including future members of Red Flag Commune, participated. Those whose lives of hardship had been economically dominated by landlords, large or small, began reversing the relationship—taking the latter's property and redis-tributing it to the poor and landless.

By the mid-1950s, many peasants throughout northern China had joined ele-mentary agricultural producers' cooperatives (APCs). These cooperatives, orga-nized under the leadership of the Party, comprised 20 or more households, which shared labor, land, and small tools for their common benefit. In Chapter 2, we will learn more of how these cooperatives were formed, who supported and who op-posed them.

In nearby Beijing, small-scale industries were also turned into economic co-operatives. Larger private industrial holdings were purchased by the state, the previous owners often receiving salaried positions in the enterprises, plus five percent annual interest on the surrendered property for a period of ten years. Foreign-owned industries had already been nationalized.

As can be imagined, the changes brought about by this transformation were con-siderable. The whole structure of economic relations between peasant and landlord, on the one hand, and urban worker and proprietors of large industries, on the other, was altered dramatically. However, among private business leaders, high-level managers, and bureaucratic officials outside the Party, political support for these economic efforts was less than enthusiastic. Yet their expertise was needed to administer the country's economic, educational, and local governmental institutions, which had been disrupted by years of war.

This issue posed a serious problem for China. Some Party officials urged that further changes be delayed. By allowing existing developments to mature, more traditionally minded leaders, workers, and peasants could be incorporated into the process. Others differed. In 1955, Mao Zedong, then President as well as Party Chairman, concluded that the process was moving too slowly. Indeed, it was tottering along "like a woman with bound feet." Progress could always be undermined. It was better that the momentum be maintained.[3]

Until this time, Party leaders had generally agreed that the low-level APCs, based on the voluntary participation of its members, were the major stepping-stone to a fully functioning socialist society in the rural areas (see Shue 1980). The steps involved in this transitional process moved from private ownership, through mutual aid teams, elementary and advanced cooperatives, and concluded with collective and state ownership of the major means of production. In this manner, it was reasoned, the continued poverty of many peasants, rooted in inequitable ownership of land, animals, tools, and machinery, could be reduced and eventually eliminated and the reallocation of resources through state planning be initiated.

In practice, of course, there were many problems. How necessary was it to have the active participation of most peasants? Should the more well-to-do peasants be encouraged to participate? What level of consensus within the cooperative was desired before moving on to a higher level of socialist ownership?

In Half Moon Village, a community we will look at in depth throughout this book, poor peasant families usually joined the cooperatives, viewing them as economically beneficial. However, when several "middle" peasant families were asked to join, they refused, preferring to work their own land with their own tools and their own labor. (Rich peasants and landlords were initially excluded from participation.) How important was it to draw these middle-level peasants into the cooperative? If the APC leaders were patient and moved more slowly in setting them up, could these households—with better land and tools—be persuaded to join their poorer brethren? Or, reminiscent of old women with bound feet, was it more likely they would hardly move at all? Even worse, might they set up roadblocks, thereby limiting the success of others?

This type of response occurred in Half Moon Village when the head of a more well-to-do family refused to allow the members of a mutual aid team (a precursor of the APCs) to construct an irrigation ditch across his land. The man recognized that the proposed water system would enhance the productivity of the team, perhaps at his own expense. The response was repeated following the formation of more advanced cooperatives several years later.

Problems of a quite different order were faced by local Party cadres newly placed in positions of leadership. Most cadres were villagers themselves, with

---

[3] Actually, in the late 1940s and early 1950s, Mao himself warned of overeagerness and "left opportunism" in completing the socialist transformation in rural areas (Mao 1949:367 and 419). His views changed in the mid-1950s (see Mao 1955:394–404).

relatives and friends in the area. Occasionally, the responsibility to implement a Party or government policy conflicted with their views and those of friends. Should one's action always be guided by Party policy determined "from above"? What if your evaluation of local conditions leads you to a different conclusion? Such dilemmas were common in Half Moon Village then and still are today.

In one incident discussed later, we find Party members being informed by agricultural officials in Beijing to have the peasants begin implementing "triple cropping" during their next planting season. Local leaders passed on the plan to the villagers, even though some of them felt it was basically unsound. The villagers definitely opposed it. Learning how the problem was resolved helps us understand day-to-day relations within the Party and between the Party and the people. Furthermore, it provides a practical illustration of a rather complex political process—the relationship between centralized planning and democratic decision making. On several occasions throughout this study we will address this important topic.

While villagers attempted to resolve day-to-day problems posed by the societal changes of the mid-1950s, China's national leaders grappled with a far more difficult issue: What direction should the country take following the conclusion of land reform and the establishment of the elementary cooperatives?

Was an increasingly more collectivized labor force the key to advancing the country's economic development—and through that effort, the people's social well-being and standard of living? Specifically, should the government encourage the consolidation of APCs into larger, more advanced units, thereby expanding the cooperative base still further? Or, was the mechanization of the country's productive forces a necessary precondition for advancing the social cooperation of its members toward a more fully socialist society? That is, should the society focus its limited energies on rapidly expanding its urban industrial infrastructure and (to a lesser extent) its agricultural technology in the countryside?[4]

The two approaches were intimately linked, both collectivization and mechanization being seen as necessary steps in the socialist development of rural China. Still, the question remained: Which should receive the greater emphasis?

Under Mao's leadership, the Party and government opted for an acceleration of rural collectivization—a "Socialist Upsurge in the Countryside" (see Mao 1978), in which mutual aid teams and low-level cooperatives (still a minority throughout the country) were to be combined into larger, more advanced units.

PROBLEMS OF DEVELOPMENT

Problems stemming from this effort to accelerate the process of socialist ownership were substantial. For the poorer peasantry, representing between 60 and 70 percent

---

[4] A good illustration of the latter perspective that mechanization is a necessary prerequisite for socialist development in agriculture is contained in a book written by an American who served as a teacher at a state-run tractor driver training school in Hebei Province. When the school first opened in 1953, the director announced to his new students: "Our task is to build islands of socialism in a vast sea of individual farming. We are the ones who will have to show the way for the whole country" (Hinton 1970:45–46).

of Northern China's rural population (Mao 1955:403), so too were the benefits.[5] Owning the least (or none at all), these people had the most to gain by furthering collectivization, since under the advanced APCs, ownership of land and other means of production ceased being a factor in income distribution. At that moment a turning point was reached. From now on, how hard the members worked rather than what they owned could be the deciding factor in the distribution of collective income.

When production was high, well-to-do peasants also gained; but when it was low, they benefited less. In addition, such peasants occasionally found that their contribution of land and other goods did not result in the compensation promised earlier by local Party officials. Finally, considerable pressure was placed on them to join the larger, more advanced cooperatives—a policy that contrasted sharply with the more voluntary nature of earlier efforts (see Selden 1982a). Such a shift in strategy not only increased conflicts between the peasants, but raised important questions about the extent of their participation in building a new socialist society.

Of the many development problems faced by the government, perhaps the most difficult one to resolve has been the attempt to unite the twin goals of socialism and modernization. The results of this effort, both positive and negative, appear throughout Red Flag Commune. Successes include the widespread mechanization of simple stationary tools collectively owned by community members; extensive irrigation canals shared by different brigades; a rural health system that provides care for every individual on the commune at a cost of less than fifty cents per individual per year; an education system that now assures a full eight years of schooling for all resident children wanting to attend; and tall shade trees that line roadways between villages like Half Moon and Little River—trees planted twenty-five years ago as part of a cooperative intervillage reforestation project.

Failures are represented by the continuation in office of highly prejudiced bureaucratic officials who look down on the peasantry as hardly able to care for their own affairs, let alone contribute knowledge and experience toward improving the larger society. They are seen in hundreds of fading revolutionary slogans staining commune walls, slogans such as "Carry the Revolution Under Dictatorship of the Proletariat Through to the End"—whose tendentious meaning probably eluded the painter as well as those villagers who still pass by these relics of an earlier era on their way to work. Such failures sometimes appear in more poignant form, as in the life history of an "educated youth" who came to Half Moon Village after trying to help develop a state farm in a province far to the northeast, or in the furious denunciation of a local Party cadre by a young woman who was unfairly passed over for a factory job in favor of the official's niece.

However, merely listing concrete examples of the pluses and minuses of China's development effort does little to help us understand the basic issues underlying these events. Much remains beneath the surface. For example, one important theme introduced shortly after the advanced APCs was Mao's call for a mass mobilization of the people to make a "Great Leap Forward." This national campaign

[5] In some areas surrounding Beijing, including Half Moon Village, the figure ran as high as 80 percent.

of 1958–1959 was partly undertaken to raise grain and steel output, and in other ways to increase the country's economic development. In its rural manifestation, it also encouraged peasants to transform their lives by mobilizing local resources and labor in the construction of water conservation and reforestation projects, and in the setting up of small sideline industries to process crops and manufacture farm tools. The profits created by these self-reliant efforts could then be used to mechanize agriculture, thereby freeing peasant labor for small-scale industrial development.

Furthermore, the Great Leap provided the impetus for one of the most intriguing social experiments in human history—a nationwide consolidation of the country's newly formed APCs into 42,000 communes. At this time, the *xiang*, or township, encompassing a population of 20,000 or more, was the lowest level of rural public administration. With the formation of communes, agricultural and small industrial enterprises came under their control, as did responsibility for commerce, the militia, education, health, and other human services. The commune soon subsumed the political administration of the *xiang* under its jurisdiction as well.

Though reduced in size and revised in form, both economically and politically, communes have continued in rural China until the present day. However, as we will learn shortly, the failures of the Great Leap far outweighed its few successes. As a result, Mao found his economic policies increasingly opposed: first by Party leaders such as Peng Dehuai (then Minister of Defense), and later by others such as Liu Shaoqi and Deng Xiaoping. In the early 1960s, China's development focused on increasing economic productivity through means more conventional than Mao's revolutionary strategy of collectively oriented mass mobilization, utilizing the spirit of hard work and plain living.

Becoming increasingly concerned over the possible resumption of power by a bureaucratic elite within the Party itself, not unlike what he perceived had happened in the Soviet Union, Mao launched in 1965–1966 his last big campaign: "The Great Proletarian Cultural Revolution." Its stated aim: to replace ingrained bourgeois, bureaucratic values with socialist ones and remove from power those individuals—"class enemies"—who would turn China away from its socialist path. In the minds of many critics, it was also an attempt by Mao to remove from Party leadership any individuals who might challenge his authority.

With this massive political movement, the door opened wide for a kind of ideological dogmatism that drenched the country with extremist slogans, promoted a personality cult of Mao, encouraged sharp attacks on many thousands of Party cadres (including a purge of China's then-President Liu Shaoqi), and in other ways drove a powerful wedge between leaders at all levels, which in turn generated factionalism among the people. Schools and universities closed down. Many young students, undirected and restless, traveled freely throughout the country, using Mao's instruction to "use society as the classroom" as their justification. Millions of urban youth volunteered or were sent to rural villages and isolated border areas to work and "learn from the peasants." Although economic production continued, the Party and government reached such an impasse that it was barely able to function. Arguments over what was the correct socialist course of action

Harvesting corn with a hand scythe, Half Moon Village.

raged. By 1967, Mao had begun to bring the politically well-disciplined People's Liberation Army (PLA) into leadership positions in many institutions in order to restore order.

Over the next nine years, until Mao's death in 1976, the Chinese people were called upon to participate in a series of related campaigns reflected in such slogans as "Criticize Lin Biao and Confucius" and "Grasp Revolution and Promote Production" (which basically meant: while pursuing revolution, don't forget production). Many people in cities and countryside had already turned away from such strident efforts, preferring to live out their lives far removed from the warlike turmoil. Others, unable to escape, were caught up in accusations, charges, and countercharges, leading all too frequently to public humiliation, beatings, and loss of life. It was only following Mao's death in 1976 and the arrest of several Party leaders associated with the Cultural Revolution—referred to as the "Gang of Four" —that China rejected active political movements in favor of an economically focused modernization program.

Today, Red Flag Commune is more flexible in its treatment of the relationship between individual and collective economic development, including the promotion of family and individual enterprises outside the collective sphere; it is more experimental in testing different interpretations of how best to increase the standard of living; and it is tentatively exploring how to encourage a more de-centralized, "grass-roots" democracy in the decision-making process at the local level. Older cadres, earlier removed from their positions in Party and government, have returned, while some of those more closely associated with Mao and his ideas have been transferred. Furthermore, most villagers appear glad to see the demise of the sharp political battles that led to such conflict and factionalism.

Still, others in Red Flag look more positively at the Cultural Revolution's goals, such as the effort of the commune to reduce inequalities between poor and well-to-do villages; the expansion and development of primary education; the bringing of improved medical care to the villages; the recruitment of peasants and workers into technical and higher education; reforms such as "combining work and study," which aimed to stimulate people of all ages to think for themselves and examine and test well-established theories in practice; and finally, the challenge to Con-fucian-inspired cultural patterns that continued to place women in a subservient status in village life. These people acknowledge that the extremism of the Cultural Revolution brought chaos to the country and personal tragedy to many. But they distinguish that result from what they think it was meant to achieve or should have achieved. Nevertheless, no matter how appealing the aims of the Cultural Revolu-tion were to some, for most, the overall result was appalling, illustrating once again the intimate connection between ends and means.

This brief historical picture of China's recent experience in socialist development provides a necessary backdrop to the unfolding of daily life in Half Moon Village and Red Flag Commune. Chapters 1 and 2 describe the people of Half Moon, the setting in which they live, and the history that brought them there. Two old peasants tell of early hardships, how land reform and the agricultural cooperative movement brought new opportunities to their lives, and how village sons and daughters are beginning to work in small sideline industries and in larger factories emerging on the outskirts of Beijing. We find that Half Moon is only one of 116 villages comprising Red Flag, a particularly large commune with a total population of over 85,000. Finally, attention is given to the important role of the Chinese Communist Party: how it is organized and how it provides leadership in village and commune affairs.

In Chapter 3, the focus is on work: how families make their living in private household, collective brigade, commune, and state-owned enterprises. We learn how income is generated and distributed in field and factory, what is appealing about employment in a state-owned factory, and why it is so difficult for rural villagers to obtain jobs in the state sector. And in both field and factory, we gain a little insight into the kinds of conflicts that divide leaders and the people from each other and how they go about trying to resolve them.

Chapters 4, 5, 6, and 7 take quite a different tack, presenting a view of the village from an ethnographic "life-cycle" perspective, tracing the process of growing up, going to school, getting married, having a family, and growing older. In contrast to the dramatic political and economic transformation described earlier, this section of the book highlights what anthropologists and other students of China have so often emphasized in the past—the importance of the family in village life.[6]

The next chapter on changing political economy brings together two themes of the book—the interpenetration of change and continuity—and how this dialectical process bears on China's effort to become a modern socialist society. We find, for example, that any decision to further mechanize the production of field crops immediately raises the question of what to do with the peasant work force.

This leads to a discussion of how to stimulate alternative forms of employment, including small village sidelines and large state-run factories. An analysis of how three villages address this question illustrates quite clearly that distinct paths of socialist economic development can be followed even within the same commune—an important reminder for those tending to view socialist society as monolithic. Nevertheless, political institutions enabling villagers to increase their input into the local decision-making process are still in their infancy.

Finally, the concluding chapter (and postscript) address several recent changes in government policy such as the re-establishment of peasant markets, maximizing individual initiative by means of bonuses, and increased shifting of responsibility for rural production to smaller economic units like the household. What advantages are gained by these changes? What problems occur? Are traditional family ties reinforced by the policy of breaking up work groups into smaller units? If so, what are the implications for the future of larger collective endeavors? And importantly, what happens when the "responsibility system" emphasizing greater household productivity is combined with the population planning policy emphasizing the limiting of family births to "only one." As we will see, the latter policy finds little favor among most people in Red Flag Commune. However, other questions need further investigation before attempting an answer.

As we come to know these people throughout the pages of this book, one point will become increasingly clear: they are "urban villagers" in a geographical sense only. Socially and culturally they retain many of their life-ways intact. Does this mean that they bear a close resemblance to millions of other peasants living on the edge of cities throughout the Third World? No, not at all. Actually, the differences are quite striking.

---

[6] Numerous studies of Chinese village life have been written since the late 1800s. Those pertaining to the pre-1949 period include: Smith (1899); Fei (1939); Yang (1945); Lin (1947); and Gamble (1954). Those focusing on post-1949 Chinese mainland include: Yang (1959); Myrdal (1963); Crook and Crook (1959, 1966, and 1979); Hinton (1966 and 1983); Chen (1973); and Bennett (1978). The more extensive post-1949 village studies of Chinese Taiwan include Gallin (1966), Wolf, (1968), and Diamond (1969).

HALF MOON VILLAGE

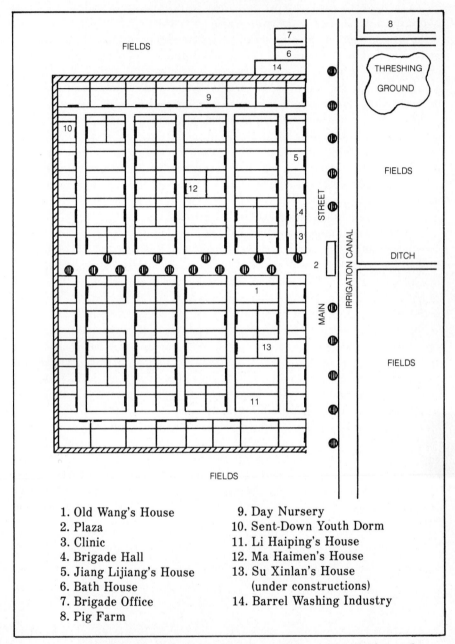

1. Old Wang's House
2. Plaza
3. Clinic
4. Brigade Hall
5. Jiang Lijiang's House
6. Bath House
7. Brigade Office
8. Pig Farm
9. Day Nursery
10. Sent-Down Youth Dorm
11. Li Haiping's House
12. Ma Haimen's House
13. Su Xinlan's House
    (under constructions)
14. Barrel Washing Industry

Figure 1. Half Moon Village, including the plaza, clinic, nursery, bridage office, bath house, and other service centers.

1 / The meeting

A BRIEF DISCUSSION

Taking one look at the pale grey December sky, the wiry rooster stood up, breathed in deeply, and proceeded to inform all those within earshot that it was indeed time to stir.

Across the courtyard in a small bedroom, Mother Wang lay quietly on her *kang*, listening as the rooster's crow faded into the background. Opening her eyes, she took in the familiar features of the room. To her right, dominating the rest of the furniture, was a tall wooden cupboard, stained a dull shade of red. On top, a dusty old cloth suitcase, unopened in years, served as a locker stuffed with family momentos, a few civil records, and other papers. Adjacent to the cupboard and flush against the interior yellow-painted wall, stood a glass-covered dresser, the drawers filled with sewing utensils. Underneath the glass top, a panorama of black and white photos of relatives and friends served as a constant reminder of earlier Spring Festivals (Chinese New Year) and other holiday occasions when family members were apt to come together.

Firmly, but with a certain gentleness so as not to disturb her husband, the woman laid back the worn quilt covering the bed and rose to her feet. Lao Wang, whose responsibilities didn't require such an early rise, continued sleeping peacefully. Standing upright, Mother Wang felt a sharp twinge of rheumatic pain in her ankles—one more reminder of increasing age. How many years now had she risen early to prepare the morning meal for her family? Too many, she had said just yesterday to her neighbor down the lane.

Taking her worn blouse, faded blue pants, and quilted jacket from the bed where they had been used for extra warmth during the night, she donned them quickly. Then, slipping her feet into two dark-colored cloth shoes buckled on the side, she glanced at herself in the dresser mirror before heading toward the central living area of the house. Brushing aside a long rectangular piece of plain cloth hanging from the doorframe, she stepped into the larger room and from there to the yard beyond. At the far end of the house, near the courtyard gate, she reentered the building through a kitchen door, turned on a small overhead light, and began preparing the morning meal.

First she removed bits of kindling and wood from a nearby box, placed them upright in a small brick-lined stove, and fired the stack with a match. Then, placing a soot-smudged iron pot on the metal grill above the fire, the woman poured several cups of water from a nearby bucket into the darkened container. In the background, through the thin kitchen wall, she heard the voice of her elder daughter calling other family members to rise. Standing quietly, waiting for the water to warm, she slowly combed her short graying hair. As the liquid reached the boiling point, Mother Wang took some recently ground corn meal from a metal container and added it and a few pickled vegetables to the pot, creating a corn-meal porridge. This, together with some steamed bread, would serve as the morning meal.

Hearing a noise outside the kitchen window, the woman watched as second son Hubao and his sister Huzeng headed across the courtyard to the family chicken pen. After vigorously brushing their teeth, the two young people dispensed the remaining saliva and paste over a low wooden fence to the waiting creatures below. The ritual was soon repeated by eldest son Hulan and his wife Chao Liling, and finally by sleepy-eyed Lao Wang.

Within minutes, the five family members had entered the kitchen. Saying little, they scooped porridge from the pot into bowls, squatted down on small stools in a rough circle, and proceeded to slurp down their breakfast in acceptable Chinese fashion. On finishing, the sons and daughters excused themselves in order to complete various chores before departing for work. Only Old Wang, now wide awake, hung back, helping his wife clean up. Once finished, he too went outside and chatted briefly with first son Hulan. Then, after climbing on his ancient bicycle, he headed through the courtyard gate toward the nearby district administrative headquarters, where he worked as a janitor.

At the opposite end of the house from the kitchen, I too had heard the morning call of the rooster, but unlike Mother Wang, chose not to get up until most of the household members had gone off to work. After washing, I heard a familiar voice calling my name through the door. Looking out the window, I recognized Zhou Xing talking with Mother Wang by the pigsty. She was pointing a hand in the direction of my room.

"Xiao Zhou, I'm here," I called, slipping on a jacket and stepping out into the yard outside.

Zhou, a friend from the Beijing Foreign Language Institute with a good comprehension of English, had first helped in translating and interviewing during the early autumn. Now, several months later, he had again offered to help me finish up the household survey. He was quite intrigued by what he called my *shehui diaocha* or "social investigation." For my part, his continuing help was most appreciated. Today, I had some special information for him.

"Zhou, there is going to be an important meeting of all field workers this afternoon following work. It was announced over the loudspeaker last night by Jiang Lijiang, the Party secretary. What do you think it's about?"

Frowning slightly, Zhou shook his head once, conveying the information that we might have to wait until late afternoon to determine the agenda. During the extremely busy fall harvest season there had been little time to hold such a gathering. Only now that the fall vegetable and rice crops were in and the winter wheat planted could such a meeting be called—most likely to report on the success of the overall production and how the results of the various work teams compared with the village quotas established in the spring in consultation with commune and municipal leaders.

As Mother Wang walked over to where we were standing, he asked her the question on both our minds.

"Do you have any idea why a meeting is being held this afternoon?"

"Jiang Lijiang is calling it?" responded Wang, the voice inflection allowing the remark to be interpreted as either a question or a statement of fact.

"Yes," said Zhou.

"Perhaps he will tell the people to work harder and maybe report on the results of the fall harvest."

"Are you going?" I asked.

Her response was noncommittal. However, she did forewarn us that if we planned to go, we should be prepared for the meeting to start late.

Actually, I was rather curious to know whether Mother Wang planned to be there. She had recently retired at age fifty from working in the fields. Now she was much involved in the forthcoming birth of her first grandchild to the wife of her eldest son, Hulan. As a retired field worker, she was no longer expected to attend such occasions, although she could do so if she wished. I thought she might go if for no other reason than to keep up with the local news.

The forthcoming gathering could offer a more unusual opportunity as well. It

Removing kernels of corn by hand in a family courtyard.

had to do with Jiang Lijiang, the Party secretary of Half Moon Brigade.[1] Although a lifelong resident of the area, he was quite new to the position, having been recently appointed to it by the district Party committee, the supervisory unit responsibile for Half Moon and fourteen other adjacent villages. So the meeting would likely offer some insight into Jiang's leadership abilities.

From the point of view of the Wang family, there was added interest in the fact that Jiang belonged to a different lineage than the previous Party leader—one without any links at all to the many Wang relatives in the village. In old China, whatever security peasants could command was intimately connected to their placement within a given lineage or clan. When someone was in need of assistance, other clan members were expected to help in whatever way they could.

Today, the expanded cooperative economic relations linking villagers together provide the basis for a shift in the locus of economic security from the extended family and clan to the collective. However, the extent to which this shift actually occurs is mediated by many complex factors, not the least of which is the way the leaders relate to the people they serve. Such relations include the possibility of continuing the age-old custom of giving preferential treatment to their own relatives.

Since significant leadership at any level is closely linked to membership in the powerful Chinese Communist Party, the problem of using one's own position for unfair privilege is a constant issue for both the Party and the people. Mother Wang knew that, and so did the village leader Jiang. I too had become increasingly interested in the issue, since it appeared to be a serious point of conflict in the village. Perhaps the appointment of Jiang to the local Party leadership represented an effort by the district leaders to weaken an old lineage power base. I hoped that the late-afternoon meeting would shed some light on the problem. At least I would find out shortly.

THE NEW BRIGADE LEADER

On the other side of the village plaza, near the main road, someone else was also thinking of the afternoon meeting. Jiang Lijiang, newly installed Party secretary of Half Moon Village, was a big-boned man in his mid-thirties. Tall, well-proportioned, and bearing a decidedly large, broad face, he easily stood out in any small group. "Big Face" was his nickname since early childhood. Neither positive nor negative associations were conjured up by its use, but everyone in the village knew the man to whom the name referred.

Jiang's day had begun even earlier than usual, since he had been awakened early in the morning by the insistent knocking of Du Yulin, an elderly peasant woman

---

[1] Half Moon is a natural village with a distinct history. It is also a "brigade," i.e., an administrative unit responsible for coordinating agricultural and sideline production and managing local educational and social service agencies, such as primary schools and day-care nurseries. The next highest administrative unit is the district, one of ten within Red Flag Commune.

who wanted his help in finding her chickens, which had "escaped" from an un-bolted courtyard gate during the night. After downing an all-too-quick breakfast of rice porridge mixed with strips of salted turnip and not-so-fresh steamed bread, he assisted Old Du in getting back her hens.

Then, at eight o'clock, he headed over to the brigade clinic just off the plaza to meet with the three paraprofessional clinic workers—"barefoot doctors"—and two of the Women's Federation members concerning how best to implement locally the nationwide family-planning program that had recently been put into effect— new incentives for limiting family births to one child and new financial penalties for having more than two. After that long discussion, Jiang hiked over to the edge of the village to see how much manure had been spread on the brigade fields. Not satisfied with the result, he urged the team leader to have his men work harder. Then, returning to the village, he dropped in on the day-care nursery, the director of which had been out ill for a week. The two older women "grannies" taking over responsibility for the sick director wanted some additional help. He told them he thought he could find someone and would let them know soon.

Now, standing by his doorway, Jiang looked at his watch and swore softly. Then, scattering chickens in his wake, he strode out his courtyard gate, turned left on the gravel roadway, and with great strides headed toward the brigade office 50 yards away. He knew he was slightly late for an appointment with Ma Haimen, the vice brigade leader in charge of grain production. They had agreed earlier to go over the agenda for the afternoon meeting. Approaching the office, he saw a group of dark-jacketed women leaving the fields and heading toward the village— a reminder that it was already lunchtime.

Cui Huifang, the team leader, nodded to him briefly as she passed. Cui was among the very best of the village field workers, skilled in her knowledge of plants, soil, and people. Such attributes had insured her election as leader of the older women's agricultural work team for as many years as anyone could remember. Jiang knew he could count on her urging her teammates to arrive promptly for the 4:30 meeting—not that such effort would have much impact, however. Why was it, he reflected, that people never come to meetings on time. If they had to go to as many meetings as he did, maybe they would change. But he wouldn't wish that hardship on anyone. Of course, there was one obvious answer: they didn't want to attend. But he chose not to dwell on that possibility.

He soon reached the brigade office. Located at the northeast corner of the village, next to the bath house, the simple 10-by-12-foot room gave little indication of being an important communication link between the village and the outside world—or, at least, not until the incessant ringing of the phone reminded one that this was the only telephone for the whole community. Jiang's eye immediately focused on a piece of scrap paper attached to a nail on the door. Penned in rough characters was a note from Ma Haimen saying that he couldn't wait; if needed, he could be found at the grain-storage shed.

Crumpling the paper in his large hand, he unlocked the door and went in. Before him stood two familiar old desks held up by crooked legs, two benches, and one *kang*, the top covered by a tattered green sheet. Leaning over his desk, he took a deep breath, puffed up his lips, and let out a blast of air, sending dust

A village leader on his way to the brigade office.

from the table to the floor beyond. This daily ritual stemmed from the high accumulation of powdery earth that regularly blows across China's Northern Plain.

Pulling up the old bench, he then sat down and stared at the phone in front of him. It was black and very ancient. There was no dial or cranking mechanism, so all one could do was pick up the receiver and wait for the operator. If there was no response—an all-too-common occurrence—the caller could at least flick the receiver lever up and down a couple of times, thereby expressing his or her frustration. When the operator, based at the district headquarters three miles away, came back from having tea, or whatever, she would politely inquire as to the nature of the call. This time, however, she responded immediately.

"*Yao nar?*" Where are you calling?

"Uh. This is Jiang Lijiang at Half Moon Village. We're low on diesel fuel. Will you tell the district supplier to bring over a full barrel? We need it by 2:00 this afternoon, if possible."

"Secretary Jiang. I can't hear you."

This time, Jiang shouted his message into the phone.

"You got that?"

"Yes."

"Now. Get me the commune headquarters?"

"I'm sorry. I can't. Something's wrong with the line. I'll let you know when it's back in service."

"Very well."

Hanging up the receiver, Jiang opened the desk drawer and took out a sheaf of papers held together by a black clip. These reports from the leaders of different production units indicating their success in meeting the appropriate quotas were, for the most part, quite encouraging. Even given the wet fall, the various teams had all surpassed their agreed-upon goals. Given the minimal increase in production costs, it meant more income for the brigade members and more money for the village accumulation and welfare funds. In his meeting this afternoon, he would wait until the end of his talk to report on this favorable outcome. That way, he could more easily hold the people's attention. Everyone was anxious to learn whether they would receive more or less income than last year, when the harvest had been particularly good.

The immediate issue, however, was that of moving large piles of manure from the brigade pig farm to the fields. The work was going much too slowly; team leaders reported that many peasants were coming to work late and going home early. Jiang knew why they were spending less time in the fields. In every peasant household, courtyard gardens were fast being replaced by large five-foot-deep earthen cellars, hollowed out of the ground by family members actively preparing for winter. Their purpose was to store brigade-grown cabbages recently distributed to all villagers as part of their collective "in kind" income.

This activity too had to be finished before the winter freeze settled in. But, thought Jiang, if the same freeze turned the pig manure into the consistency of hard rock, the spring crops would be seriously damaged. Which should come first—the storing of household cabbages or the protection of the brigade-owned crops? As far as he was concerned, the brigade responsibility came first, especially during work hours. He would have to speak sharply about it at the afternoon meeting. Those villagers who refused take the work seriously now should receive fewer work points when decisions on such matters were made later in the month.

Such reflections were cut short by someone opening the door and walking in. It was caretaker Wang. An older man in his sixties, Wang Baoshun had been permanently assigned responsibility for the brigade office some time ago. Like workers in the fields and sideline industries, Wang received eight work points a day from the brigade for his job in the office, points that twice a year were added up and then translated into his share of the collective brigade income. On many days, he also took care of his grandson while his daughter worked in the fields. But mostly he sorted out and delivered papers and mail, watched over the public bath house next door, answered the phone, and delivered messages—especially delivered messages. Much of his day was often spent tracking down one of the brigade leaders, a clinic "barefoot doctor," school teacher, or other village cadre with one communication or another.

Jiang, looking up from the desk, spoke first.

"Lao Wang, I'm going home for a quick bite to eat and a little work around the house. If Ma Haimen shows up, tell him all the brigade leaders are to come here at 4:00. Then we can go to the meeting together. I'm also expecting some diesel oil around 2:00. Zhang Yanzi may need it before plowing the southwest field."

"All right. I'll be here all afternoon. If I see Ma, I'll tell him."

As Jiang went out the door, he turned to caretaker Wang and added, "Is it true that the women's bath-house key is lost again?"

Wang, appearing not to hear Jiang's question, stared intently at a crack in the floor.

"Well, they will want the key to the men's shower room. But you remind them about the meeting right after work. If they start showering after the men are finished, we'll never begin the meeting. So tell them to bathe later."

Wang acknowledged the instruction with a brief nod, knowing full well that if the women wanted a bath after coming in from the field, they were going to get it. Nor would he refuse them access to the men's shower room—especially since he had again misplaced the key to the women's side of the bath house.

A little later, after cleaning up the room, Wang Baoshun heard the sound of a diesel engine. Stepping out the door, he looked down the main roadway. Far away, a large red tractor appeared, moving slowly toward the turnoff to Half Moon.

Zhang Yanzi, a sturdy woman in her late twenties, hunched her shoulder forward and, after reaching for a firm grip on the steering wheel, pulled sharply to the right, sending the tractor in the direction of the village. Zhang was proud of being a tractor driver, and for good reason—her skills in driving and mechanical repair were known throughout the whole district.

She was one of millions of urban educated youth who had left the city for the much harder life of the countryside. Serving first as an agricultural worker on a state farm, she was soon offered a job teaching primary school. Aware of the serious difficulties teachers and other intellectuals had encountered in 1966, the first year of the Cultural Revolution, including the bad treatment her educated father had received, Zhang did not want the assignment, but she had to accept it for a while. Only after many requests for transfer was she finally relocated to a production unit, first feeding pigs, then serving as a cook, and finally being trained as a tractor driver. In the mid-1970s, her health deteriorated, causing her to return to the Beijing area. She was then posted to this suburban village. Given the easing of government restrictions, enabling many Beijing youth to return to the city, Zhang could probably go back too if she applied. But she enjoyed being a tractor driver, and so decided to remain.

Arriving at the brigade office, she switched off the diesel engine, stepped down from the tractor, and seeing caretaker Wang in the doorway, waved hello.

Wang Baoshun spoke first.

"Secretary Jiang left just a little while ago. He said you might need some fuel before going down to the southwest field. Only it hasn't arrived."

Zhang responded, "I've got enough for this afternoon, so don't worry."

"I'll tell Jiang. By the way, if you haven't heard, there's a village meeting at 4:30 this afternoon after work. Most field workers will be there."

"O.K."

Wang watched as the newly painted diesel tractor again sprang to life and moved toward the southwest corner of the village. Being a tractor driver is an important job, thought Wang. He remembered a recent discussion with the district purchasing agent, who said that in some parts of China, tractor operators wouldn't drive unless they were given a good-tasting, high-quality cigarette. And if they were contracted out to drive for another brigade or commune, they expected a delicious meal in payment. Without it, commented the agent, they would only plow the middle of the fields and leave the edges untouched. Caretaker Wang knew that was not a common practice in the Beijing area, and he hoped it wasn't elsewhere either.

A CRITICISM OFFERED

Around 4:30 in the afternoon I walked over to the village plaza and waited for Zhou Xing. Jiang Lijiang was already there, as were the other village leaders, having just concluded a brief meeting in the brigade office down the road. Except for a few children playing cards on the corner, no other villagers were in sight, a fact that reminded me of Mother Wang's morning comment about meetings like these always being late.

I waited on one side of the plaza and Jiang and the others stood opposite me, looking down the roadway. After a while, Zhou arrived, followed by several peasants carrying small wooden stools. Chatting, we watched as the plaza slowly filled with men and women. Some stood talking together in small groups of three or four. Others came and stood along a plaza wall that offered some protection from the chill of a late afternoon wind. Once satisfied that all had arrived, Jiang Lijiang went over to a door of a large rectangular building, pushed it open, and stepped inside.

Soon the room was fully occupied with peasant villagers. When it looked like the meeting was about to begin, Zhou and I also stepped inside and looked around. The structure was completely barren, from packed earth floor to unpainted walls and ceiling. At one end, a boarded-up interior window frame with a metal hasp and lock gave little indication of protecting the village television set enclosed in the closet behind. On warm summer evenings, as many as two hundred or more local residents would be found outside the building lined up eight to ten feet deep, watching the latest offerings from Beijing and elsewhere through another window facing the main road. Now, in winter, few individuals were sufficiently interested in the evening fare to brave the chilled air. However, as a community building, it was an obvious meeting place for events such as this.

Big Face Jiang watched carefully as we came in and sat down, our backs resting against the cold adobe wall. He observed me even more closely when I brought out a small portable tape recorder, propped it upright on the earthen floor, and pushed the appropriate switch. I offered in response my most disarming smile. Other villagers either nodded in recognition or disregarded us completely. There were quite a few children in the room. Some stayed close to a parent, while others ran around with little or no supervision. What struck me particularly was the spatial division by sex: men at one end of the room, women and children at the other. Clearing his throat, Jiang Lijiang began.

"I announced on the loudspeaker that we would get together at 4:30, but as you came here later, we have had to start after 5:00. Now, we should pay attention to this and not be late the next time.

"The main purpose of today's meeting is to ask you to make good use of your time. Don't waste time in production work. This afternoon all the brigade leaders

An old man and a boy at a village plaza.

came to my office and talked. We discussed the situation over the past few months and at present. All the leaders said we have a big problem. Too many people are going out to work late and coming back early. That won't do. It won't do any good for all of you."

At that point a child burst out crying, and most of the peasants in the room began to laugh. Turning toward a woman who appeared to be the child's mother, Jiang Lijiang spoke sternly.

"Don't let the child cry. If it cries, take it outside."

I watched as the woman drew the crying child to her.

Jiang continued.

"This sort of thing happens every year. It's because we don't have a lot of work to do in the fields and because it's cold outside. On the one hand, the leaders don't pay enough attention to the situation. They are just interested in keeping track of their accounts and similar problems. This is a natural tendency. On the other hand, you brigade members don't pay attention to your work either. You come out late and go back early. Today, at our brigade leader's meeting, we all agreed that something must be done. If the situation goes on like this, it will be bad for you."

A few peasants listened carefully, while others appeared largely uninterested, watching children play or whispering among themselves.

"Tomorrow, the weather is expected to be good, quite warm. Not as cold as today. So we must seize this good opportunity to finish all kinds of work. Don't let this chance get away."

Across the room, two young men began talking quietly. Jiang stopped his remarks and stared at them. Not realizing they were the object of his attention, they went right on with their conversation. Angrily, Jiang responded.

"If you two want to talk, go ahead. I have no objection. You talk to the other brigade members."

The two men, realizing that they were the focus of Jiang's remarks, stopped speaking and turned attentively toward him.

"We should finish our work now in warm weather so when it becomes cold we can have some holidays, have some meetings, or something like that. If you don't work now you will have to do it later when it's much colder, and that's not good. We have 200 piles of manure, and we have to plant some vegetables. First, we have to get the manure to the fields. We also have to put rice stalks in the pig sties along with ashes and dirt to make more fertilizer. This is also the advice from the district."

By this time, several other of the younger men were talking among themselves. A few children had also begun to run around the room. Jiang became frustrated.

"What is wrong with you?" he demanded, turning toward the men.

"Don't you realize what you are doing is against what I am saying?"

The young men stopped talking.

"Some people think there isn't much to do and therefore don't work hard. But this won't do. Others may have heard that the total income of our brigade has decreased from last year and are therefore in low spirits. You think you work hard all year but achieve less than before. Still others of you want to go out to make some money on your own and because you can't you are upset. Therefore, you slow down, get mixed up, or do nothing. But that won't help. Remember, the state won't give us money to support ourselves. It depends on us. We can't count on state support or a state loan. Most people work hard. Only a few are lazy. But the effect is quite strong. It undermines the people's spirit.

"Do not think we cadres are unaware of what you are doing, even though we can't go to the fields and work with you. Of course, it is not good to criticize you in this room by name, but we know those who work hard and those who do not. In a few weeks we are going to evaluate your work points, and at that time you will realize the consequences. That's why we think it's important to have a meeting here and tell you beforehand—so you will repent by the time we evaluate the work points. And remember, if you come out to the fields late you will waste a steambread."

Jiang's effort at introducing a little humor largely went unheeded, although a few smiles greeted his remark. Zhou whispered in my ear that most peasants like to eat three steambreads before going to work in the fields, although they only need two if they are not working. So, if they eat three and go out late, they are wasting one.

Jiang went on.

"We must complete our work before the cold sets in. If the manure becomes frozen it will be hard to spread. In this way we waste our labor. Two years ago we had 270 field workers. Last year it dropped to 240. This year there are only 190 people working in the fields. This is because some of us have become contract workers, working in the chemical plant and elsewhere. Remember, the profit you make is less than those who are employed under contract in the factories. So they are making more money for you and you have to work harder also.[2]

"On the whole, the total income this year is very good. Today, we checked both income and expenses. We found that, overall, we will perhaps reach 240,000 dollars [1 Chinese dollar or *yuan* is equivalent to .65 American cents] for the whole brigade. The total expense is 130,000 dollars, so we will still have 110,000 left. This is our net profit. This income is even a little better than last year. So don't think our overall income has decreased.[3] Don't be in low spirits. Our living standard is slowly improving. Remember, it is the economic base that determines the superstructure. This is the same in the family. If the family is rich or has no economic problems, then the family members will be in high spirits. If you have money, your life will be easy. So if you work hard in the fields, it will be good for you. But if you come out late, the team leader should see to it that your work points are cut. Even if the team leader doesn't do that, many brigade members will criticize you. That is all I want to say. Are there any announcements?"

Vice brigade leader Ma Haimen spoke first.

"This year each person will have 135 *jin* [one *jin* equals 1.1 lb] of rice, so

---

[2] Contract workers are temporarily employed outside the village by the commune or the state, usually in construction or factory jobs. Though receiving a higher income, the excess is allocated to the brigade accumulation fund rather than the individual.

[3] Although the total income was higher than that in 1978, a more detailed study of brigade income suggests that net income was slightly less (see Chapter 3).

please get your sacks ready. The brigade will bring the grain to your family so you won't have to come to the threshing ground to get it."

Another young man stood up.

"All Communist Youth League members meet at the nursery at 7:00 this evening."

By this time, most peasants were pouring through the doorway into the rapidly darkening evening. A few carried their young children. Others walked together with stools under their arms. As Zhou and I got up to leave, no one paid us any attention. All appeared anxious to get home and begin the evening meal.

Following dinner, Zhou and I went to my room to transcribe the tape into the field notes. After a while, I realized that Mother Wang in the adjoining room was listening intently to the tape. I was curious as to why she appeared so interested. I invited her into the room, but she declined. She did offer one comment, however, following the portion of the tape where Party secretary Jiang warned those field workers who had been coming to work late and going home early: "In a few weeks we are going to evaluate your work points, and at that time you will realize the consequences. . . ."

Mother Wang spoke out sharply. "Who does he mean by 'we'? All the peasants in the brigade evaluate. Then the leaders check it."

"Could a leader change an evaluation without talking with the peasants about it?" I queried.

"No. They have to ask the opinion of the brigade members."

"What if all leaders agree?"

"One leader can't change an evaluation. But if they all agree, then they don't have to discuss it any more."

"How do the villagers feel about that?" I then asked.

Looking at me briefly, she then turned away and headed toward the door. Just before going outside, she paused, turned again, and said quietly:

"*Zhong kou nan tiao. Na neng renren chengxin.*" People have different opinions. Some are satisfied and some are not.

At that moment, I didn't feel it appropriate to inquire further. It was clear how she felt. After she left, Zhou Xing and I turned back to the transcription, finishing about an hour later. Thanking Zhou and saying goodnight, I took a brief stroll through the now silent village. It was quite cold, and the winds were picking up. Quite possibly the 200 manure piles would freeze overnight. But if others were concerned, I would never know—except perhaps Jiang Lijiang. Looking down the main roadway, I saw the soft light of the brigade office shining through the window. Inside, Jiang was sitting at his desk, writing. Slowly, I turned away and headed back toward the warmth of my own room.

2/Half Moon Village

THE SETTING

China's capital city of Beijing has myriad government offices, tall apartment buildings, paved streets, crowded buses, historical sites, lovely parks, and almost six million residents—all of which are far removed in sight, sound, and smell from the quieter, slower-paced, agriculturally based community of Half Moon. Situated on the city's outskirts, the village is located over 25 miles from the urban center—almost two hours by bicycle, a common form of transportation to and from the city. Although contained within the municipal boundary, the community is surprisingly rural in character, as are most other villages that comprise Red Flag and other nearby communes. It is also fairly small, with a total population of 543.[1]

In summer and early fall, bright rays of the morning sun warm the ten-foot-high courtyard walls that define both the outer perimeter of the village proper and the family residences within. In winter, these same walls deflect the occasional snow and more frequent wind that sweep across China's Northern Plain. Winter mornings bring another feature unique to that season—a soft blanket of smoky haze from one hundred cooking fires that hangs over the village until dissipated by the thermal-producing heat of a bright sun or a light gust of wind. With arrival of spring in April and May, courtyards are bathed in profusions of white lilac blossoms and the pale red flowering plum. Nearby, looking almost like a huge abstract painting, criss-crossed mosaics of sparkling green edged in brown define the village's irrigation ditches, freshly lined with new grass. Each square marks one border of the six collectively owned fields.

Several features distinguish Half Moon's rural character. Most obvious are the flat agricultural fields bounding the living area. Depending on the season of the year, these fields produce rice, wheat, and corn as well as many varieties of vegetables. Rice is the major crop, closely followed by wheat and vegetables. A little over 50 percent of the village holdings of 800 *mu* (1 *mu* = $\frac{1}{6}$th acre) are used to grow rice, which produces an average yield of 1000 *jin* per *mu*.

For many years, the poor quality of the soil seriously limited the peasants' ability to produce adequate crops. Situated on an alluvial plain near a meandering river, the land is low-lying, with a high water table and a high alkaline content. As such, until

[1] Beijing Municipality comprises nine districts and nine counties. Four districts are urban, four are "near urban" (*jin jiaogu*), and one is a special mining area. Red Flag Commune is located in a more "remote-suburban" (*yuan jiaogu*) area of Daxing County.

26

Early morning at Half Moon.

commune-wide efforts were made to control the water through better drainage and irrigation, the land suffered from waterlogging and was therefore quite barren and only minimally productive for farming.

The ruralness of the community is also emphasized by the nature of its housing: peasant dwellings of adobe and brick whose joined outer courtyard walls abut the agricultural fields. Within, well-worn dirt lanes define the routes used by residents to visit and carry on their daily village activities. At regular intervals along these roadways, tile-roofed arches shelter swinging doors opening into each family courtyard. Looking inside, one sees small gardens planted with Chinese cabbages, onions, string beans, and other vegetables for winter consumption. Date trees provide fresh delicious fruit. Persimmons too are grown, though less satisfactorily. And always, special fenced-in areas are set aside for raising chickens and fattening pigs.

Stacked piles of twigs next to every courtyard wall serve as kindling for household fires. Once trees were the main source of peasant fuel, but now timber has become a scarce item throughout China's deforested Northern Plain. In Half Moon and similar villages of Red Flag Commune, wood chips and compressed coal have become the common cooking and heating fuel. Those few households that are fortunate enough to have obtained a sizable pile of cut wood or sawdust are likely to have a resident carpenter as well.

Finally, water is a precious commodity. In Half Moon, water is pumped from a well into family courtyards, where a single spigot controls the access. In poorer villages like Little River, a half mile away, the peasants carry water to their homes from a common well. But all use it sparingly. Whatever is left after cooking, washing, and laundering drains into the garden to nourish growing food and flowers. Only in late fall, when the family garden has been transformed into a root cellar for winter storage of vegetables, does the remaining water trickle through a small hole in the bottom of the courtyard wall to the lane outside.

Although visitors are occasionally entertained in family courtyards, more informal socializing occurs in the small plaza located in the village center. Here, dur-

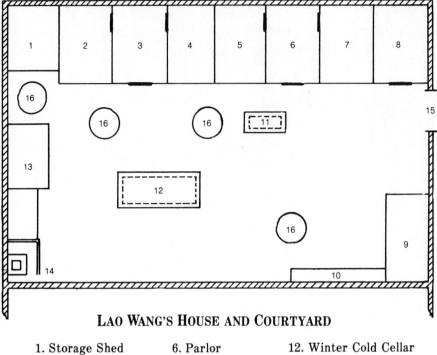

LAO WANG'S HOUSE AND COURTYARD

1. Storage Shed
2. Bedroom
3. Parlor
4. Bedroom
5. Bedroom
6. Parlor
7. Bedroom
8. Kitchen
9. Chicken Pen
10. Woodpile
11. Water Drain
12. Winter Cold Cellar
13. Pig Pen
14. Latrine
15. Roofed Gate
16. Tree

Figure 2. The Wang family house and courtyard.

ing the day, children and youth come to play. In summer evenings after work, as many as 100 villagers of all ages join together and watch the news, opera, and other programs from Beijing on the large black-and-white brigade-owned television set purchased in 1978.

Through this same plaza passes the main gravel road linking Half Moon with nearby villages and with such institutions as the district administrative office, food and general store, elementary and middle school, hospital, and a small jade-carving factory. Bordering both sides of this roadway, tall young trees planted two decades ago during a major reforestation program offer valuable shade from the heat of the summer or protection from the biting cold of a winter wind. A twenty-minute bicycle ride down this road, past numerous other small villages and fields, brings the local traveler to the headquarters of Red Flag People's Commune and the old market town that lies adjacent to it. From there, buses leave regularly for Beijing and the outside world.

At the edge of the village, near the brigade office, stands one very modern-looking structure: the local bath house. Its completion a year ago was quite an event in Half Moon. Not only is it contemporary in design and large in size, providing showers

The author bicycling on the main road between the village and commune headquarters.

for over 20 people at a time in both the men's and women's sections, it is solar heated! Hearing from some factory workers about a passive solar bath house that had been built in Beijing, several village leaders went to the city to learn more about it. Reporting back home, they concluded that with money from the brigade accumulation fund and bricks from an old building, along with some financial and skilled help from the commune, they could construct their own solar bath house. After several years of discussion by the villagers and commune leadership, the brigade received approval and decided to go ahead. Now everyone is quite proud of it— except perhaps when the sun goes behind the clouds for several days at a time.

Although Half Moon may have a rural character, its location near the nation's capital sets it dramatically apart from tens of thousands of communities situated in more isolated areas of North China. For example, its close proximity to Beijing greatly increases its economic potential, particularly in vegetable production. In addition to growing vegetables for city dwellers, an immediate and constant market for the villagers' produce, residents are employed in nonagricultural pursuits as well.

Such employment includes work in sideline industries, small factories and service agencies that comprise a rising secondary layer of the economy characteristic of suburban communes located near cities. Many villages within Red Flag Commune have developed small local enterprises producing consumer goods ranging from light bulbs and parts for electronic switches to machine nuts and rice planters.[2]

[2] However, Half Moon has participated only minimally in this economic endeavor. A comparative analysis of factors influencing the development of sideline industries in Half Moon and two other commune villages is presented in Chapter 8.

One might suppose that the more developed transportation and communication technology associated with urban life has an important impact on the adjacent rural sector. And indeed, it does. But this impact is still far less significant than that found in the industrialized West, where advanced transportation and communication facilities immediately involve city and countryside in an extensive network of social and cultural linkages.

Half Moon, for example, has no direct access to any bus service or other scheduled means of transport. When needing to travel somewhere nearby, a resident will commonly use a bicycle or simply walk. Shortly after my arrival in the village, a peasant commented that unless I could get a bicycle I would have to rely on the number 11 bus. After several days of keeping an eye out for a passing bus, I asked a neighbor when it came to the village.

"The number 11 bus?" he repeated, a big grin spreading across his face. Then, bursting with laughter and slapping his thigh, he pointed toward my legs. "That's the number 11 bus. Your own two feet!"

There is one other form of transportation well recognized throughout rural China: catching a ride on the back of a wagon. In Half Moon and similar more prosperous villages surrounding Beijing, the old horse-drawn wagon is being replaced with large two-wheeled hand-held "walking tractors." Although originally designed for agricultural purposes, these machines can be easily converted into motorized four-wheeled vehicles by attaching a cart or wagon to the frame. Without access to cars, and with very limited availability of trucks and motorcycles, the noisy but adaptable two-cycle mini-tractor serves admirably.

A brigade walking tractor with the solar bath house in the background.

For communicating news to the village, Half Moon relies heavily on its six conveniently placed loudspeakers. Direct contact outside the village is limited to the single telephone located in the brigade office. However, the quality of the line is so poor that its effective range extends only to the commune perimeter. Anyone wishing to place a call to Beijing or elsewhere usually goes to commune headquarters. Actually, peasants oriented around agricultural production have few reasons to either call or visit the city except on rare occasions such as attendance at the funeral of a close relative, a special holiday, or some other similarly important event. So the direct cultural influence of the city on this segment of the village is more limited than one might imagine.

Still, economically speaking, some residents of Half Moon and other nearby communities are not really peasants at all. Some are employed in small industries and factories located close by. Others work in commune and state-owned suburban factories. One man even works at a large auto assembly plant in an urban district of Beijing. Living in a factory dormitory during the week, he returns home to his family on weekends or whenever he has time off from his workplace.

More important, two very modern state-controlled industries also provide jobs for local villagers, including quite a few from Half Moon.[3] One produces chemicals, including fertilizer, and the other processes grain for animal fodder. Since both are partially automated, they offer rural-based workers their first glimpse of a technological future unheard of in their own communities. As employees in these plants, such individuals bring back to their villages important knowledge about advanced production techniques and methods. As they form friendships with city workers, they bring news of urban life ways and culture as well.

One other group has contributed significantly in bringing urban knowledge and experience to Half Moon: the so-called "sent-down educated youth." Beginning in the mid-1950s and dramatically expanding during the Cultural Revolution, the *shangshan xiaxiang* campaign ("Up to the Mountains and Down to the Countryside") assigned millions of young urban middle school students to work in villages and towns throughout rural China. Urged to learn from the peasants the values of frugality, hard work, and self-reliance, these young people were assigned to the fields. Occasionally, when feelings of trust had developed between them and the rural populace, relocated youth were also asked by village leaders to teach primary school, become production team accountants, or serve as "barefoot doctors."

Although this nationwide relocation movement did much to minimize urban unemployment, it presented the government with a great many political problems, not the least of which concerned severe social and psychological disruption on the part of many youth and their families—particularly those who were separated from

---

[3] A household census taken by the author and others in 1979 showed that over one-third of Half Moon Villagers are state employees—a much higher than usual percentage, which helps to account for the village's relative affluence vis-a-vis most commune villages. Red Flag itself is atypical in having state-owned enterprises of both an agricultural and industrial nature within its borders. These include dairy and duck farms providing milk and meat to the city, a tractor repair facility, a machine nut shop, and two modern chemical and grain-processing factories.

family and friends for long periods. However, it was not until the late 1970s, several years after Mao's death, that the new leadership brought the movement to a close.[4]

At Half Moon, except for the few young men and women who married into the community, the one physical reminder of this dramatic social experiment is a vacant brick building located near the far corner of the village. Its construction was initially paid for with state funds, the eight rooms serving as dormitory quarters, lounge, library, and kitchen for twenty or more educated youth from the Beijing area who were regularly assigned to work in the village. Today, an outsider walking past the abandoned structure cannot help but be struck by the almost ghost-town quality of the place. An impressive solid cement pingpong table, unused for years and surrounded by weeds, stands in the center of the courtyard under a large lifeless tree. Locked dormitory doors and torn or broken paper and glass windows add to the forlorn atmosphere of the place.

Curious about such an unused facility in an otherwise lively village, I decided to explore the area more fully. Late one fall afternoon, after walking around the courtyard, I looked in the window of what was once a library. On the other side of the glass I saw row upon row of paperback books resting on four homebuilt bookcases. Close by were two well-made straight-backed chairs, one lying on its side and the other standing next to a dusty wooden table. On the wall were tacked several bright-colored pictures of highly motivated-looking youth in various work settings, obviously taken from a popular magazine of the day. And next to one of the pictures, written in bold letters with a dark thick-lead pencil on the faded plaster, was a long poem. From my angle of view outside the window, it was almost impossible to read. Still, I took out pen and paper and began writing down some of the words. Then, hearing a sound behind me, I turned around to face a handsome man in his mid-thirties, standing in the middle of the roadway forty feet away.

Frowning and looking firm, he said nothing. But with a series of brusque movements of his arm he made it clear that I was not wanted there. I quickly moved away from the building and the strange man, who was unknown to me. Neither of us spoke. For my part, I was still very caught up with what I had seen on the wall. Unable to clearly read the poem due to the angle of the window and the locked door, I could only barely determine its general content. As best I could tell, it was a pessimistic commentary on the future of Chinese youth. But what fascinated me the most was the language in which it was written: English!

In summary, any outsider looking at Half Moon and other villages of Red Flag Commune can easily see that they have advantages not characteristic of communities located in more remote settings of northern China.[5] Economically, the opportunity to produce vegetables for the urban market offers a steady source of income. Electrification, introduced in the 1950s, brings important benefits to local agriculture, in-

---

[4] Seven thousand came to Red Flag Commune alone, most to work in the state sector. Others served in large state-owned farms, particularly in China's isolated border areas. A brief life history of one such educated youth is described in Chapter 5.

[5] Of Red Flag's many villages, Half Moon is particularly clean, attractive, and affluent. This is without doubt the major reason why it was chosen by the commune leadership as the research site. However, in Chapter 8, a comparative study of several different villages will show that Half Moon is not the most affluent.

dustries, and homes. Improved means of transportation continuing to expand out from center city now enable a few villagers to work in and around Beijing, returning on weekends. In the not-too-distant future, daily commuting will become feasible, with all the economic and cultural benefits and problems that it entails.

Half Moon also has two distinct qualities that set it off from surrounding communities. One is the newness of its buildings, the large majority of which have been constructed within the past two decades. Equally eye-catching is the way in which the village is laid out—to resemble a half moon. Why the recent construction and unique shape? The reason is interesting.

LOCAL HISTORY

In the early twentieth century, the place that became Half Moon was part of the Emperor's private hunting grounds. To keep the game in and unwanted people out, the land was protected by large adobe walls. Access was by means of one of four large red gates located to the east, west, north, and south. Following the collapse of the imperial dynasty in 1911, a few government officials and private entrepreneurs sought and eventually obtained control over the area. At the same time, squatters from famine-stricken regions of Hebei and other nearby provinces began moving in.

Carrying their few possessions on baskets strung between shoulder poles, these landless peasants and beggars came to build small mud houses and make arrangements with the newly installed but largely absentee land owners to raise grain, cotton, and other crops. Additional work opportunities included the extraction of saltpeter from the alkaline soil in spring for the making of gunpowder. In winter, most peasants moved outside the old walls, since there was nothing available to live on at that season of the year and the earlier harvest was too small to tide them over. Hardships also came in the form of bandits who continually preyed on the vast countryside of North China. Beholden to landlords for their livelihood, continually threatened by the ragtag bands of robbers that surrounded them, and attempting to eke out an existence from the unforgiving soil, these poor peasants became the pool from which Half Moon Village was eventually formed.

It should be noted that under these circumstances, the more common type of rural Chinese residence pattern, which utilized extended clan networks within and between villages, was difficult if not impossible to establish. The new settlers came from different provinces, some having no relatives at all and others very few. The tendency was for individuals and small nuclear or at most three-generational families from a given area to join together as best they could, often without more extended kin. During the war with Japan, a more structured and integrated form of village organization (*baojia*) was encouraged by the military occupation forces in order to exert civil control more effectively. Nevertheless, most of the low mud houses remained scattered across the landscape, thus limiting any efforts to instill greater social cohesion. Intervillage clan ties were correspondingly weak or nonexistent.

The area was declared liberated in 1948, after the fall of Japan and somewhat before the complete victory of the communist forces over Chiang Kai-shek's

Kuomintang government. Soon the peasants, with the help of several young Party members assigned to the area, organized a new village government. The next ten years brought significant economic and social changes, beginning with the implementation of land reform and concluding with the emergence of Red Flag Commune in 1958.

The stated purpose of land reform was first to break the back of the traditional elite by redistributing the land more equitably—though not equally—among the large number of peasants who had little or none, and through this initial change in the social relations of production to encourage greater cooperation that could substantially increase agricultural productivity. Underlying this goal was a second: by actively participating in the redistribution process whereby landlord holdings (and to a lesser extent those of rich peasants) were divided among the poorer peasantry, the latter could gain an understanding of themselves as a force for change. This effort to create a new class consciousness through active struggle against the powerful landlords, and the social and economic responsibilities that emerged from it, came to be known as *fanshen*, or literally, the process of "turning the body over."[6]

Wanting to know more precisely how this process was implemented in Half Moon, I asked several villagers early in my stay who could give me that information. Their response was almost universal. "You want to know about the old days? Go see Old Li. He's retired and has plenty of time. But watch out, he'll talk your head off." And they were right.

After meeting Li Haiping several times, I knew more than I needed about his early childhood in Hebei Province and what he had done after moving to Half Moon in the early 1940s. He first worked as a laborer for an absentee landowner; then he found a job with the Japanese—"under duress," he assured me—and finally became active in the peasant movement. By 1950, he was a leader of the local Peasant Association and shortly thereafter joined the Party. Now retired due to a heart problem, he continued to assume small duties around the village. I often saw him running errands or shopping for someone at the district food store.

One afternoon, we talked specifically about the land reform movement in the village. It was obvious Old Li was looking forward to sharing his story by the lively way in which he greeted me. Others said he knew it well, having talked before middle school students as part of a general series on the political history of the commune. We were joined by Yu Futian, a friend of Li Haiping who had lived in the area even longer. Sitting under a small shade tree along the roadside near the edge of the village, Li began by pointing to the fields and waving his arm in a half circle. I immediately turned on my small tape recorder.

"This whole area was liberated in 1948, and land reform began a year later. Before that I worked at almost every kind of job—like making gunpowder and growing wheat as a farm hand. I even rented some land once, one dozen *mu* from a small landlord. At that time life was very hard."

---

[6] A detailed ethnographic portrayal of how this process was carried out in the North China village of Long Bow is contained in a book by William Hinton (1966). A follow-up study by the same author (1983) is also well worth pursuing.

An old village leader.

"How did land reform begin?" I inquired, hoping to focus the questioning on several key points.

"First we had to decide who to include and who to work with. There were no Party members in our village, so we asked two nearby cadres to come over and help. They suggested that we get the peasants together and have a big meeting and they would come too. At that meeting, they told us the Party's basic policy for land reform was 'to rely on the poor peasants, unite with the middle peasants, isolate the rich peasants, and overthrow the landlords and wipe out feudalism.' Well, it took us some time to figure out what they meant by that statement. It wasn't until much later that we really began to understand."

"When it came to actually dividing the land, how was it done?"

"At that time, about 90 percent was under control of middle or rich peasants and landlords. When it was finally divided, the poor peasants received their share according to the number of persons in the family and the quality of the soil. If there were four or five persons in a family they got about 20 *mu*. But it could have been more or less according to the quality."

"And the landlords?" As I asked the question, Yu Futian took a worn leather pouch out of his pocket, opened it, and shook some tobacco into the bowl of his long-stemmed pipe. After watching Yu light it, Li continued.

"The landlords were given a share of the land according to their family size, just like the others. Their houses, animals, and tools were divided up among all the people, and they were given their share too. But with the rich peasants, we did not take all their lands. We only took the part that they had rented out to others. We let them keep the land they worked themselves. For the next few years, all the families did their own individual farming. Of course, some made out better than others. But by 1952, several had become bankrupt, due partly to poor management of their land. They even received a little state aid, but it didn't help enough."

"How did you distinguish between well-to-do, middle, and poor? There must have been a lot of disagreements among the peasants?"

"It was easy to determine who the landlords were. They didn't work the land at all. Rich peasants did some work in the fields, but they made more of their income renting land to others. In this area, if a family got 30 percent of its income from the work of others, it was defined as a rich peasant family. In some other places not far from here, it was 25 percent. As for the middle peasants, they worked in the fields, but not for landlords. Only the poor worked for them. Most poor peasants rented land, and a few owned a small amount. And, of course, the tenant peasants were the worst off—they owned nothing."

"What about the mutual aid teams?" I asked. "Were they very helpful?"

I knew that following land redistribution, voluntary cooperative work groups were formed, which pooled labor in a manner not dissimilar from earlier forms of cooperation common in the past. However, newly distributed land and peasant tools remained under the ownership of individual households.

"Yes, although there was opposition from the landlords and rich peasants, naturally, and also from some of the middle peasants. They had a better situation—more land and more tools and animals. For that reason, they had no interest in joining the rest of us. But they did spread rumors that the KMT government would return and take the land back. They also kept their old deeds carefully hidden in jars underground, hoping they would become usable again sometime in the future. And later, when we built several irrigation ditches, one household head tried to sabotage us by not allowing a right-of-way access through his land."

"What did you do?"

"We built them anyway. By this time the mutual aid teams had become pretty successful. That is, production increased. Even some of the poor peasants who at first were afraid to join began to participate. Also, there was a lot of talk in the area about starting a cooperative farm. Not too far from here, near East Gate Village, 60 households organized themselves into such a farm. It became quite well known. Yu Futian knows all about that."

Yu had been listening attentively, though somewhat restlessly. I could see that

Li Haiping was not the only one who liked to talk about the early days of the cooperatives. I turned and watched as he relit his pipe. As he began talking, I again turned on my recorder.

"I am uneducated. I've never been to school. I first came here with my parents when I was six. I've been here now for sixty years. When I was eleven I began working for a landlord and received food in return. Nothing else. Later, I was a tenant farmer. During land reform, I lived a little north of here, in a village that had less land than most places. We received just three *mu* of land per peasant. We grew crops, but the harvest was not good. Only those who had better land could get a yield of 100 *jin* or more per *mu*. The rest of us got around eighty.

"Then, in 1954, we organized our first agricultural cooperative. That's when things really began to improve. Harvests increased, and our living standard went up. In the following year, every member of the cooperative received 100 *jin* per *mu* of corn and wheat. Ten percent was wheat and the rest corn. With poor land and no irrigation, we couldn't improve much more. Still, just about everybody supported the cooperative."

"How many?"

"Around 80 percent. Some were excluded, like landlords. Others simply didn't want to get involved. But most did."

Old Li had told me earlier how his village had moved from the mutual aid teams to the elementary APCs. It apparently began with 15 families volunteering to form a work team. Ownership of land remained in the household, but payment for work completed was calculated on a dual basis: combining the size of land holding contributed and animals donated with the amount of labor performed.

Then, in 1956, several lower-level cooperatives in the area were consolidated into a larger one. This advanced cooperative was organized into "production teams" of about 20 households each, and then further subdivided into work groups of five to ten households. But what made the higher-level cooperative qualitatively different from the earlier ones was that the contribution of land, animals, and tools no longer influenced the income received. Rather, income was determined solely by one's own labor, measured in number of "work points."

Needless to say, not all the area residents were pleased by this plan, a point Li Hiaping readily acknowledged. But was coercive pressure placed on the more reluctant villagers to join the advanced APC? I was not able to obtain from Li, Yu, or anyone else I spoke with any specific illustration that collectivization had been forced on anyone. Of course, fear of being called a "bad class element," accompanied by appropriate reprisals, may have led some of the more well-to-do peasants to keep any complaints to themselves. But in this area there were very few well-off peasants (and few absentee landlords remained in the area). In other North China villages, with a larger number of well-to-do peasants, coercive pressure was certainly applied, particularly when economic advantages were not forthcoming (see Selden 1982a).

Of course, the government didn't limit its support of these developments to verbal encouragement or persuasive pressure. It regularly provided direct incentives, such as the opportunity for cooperative members to borrow money from government-backed loan funds. If Half Moon villagers had not perceived it to be in their own interests, they would not have participated so actively. Still, I wanted to know exactly how much of an economic advantage resulted from this cooperation. Yu answered my question.

"From the beginning of the cooperative movement in 1952 to the time the communes were formed in 1958, our average corn and wheat harvest production grew from slightly less than 100 *jin* to 500 *jin* per *mu*. In 1957, we even began to grow rice—a little over 500 *mu* of it. The yield was between 400 and 500 *jin* of rice per *mu*; and believe me, the peasants were very happy to eat more rice and less corn."

Li Haiping and Yu also stressed that following land reform and the establishment of the mutual aid teams, the one other factor enhancing the cooperative's productivity was a revision of old land-use patterns. Traditional inheritance customs required that sons share in a father's estate, often resulting in noncontiguous miniscule plots of "patchwork" land being farmed in a highly irrational manner. Tiny scattered hamlets, such as were found at Half Moon, were equally inefficient as economic units. It was thought that if such land could be combined into larger productive parcels, it would not only enable the peasants to increase their productivity, but, in addition, set the stage for an even more significant increase in production through the development of mechanized agriculture. Finally, larger economic units like the newly emerging agricultural producer cooperatives could also help the peasants undertake community-wide tasks of benefit to all the members, such as extending irrigation ditches and encouraging local reforestation.

In early 1955, members of the Rural Works Department of the Beijing Municipal Party Committee, in conjunction with the Agriculture, Forestry, and Water Conservancy Bureau of Beijing's People's Council, undertook a detailed investigation of an area surrounding Half Moon in order to determine what factors were limiting the economic growth of the region and what steps might be taken to develop it. The results of their study, published in the October 10, 1955 issue of the *Peking Daily* newspaper, reaffirm the experience of Li Haiping and Yu Futian:

> The dwelling places of farm families are widely scattered because the villages and homes were built in a planless and arbitrary way near the peasant's own plot of land. As a result, small hamlets of two or three households dot the fields, hampering mechanized farming and increasing costs for such construction work as building roads, installing electric power lines and setting up cultural and recreational facilities. . . . [The report concluded with a plan that was carried out several years later.] Villages which are small and scattered will be gradually evacuated . . . with farm members moving in from other places if their old houses have become ramshackle, and if they themselves are willing and able to do so.

A short time later, Li, Yu, and the other ex-squatters from Hebei Province decided to relocate their scattered homes into a more homogeneous settlement nearby. However, in contrast to similar poor peasants elsewhere who decided to move, this group proceeded to design the plan of their relocated village in such a manner that it took on a crescent-like form similar to the geographic shape of the province from which so many of them had come—a half moon. Thus was the new beginning of Half Moon Village.

RELATIONS WITH THE COMMUNE

Red Flag Commune was formed in 1958. The poor nature of the marshy and alkaline soil and the accompanying low population density had earlier drawn the active attention of the Beijing municipal authorities. A state-owned and managed tractor station was set up earlier to assist in upgrading the land and improving agricultural production. Other state-owned agricultural and industrial enterprises followed. By the spring of 1958, when the commune movement began, the area had seven large advanced cooperatives and an even larger state farm, the latter employing nearby peasants in agricultural activities, some of which were experimental in nature.[7] In late summer of that year, these different enterprises joined together to form Red Flag People's Commune.

Today, Red Flag has become one of the largest communes in the country, comprising nearly 62 square kilometers in area and 85,000 in population. It has over 17,000 households, grouped into ten administrative districts and 116 production brigades, most of the latter equivalent with the older natural villages. The agriculturally based brigades use much of the commune's 160,000 *mu* of cultivated land for growing rice, wheat, vegetables, and other produce, mainly for the city. The remainder of the land is used for dairy, pig, and duck farms run by the commune and the state. Additional commune enterprises include fish ponds, orchards, grain- and wood-processing shops, an agricultural machine repair plant, and many small factories, which make such products as fertilizer, bricks, and powdered milk.

Of the total commune work force comprising 40,306 people, 61 percent are employed at the village-brigade level, mostly in agricultural field labor. Another 15 percent work at one of the ten district-level enterprises such as the jade carving factory located close to Half Moon. Three percent are employed at the commune level itself. These are commune members who work in the state sector. The remaining 21 percent are regular state workers in enterprises located on or close to the commune.

Clearly, Red Flag Commune serves as a highly interesting case study of a unique experiment in human history. Economically, it has survived several rather outlandish policies that threatened basically sound efforts to increase agricultural production through the cooperative interchange of different sectors of the work force. Socially, it has provided an enlarged structure for the development of a broad range of human services, including clinics and hospitals, day-care centers, and primary and middle schools. Organizationally, it has established an administrative structure that includes a director and several vice directors, an administrative committee, and other groups such as the Women's Federation and the militia that deal with various matters of concern to the commune and municipality.

---

[7] This research station is still maintained. Two American scientists-technicians, commune residents for over a decade, were until recently among its active advisors.

Parallel Party committees formed at each of these levels of organization determine basic policies, which are then put into effect by the appropriate administrative committees. Similar forms of decision making are maintained at the brigade level. To effectively administer a commune the size of Red Flag, it was decided to establish ten separate districts, eight of which are in the collective sector and two in the state. The eight districts serve as intermediate agencies linking the commune headquarters with the 116 village brigades.[8]

Of the greatest significance in all this activity is the role of the Chinese Communist Party. Who is involved? Through what organizations does it function? What are its relations with the people? And what are its goals and its methods of attaining them?

THE PARTY AND THE PEOPLE

In Half Moon, the village leadership consists of a formally defined brigade committee composed of the Party secretary, an administrative head (a separate position from that of the Party secretary), three vice directors in charge of grain, vegetable, and sideline production, and one of the work team leaders.

In principle, the Party elects its members of the committee, and non-Party villagers do the same, the specific number of representatives of each group being left undecided. In fact, the Party has always selected all the committee members, after seeking advice from the villagers on the proposed candidates. Given continuing complaints about the lack of democratic input by non-Party members, various ways to deal with this criticism are being explored. The most significant is a proposal to establish electoral procedures in which villagers can vote for both Party and non-Party candidates on the same ballot, with the number of candidates exceeding the openings on the committee. If this step is accomplished, it will clearly represent a qualitative change from existing practice.

The Party secretary always serves as the chair of the brigade committee. In Half Moon, the administrative head of the brigade and the vice director in charge of vegetable production are also Party members. The vice director for grain production, Ma Haimen, is a probationary Party member. Assuming he receives a positive evaluation at the end of the year, he will then become a full member. In other words, four out of six members of the most important local administrative committee are directly affiliated with the Party. As such, the Party has major control over the decision-making process for day-to-day affairs in the village.

Anyone wishing to join the Party may apply to the brigade Party branch, which represents the leadership locally. Of the twelve Party members presently in Half Moon, six belong to the local branch. All applications are reviewed by this group, which then offers its recommendation to the next highest body, which makes the

[8] It should be noted that Red Flag Commune no longer has the formally designated village-level production teams characteristic of most communes in China. In Half Moon and other commune villages, the brigade is the unit of accounting for purposes of distribution of income, goods, and services obtained through collective work.

final decision on the applicant. At Half Moon, that higher body is the district Party branch.

Cui Huifang, the older women's work team leader in the village, has applied several times for Party membership, but she has yet to be approved by the district. In 1977, there were six women Party members out of a village total of fifteen— one of whom was the Party secretary. This much higher than usual proportion of women members is a reflection of a policy undertaken during the later years of the Cultural Revolution to bring more women into positions of leadership. All have since been transferred outside the area, leaving the brigade without any female members at all. Cui thinks this imbalance will be of benefit in her present application.

Criteria for belonging to the Party involve a commitment to build socialism, an ability to work hard and selflessly, and a willingness to support the policies of the organization even when the individual member is in disagreement. This latter feature of Party discipline, known as "democratic centralism," is integral to the unity that the Party tries to achieve. Members are encouraged to fully express their views on any proposed policy for as long as it is under active discussion; this is the democratic aspect.[9] However, once a course of action has been determined by the leadership at a given level, Party members are expected to support that policy irrespective of their own position on the matter; this is the centralist aspect.

The village also has three other formal organizations: the Communist Youth League (CYL), the Women's Federation, and the militia.[10]

Membership in the CYL is drawn from politically active middle school students and other youths in field and factory who wish to work with the Party in the workplace, in sports and other recreational activities, and in political study groups. The political socialization of many Party members began with their membership in the CYL.

The Women's Federation, like the CYL, is really a Party-led organization in the sense that while taking up issues of direct concern to women, such as improving opportunities for educational and technical training, it explicitly represents the Party's views on these issues. Today, in keeping with the national emphasis on the "Four Modernizations" and a corresponding need to limit population growth, the major task of the Women's Federation is to popularize family planning in order to reduce the number of births per family to one. It also takes part in sanitation and other public health programs.

Though defined by the Party as a mass organization involving all village women,

[9] The open manner in which so many Party informants addressed the issues I raised in my research and the varying answers they gave in response to my questions was no doubt partly due to the active debate and reevaluation of basic Party policy occurring throughout much of 1978 and 1979, following the death of Mao and removal of the "Gang of Four."

[10] There was once a fifth: the Poor and Lower Middle Peasant's Association. It was organized in 1964 as part of a nationwide "Four Clean-up" (siqing) campaign to deal with problems of theft, corruption, profiteering, and other illegal activities of local cadres (see Baum and Teiwes 1968). A Party work team from the city was sent to the village to investigate (i.e., "clean up") possible corruption. Since no major problems emerged, the work team moved on, and the Association disbanded shortly thereafter.

A probationary Party member being interviewed at the clinic.

the actual participating membership is considerably smaller. In a household survey taken in the fall of 1979, less than 10 percent of the women interviewed responded positively to a question asking whether they belonged to the Federation. Such lack of identification seems clearly associated with the village's limited support for the new birth-control policy.

Finally, the active militia consists of all brigade members from 18 to 25 years of age. Men 25 to 45 and women 25 to 40 are inactive members. Annually, during winter when agricultural responsibilities are at a minimum, PLA representatives come to an area just outside the village and offer a short refresher course on firearms, including rifle practice. Except for a brief period in 1972, all arms and ammunition have been kept at the district headquarters rather than in the village. The villagers are taught that the purpose of the militia is primarily to protect the country from foreign invasion—an experience vividly etched in the memory of many residents—and, secondarily, to prevent sabotage at home.

The village leaders of these three organizations are usually active Party members. In Half Moon, the one exception is the Women's Federation, where the local person in charge is now being considered for membership. It is significant that she is highly respected not only by the relatively few Federation women who elected her, but by the other women in the village as well. However, what may be surprising to those unfamiliar with political life in rural China is that, with the exception of the Party, these three organizations and the administrative brigade committee are the only ones in the village. There are no others, no informal voluntary organizations such as are found throughout small-town America (Hsu 1981:394–395). Under such circumstances, the Party is not just the ultimate village authority; in many respects it is the only one. The brigade committee, for example, though a distinct entity in its own right, never takes an administrative action opposing Party guidelines.

What happens when a villager is caught stealing? When a husband beats his wife? When a local Party cadre is accused of embezzling?

Actually, crimes such as these are very rare. When they occur, they are investigated by the Public Security Bureau attached to the district headquarters and run by a Party-led district committee. Several years ago, a young couple took some vegetables from the collective field for their own use. Shortly thereafter, they were caught stealing a few boards of wood. Brought before a mass public meeting of the village, they were required to offer a thorough self-criticism of their wrongdoing. Here, the usual custom of separating public and private is purposefully reversed. However, if the offender is a Party member, the Party rather than the brigade committee has (until very recently) determined the individual's fate. Such was the case in Half Moon in the fall of 1979, when a district leader was accused of misusing public funds. Significantly, that same fall, China introduced for the first time a legal criminal code, which now enables the people to deal with issues of crime and punishment in a formal prescribed manner, separate from the actions of a local Party branch or brigade committee.

Given the extent of authority and power held by the Party, its responsibilities are rather awesome. There is a distinct nationwide governmental structure operating at the municipal, county, prefectural, provincial, and national levels. But such agencies still function in concert with the Party, largely as an administrative arm rather than as a separate policy-generating body—similar to the way in which the Half Moon brigade committee operates in concert with the local Party branch.

We can see from these examples how the interrelated economy of Half Moon Village and Red Flag Commune is intimately linked to its political structure. There are many ecological, technological, and cultural factors limiting the area's economic development. These constraints require difficult decisions in the allocation of human and material resources, in establishing an effective economic infrastructure that can raise the productivity of the people, and in providing for the education, health, and general welfare of the populace. The Party, drawing on the theories of Marx, its own experience, and that of the people, is the political instrument that makes these decisions.

With the above remarks in mind, it would be easy to see the Party as monolithic. But it is not. In Half Moon, members regularly disagree with one another. This shouldn't be surprising, since their ideas are based on the same diverse experiences as those found outside the Party. Members also find themselves in disagreement with their own leadership. This may be due to simple differences of opinion or to conflicts generated by Party policies that clash with the views of family and friends.

Several years ago, the Beijing Party leadership in charge of agricultural production for the municipality urged that villages within its jurisdiction change from a two- to a three-crop system, stating that recent research on experimental plots elsewhere had demonstrated its feasibility for the area. Asked to carry out the policy in Half Moon, Party leaders soon found themselves at odds with just about all the field workers, who said the plan wouldn't work, that the soil simply wasn't adequate to the task. The leaders, largely agreeing with the field workers, were caught in a classic dilemma. Eventually, the villagers did agree to try the three-crop plan. They understood very well the pressure that their local leaders were under. But as it turned out, their initial evaluation was correct. Crop production temporarily decreased, city officials admitted their error, the peasants went back to their earlier practice, and the local Party leaders resolved their dilemma. But the illustration shows rather clearly the kind of pressure the village cadres are under as the interface between the higher leadership of the Party and the people.

The example also suggests that Party officials residing in Beijing city have limited experience and understanding of the life and problems of peasant-farmers living within their municipality. And without that knowledge, their ability to offer sound planning strategies is severely limited.

3 / Working

HOUSEHOLD ECONOMY

In Red Flag Commune, most economic activity occurs within five institutions: the family, the work team, the village brigade, the district, and the commune industries. Beyond this outer perimeter lie economic and political structures of larger scale, including the municipality, the county, the province, and the national (state) government, all having less immediate relationship to the daily lives of most residents.

Although the economic role of the family in Half Moon Village has been transformed by collective ownership of land and machines, important continuities with the past remain. Courtyard gardens are still used to grow vegetables and fruits. Chickens continue to be raised, surplus eggs being purchased by neighbors or sold at the local district store. One Half Moon family used their courtyard to produce eggs commercially, earning 400 *yuan* or more a year for their effort.

Almost every courtyard contains a family pigsty, an adobe-walled, lean-to-shaped enclosure that opens into a big pit. Here, one or more porkers savor their daily helping of corn mush mixed with scraps of food left over from the family meal. This low-protein diet extends the pigs' fattening time to a year—four or five months longer than that taken by the better-fed collectively owned brigade pigs. Still, a family can add 100 or more *yuan* per pig to its annual private income by selling these animals at the district store or local market. Pigs, of course, produce more than meat, which is why they were once jokingly referred to as "little fertilizer factories," a phrase attributed to Mao. Manure mixed with dirt is periodically removed through a large hole in the exterior courtyard wall and sold to the brigade, increasing family income even more.

In each courtyard, a separate walled enclosure hides a slit trench. Here, human manure—night soil—is occasionally collected by the village "honey man." Sitting next to a holding tank on a mule-drawn cart, he makes his regular rounds down Half Moon lanes. Obtaining night soil from each household, he first hauls it to a large earthen pool, where it is mixed with pig manure and allowed to ferment until ready for use as fertilizer in the brigade greenhouse. Sound public health practice precludes human manure from being spread directly on the fields. For its contribution to the collective welfare of the brigade, each household receives an additional 12 *jin* ration of grain per person per year.

A peasant selling small eggplants on the road to the district headquarters.

Of great importance to many household economies in Red Flag Commune is food grown on private plots—the total holdings equaling approximately five percent of each brigade's land base.[1] From this private enterprise, families can significantly increase their source of fresh vegetables for home consumption. Or, they can increase their income by selling them to the state or at a nearby peasant market. Thirty-six thousand of these so-called "free" markets are scattered throughout rural China. None are found within Red Flag Commune itself, but a large one is located along a side street in the old market town that borders commune headquarters.

Here, fresh vegetables, chickens, and other meat and produce are sold from the backs of carts and on blankets spread in rows along the ground. Adjacent to the household offerings of these peasant traders are wooden stalls where white-jacketed state workers sell their competing produce. Privately sold vegetables are usually fresher, but also cost more. On the other hand, chickens are looked over very carefully to make sure the buyer hasn't resolved someone else's problem of what to do with a sickly hen.

COLLECTIVE ENTERPRISE

As important as these economic efforts are to the average peasant family, income gained from the collective effort of Red Flag's 116 brigades is much more

[1] In some parts of China, this percentage has now grown to as high as 15 percent (Domes 1982:261). However, such a great increase has not taken place at Red Flag Commune.

significant.[2] That is, even though opportunities for expanding privately generated income are increasing, the overall basis for determining the living standard of a given family is still more closely linked to its collective work in brigade, commune, or state-owned field and factory than in its individual entrepreneurial activity.

The most significant collective activity of the 116 brigades within Red Flag Commune is agricultural. Half Moon, for example, has 795 *mu* (132.5 acres) of irrigated fields. Crops planted at different times of the year include rice, wheat, corn, peanuts, rape (for rapeseed oil), and many vegetables, such as string beans, squash, cabbage, spinach, turnip, radish, and fennel. Due to the flatness of the land and the increased availability of large diesel tractors, a great deal of the plowing and planting is mechanized. Yet cultivation is done almost entirely by hand. Rice transplanting is accomplished both by hand and by machine, the latter becoming more prevalent as brigades increase their purchasing power (which is channeled through the accumulation fund) and the technology becomes more proficient.

Finally, harvesting also utilizes machine and human labor. Rice harvesting is particularly difficult to mechanize, due to the amount of water that must be left in the field until just before the rice is cut. The resulting damp earth is too soft for the use of heavy machinery. Therefore, an intensive effort is required of every field worker. Using small scythes, all available villagers, young and old, middle school student and retired, are asked to come out to the paddies, cut the rice, tie it in small bundles, and then carry it to the edge of field, where it is stacked prior to being removed for later threshing. Only in the harvesting of wheat, and to a lesser extent, corn, is the use of commune-owned combines possible. Yet even here, there are problems limiting further mechanization.

One has to do with the nature of the two-crop system of wheat and rice under the climatic conditions of the Beijing area. One of the two busiest times of the year for agricultural workers is in spring, when winter wheat is harvested and rice, vegetable, and corn crops are planted. The other especially busy season is fall, when the large rice crop is harvested and the wheat planted. Most vegetables are harvested during summer and early fall, although a few grown in greenhouses become available during winter.

The problem for mechanization has to do with the speed with which both harvesting and seeding must be accomplished. If the wheat is not planted by October 10, it will not have adequate time to mature before harvesting. However, early October may be too soon to cut the rice mechanically. Even if the water were to be drained early, allowing heavier equipment to run on the damp earth, the rice is still too green for the machinery to accept it without becoming snarled. So it must be cut by hand. If poor weather slows down either harvesting or planting, a a corresponding loss in productivity occurs.

The mechanization of wheat production is similarly limited by the two-crop

---

[2] Collective income is generated by the shared effort of a particular production unit. In Half Moon and other villages of Red Flag Commune, that unit is the brigade. In most areas of rural China, the accounting unit is the "production team," a working group of smaller size. The collective also refers to a type of ownership of the means of production, the other two types being private and state ownership. A thorough discussion of these differences and their implications is contained in a later chapter.

Distributing grain at harvest time.

system. In contrast to the United States, where harvests can be completed over several weeks, in Red Flag the wheat must be cut much more quickly in order to plant the rice. For the commune to fully mechanize the wheat harvest would require the purchase of several times the number of combines needed to harvest a similar amount of wheat over a longer period of time in the United States. But to obtain this many combines for five to ten days' use, and have them sit idle for the rest of the year, is financially unfeasible. Therefore, the harvesting of wheat, as well as that of rice and corn, is still done partially by hand.

What happens after the rice, wheat, corn, and vegetables are harvested? Some produce is sold to the state, some distributed to the villagers, and some set aside for seed and as a reserve. The amount allocated to the state is determined by a contract negotiated between the commune and the municipality. The method used to distribute income to the brigade members entails a choice between two alternatives.

One is the "work point" system used by Half Moon villagers, in which an individual earns up to 10 work points per day. The total number of points earned per year is then used to calculate what portion of the distributable income will be received by that individual. The other alternative is the "piece work" system. Under this arrangement, values are assigned to given tasks and individuals receive their share of the income based on the specific work accomplished. In East Gate, a large and well-known brigade in Red Flag, the villagers decided several years ago to use the piece work method of distribution. Once the value of the given task was determined to everyone's satisfaction, the accounting process was direct and simple.

The work point system is a little more complicated. Once a year in Half Moon, and sometimes twice in other villages that use this system, the brigade holds a mass meeting for all field workers. At this meeting, the workers appraise their own worth as defined by the number of work points they think they should receive based on a scale from 1 to 10. Other field workers at the meeting then discuss the appraisal, sometimes suggesting that the amount be raised or lowered. It is possible to receive 9 points one year and 7 or 8 the next if the individual is considered to be less productive due to either age or laziness. In most group discussions, however, work point evaluations are increased rather than decreased, since the Chinese value of modesty requires a lower self-appraisal than what is generally recognized as the person's true worth. By contrast, those few who try to overrate themselves are soon informed of their misguided self-perception. Of course, as Mother Wang informed Zhou Xing and me following the December meeting of brigade field workers, the village leaders do review individual work point ratings and make changes when they think it necessary.

Why don't Half Moon villagers use the piece work method? They found that when distribution was determined by work completed—such as the cutting of a small rice paddy—the field workers were more likely to quit for the day at the conclusion of the particular task. On the other hand, when they were paid according to the number of hours spent in the field, they worked longer. After reflecting on the advantages and disadvantages of the two systems, they decided that the work point method was best for them. Once that decision was made, they still faced the problem of what to do when brigade members showed up late, especially during the busy harvest season. In an effort to resolve that problem, it was decided that anyone not working at harvest time without an acceptable excuse should be penalized three day's work points—one for the specific day missed, plus two additional ones.

Recently, Half Moon villagers have explored several other variations on this theme. Until a year ago, they followed the usual arrangement of up to 10 points a day. Now they are experimenting with a new policy in which work from December through February is awarded a maximum of 6 points; March through April, 10 points; June through August (the busiest season), 14 points; and the rest of the year, 10 points.

Whatever the specific arrangement used for distribution, all brigade members in each village in the commune meet twice a year to divide up the income derived from their collective work. This includes a certain amount of cash received from the sale of agricultural and sideline industry products to the state, and "in kind" income—including grain, vegetables, and additional foods produced by the peasants themselves. It is shared as well with other work point earners, including health clinic personnel, day-care workers, and school teachers, who provide important human services for the community, and with the temporary contract workers mentioned previously.

A far smaller collective activity of Half Moon Village is the development of its modest sideline industry: one, a barrel-washing enterprise that cleans 50-gallon diesel drums for later reuse, and the other, a chemical-mixing operation. When fully operative, they utilize the labor of twelve villagers. Between contracts, these sideline workers join other brigade members in the fields. Additional collective income is generated from two brigade-run farms, which raise 450 pigs and 150 chickens at a time. (The local pig farm is especially popular, since it provides the villagers with healthy piglets at low cost, which are then fattened and sold for additional private household income.) In addition, the brigade has a small reforestation enterprise that brings in a little income, and it rents out the village truck for local transport.

Another collective activity of importance to the village is the contracting of local residents to work on commune construction crews, on water conservation projects, or as temporary factory workers in commune and state-level enterprises. At present, 23 men and women from Half Moon hold jobs as contract workers, an arrangement that is particularly beneficial to the brigade. That is, wages earned by these temporary employees come directly to the brigade, which continues to pay the contract worker his or her previous income. Since commune and state wages are always higher, and in the latter case sometimes even double that of local income, the brigade always benefits—a point Party Secretary Jiang Lijiang reminded the villagers in his December meeting with them. Of course, the brigade must continue to provide these temporarily relocated village workers with their share of the collectively owned grain, vegetables, and other home-grown produce. As for the contract workers themselves, they can at least hope that a temporary job might lead to a more permanent one—though the prospects for such a move are minimal.[3]

In Half Moon, the total income from the brigade's collective production for the year 1978 (the last year for which statistics are available) was 226,000 *yuan*. Of this amount, approximately 58 percent (130,000 *yuan*), came from agriculture—including the sale of grain and vegetables to Beijing municipality for its urban residents. To encourage higher production, the municipality initially sets a low production quota in its contracts with brigades. Agricultural goods sold to the city above that quota bring a 50 percent higher payment, an obvious incentive to produce more. Another 5 percent (12,000 *yuan*) was earned by the brigade from its sale of pigs and chickens. Nonagricultural collective activities, including sideline production, the loaning out of contract workers to the commune and state, and other miscellaneous efforts brought in another 37 percent (84,000 *yuan*). The year's total income of 226,000 *yuan* was an impressive increase from the 90,000 *yuan* that was their total a decade earlier.

As for the brigade expenses, from their income of 226,000 *yuan*, they subtracted approximately 48 percent (108,000 *yuan*) for production costs (not including payment for labor), almost 11 percent (23,596 *yuan*) for the accumulation fund, 3 percent (5988 *yuan*) for all taxes, and a little over 1 percent (3300 *yuan*) for the welfare fund.

The accumulation fund is used for capital improvements, such as agricultural

---

[3] The difficulty in obtaining a permanent state position is greatly magnified by having to change one's category of "residence," a problem with many complexities, as will be seen shortly.

machinery and construction of the new bath house. Next year the village hopes to buy a rice transplanter with its annual earnings. The state agricultural tax is a fixed amount (a specified number of *jin* of grain) rather than a percentage. Therefore, as the brigade produces more, the proportion of tax paid to the state decreases. In 1978, the tax came to 2.6 percent of the total income.[4] The welfare fund uses its annual allottment for programs of community benefit, such as child and health care. If there are childless elderly people in the village with little or no income, this fund is used to assist them as well.

The remaining 85,390 *yuan*, or almost 38 percent of the total income, was then distributed to the brigade members in cash, grain, and vegetables. The grain is allocated so that each member receives 450 *jin*, which is more than adequate for an average adult diet. (Some is used for fodder.) Those field workers with a work point rating of 10 receive a little more. In 1978, the value of each 10-work-point day came to 1.3 *yuan*, or about 35 *yuan* per month maximum income from the collective. The following year, when the state increased its purchase price of many agricultural products by 25 percent, the brigade income increased proportionately.

Today, the average Half Moon brigade member employed in the collective sphere has an annual income of a little over 400 *yuan*, including that derived from noncollective household enterprises. Although this income is more than adequate to purchase all the necessities of life and some of the luxuries, including the "four jewels"—bicycle, wrist watch, radio, and sewing machine—it is considerably less than the average annual income earned by most state factory workers of comparable age (720 *yuan*). To become a factory worker is the goal of almost all village young people today. Why this is the case is not difficult to understand.

FROM FIELD TO FACTORY

Most young people begin their working lives in the fields, being assigned that position by the local brigade production committee. Some prefer to find a job in Beijing, but are restricted from doing so by a government policy put into effect in 1954 that effectively limits anyone from moving away from their established residence and workplace unit (*danwei*) without official approval. By means of this legislation, the Chinese government has effectively resolved one of the most pressing problems facing Third World countries today—the migration of large numbers of peasants from their own villages into overcrowded urban slums seeking largely nonexistent jobs. Obviously, they have done so at the expense of an unprecedented restriction in freedom of movement.

Of course, various efforts can be made to obtain a city job. But such a move is seldom achieved. To be an unemployed peasant youth living off one's parents is practically unheard of; to find work elsewhere is almost impossible. So rural young people accept what they are assigned. Still, in the back of their minds is the realiza-

---

[4] Except for people wth very high incomes, there is no individual income tax in China. However, licenses are required to run brigade sideline industries.

tion that one's first assignment may also be one's last. In the forefront is the commonly accepted belief that "It is far better to be a worker than a peasant." What are the prospects of commune youth getting a factory job?

In Half Moon, one of the most likely places to obtain such a position is in the two-year-old jade-carving factory owned by the district. Located a few minutes bicycle ride from the village, it is presently housed in the district auditorium, to be vacated when a new factory building is completed several years from now. Inside, row upon row of tables provide work space for many of the 370 employees, 90 percent of whom live in the villages contained within the district. These workers spend each day grinding and polishing small jade figurines, which when finished are sold to the state export bureau for amounts ranging from several *yuan* to 400 or more.

Several years of negotiation between the district and the Beijing municipal bureaucracy eventually led to the formation of this enterprise.[5] Once the district had obtained the necessary used motors, belts, and grinding and polishing machines from the city jade-carving factory, they hired a retired master craftsman to train the local workers. These new employees were almost all recent junior middle school graduates, recommended to the factory by teachers from the district middle school. Criteria for selection included level of educational competence and ability in drawing, painting, and "completing meticulous tasks with care."

The basic monthly wage of these workers ranges from 33 to 41 *yuan*, with an average of just under 40 *yuan*. In addition, all the jade-factory workers are eligible to receive a bonus of up to 10 *yuan* a month if the factory exceeds its state quota. As with the brigade agricultural contract, the initial goal is purposely set at a low figure, enabling factory workers to easily exceed it. Section leaders in charge of particular workshops earn incomes that are little different than those of the regular workers, 41 *yuan* a month, plus a bonus that is based on the average output of the workers in their shops. The factory manager receives a monthly income of 44 *yuan*, and a comparable bonus based on the average output of all 370 workers.

A totally different kind of operation is the Red Flag chemical factory, a large state-owned and commune-run enterprise covering 40 acres and employing 810 workers, slightly less than half of which are women. Several of these employees come from Half Moon. Originally set up in 1958, at the beginning of the Great Leap Forward, with 10 new workers and one old horse stable, it has now become a highly modern enterprise, turning phosphorus ore into chemicals including formic acid, phosphate fertilizer (which is sold to the commune), and ash for cement. Its annual output of chemicals is valued at over 15 million *yuan*, 3.95 million of

---

[5] The amount of effort required to establish this small factory illustrates rather well the immensity of the Chinese bureaucracy. Before setting up the factory, the district leaders had to obtain formal approval from the following government organizations: the Commune Economic Planning Committee, the County Committee in charge of Commune Affairs, the Beijing Municipal Export Bureau responsible for overseas sales, the Beijing Municipal Planning Committee (the highest authority), and the Industries Bureau. After each had granted its approval of the application, the district was allowed to contact the factory to obtain the needed equipment. Of course, they had informally contacted the factory long before to make sure that it was willing to lease and later sell its old surplus machinery.

The district jade factory.

which constitutes the annual profit for the factory. Before 1980, all profit was turned over to the state treasury. Today, due to a change in government policy, the factory keeps 30 percent to use for capital improvements, bonuses, and facilities for the general welfare of the factory personnel, including a clinic staffed with six doctors, a canteen, dormitories, and a nursery. Many of the younger unmarried workers, including several from Half Moon, live in the large men's dormitory during the week, returning home on Sundays or for holidays.

Worker incomes in this state-owned factory range from 30 to 80 *yuan*, with an average of approximately 45 *yuan.*

An additional 12 *yuan* in monthly bonuses are earned by most of the work force. Five criteria have been established for these bonuses: individual level of output, quality of work, avoidance of waste, cost efficiency, and attention to safety. In addition, there are three important attitudes that are part of every worker evaluation: labor attitude (approach to work), political attitude (political knowledge), and communist spirit (willingness to help others). These "five criteria and three attitudes" were first decided on by the employees at a six-day-long Worker's Congress held at the chemical factory in 1978. They now serve as the guidelines for determining bonus eligibility. Such decisions are made collectively in face-to-face workgroup meetings, not unlike similar discussions held in village brigades that utilize the work point system.

Although Half Moon has only a few regular (state) employees in this chemical factory, another 20 have been hired recently as contract workers. Under this arrangement, the brigade receives 75 *yuan* a month from the factory, approximately 35 *yuan* of which is then paid to the contract worker as a wage. The other 40 *yuan* remains in the brigade's collective treasury. Each year, the brigade committee determines the amount of wage to be given to the contract worker based on the average income of the other brigade members. For the year in question, the brigade average was 35 *yuan*. By such means, potential conflicts within the collective generated by some brigade members receiving much higher wages than others are resolved. Furthermore, the brigade benefits financially. All in all, it is quite a successful arrangement for both factory and brigade.

Several other factories in Red Flag Commune employ Half Moon residents. One, a state-owned grain-processing mill undergoing a large expansion, is situated about ten miles away. Liu Ming, a young villager in his mid-twenties, gets on his bicycle at seven in the morning and arrives 45 minutes later at the factory. While maintaining a room at home, he also has free housing in a factory dormitory. As a permanent state worker receiving a regular wage of 50 *yuan* a month, he has numerous other benefits, including free health care, access to technical courses offered by the factory, participation in the local trade union, and a generous pension upon retirement. However, he is no longer formally designated a brigade resident, which means he no longer receives grain or other rations from the village, and if he were to join the CYL or the Party, his affiliation would be through the factory.

Between the temporary contract worker and the permanent state worker lies one other important category of factory employee—the so-called "commune-member-worker." Half Moon has over 100 such workers. So do many other villages in Red Flag. These men and women are employed by the state sector of the commune rather than the brigade, and receive benefits similar to those of other state workers. One such enterprise is a small electrical-parts plant, located at the same district headquarters as the jade factory. It has 465 workers, 80 percent of which are women. However, instead of these workers receiving factory coupons enabling them to purchase grain and other commodities from state stores, as is the case with other state employees, the ration continues to be received "in kind" from the brigade.

Why this special arrangement? Why not just allow brigade workers to become state workers? Basically, the answer has to do with the question of residency referred to earlier. At birth, one is given a particular residency status (*hokou*). The designation, urban or rural, follows that of the mother. Rural residents are not usually eligible for employment in the state sector. They cannot place their children in the higher-quality urban schools, or gain other benefits commonly associated with urban residency, for example, a coupon enabling the individual to purchase a television set. Due to the 1954 residency policy, Half Moon and other peasants are restricted to their present environment, and cities are spared the problem of a massive influx of unemployed rural residents.

To resolve potential conflicts between brigade, state, and commune workers generated by different income levels, the state, through the commune-run factory, pays the brigade 120 *yuan* a year for each commune-member-worker it hires. The brigade then uses those funds to provide the grain ration for the worker, who is technically no longer a member of the brigade. By this means, the state is relieved of the responsibility of providing grain coupons (and thereby the guarantee of foodgrain) to its newly hired workers. Complicated? Yes. But it is also effective in enabling the state sector of the commune to deploy its financial resources in a manner that heightens its industrial development without having to drain off capital to provide a guarantee of grain for its workers.

RESOLVING CONFLICTS

As important as it is to analyze village-level economics, such a study sometimes plays down the human element: those who actually do the work. Anthropologists, broadly concerned with the lives of the people they study, often spend time in the workplace—whether it be in agricultural field, factory, or elsewhere. Immediately on arrival in Half Moon, I made arrangements to spend six or more hours each week working in the fields with the villagers. As the research progressed, however, this plan appeared less and less practical. In some weeks, only two or three hours were devoted to such work. Admittedly, my minimal participation didn't bother the villagers in the slightest. Indeed, on more than one occasion they amusedly suggested that I was spending too much time in the fields.

One day in particular, Ma Haimen, the brigade vice director, strolled over to where I was thinning spinach and after watching me for a few minutes offered the comment "You must be tired. Why don't you stop now." Since Ma knew that I had only been there for a short time, he was clearly aware that I couldn't be tired. Obviously something else was on his mind. Comments offered out of context carry hidden meanings—often of a critical nature. But if that was so, what was he criticizing?

"Ma Haimen? How can I be tired? I just arrived a few minutes ago."

Squatting down beside me, Ma began pulling small green shoots out of the ground, leaving the healthiest-looking spinach to grow.

"Look," he said, answering my question in a highly indirect manner. "See how I do it. It's not hard. But you should be careful not to take too much of the plant out at the same time."

With that remark, several nearby field workers burst out laughing. Ma, now smiling as well, pointed to the extremely sparse row of green shoots behind me and then at the much thicker rows of the other workers. "Look behind you. Most of us are thinning the spinach, but you appear to be harvesting it." At that point, I joined in the laughter, promising to be more careful in the future.

Several weeks later, while I was helping one of the men's work teams harvest corn, another conflict occurred. But this time it was not resolved through the use of humor. Since it was harvest season, everyone was working hard. That morning, over the loudspeaker, Jiang Lijiang had encouraged state workers with the day off, middle school students, and others to spend part of it helping in the fields. There was no question in my mind that those "others" he was referring to should include me.

Finishing a quick breakfast with the Wang family a little before 7:00, I headed down the dirt lane toward the main road. At one end of the village, members of the young women's work team were beginning to congregate. A few were bending over, sharpening wooden-handled scythes with a file, while others chatted informally. Su Xiulan, the team leader, was talking with Cui Huifang, head of the older women's work group—probably coordinating team assignments for the day. Su, a robust and active woman in her late twenties, looked tired this morning, which was not surprising given the long evenings she and her family had spent this past week laying adobe and brick walls for their new house.

At the other end of the village, on the road leading to the district store, the 45 members of the young men's work team had also gathered. Ma Haimen, standing with several of the men, laughed at a joke being told him by another peasant. Others, dark jackets set off by light blue baggy pants, simply lounged against an adobe wall watching a "granny" push a tandem baby carriage toward the day-care nursery around the corner.

"Hey, Granny. You have to work today too, huh?" one of them teasingly shouted as she passed by.

"More than you," she responded, drawing an amused grin from the lips of the earlier speaker.

"Ah, old woman, life is hard, all right. But at least you have grandchildren to take care of, and that will keep you out of trouble."

At 7:00, the tempo quickened. Crossing an irrigation ditch to a nearby field, Su Xiulan's small group moved efficiently down the rows, cutting stalks of corn at their base with long-handled scythes. Cui's larger group followed the same pattern in the next field. I joined the men's group as they picked up their tools and headed toward the back side of the village, out of sight of the women's teams. Approaching our work site, we saw two peasants from another work team holding metal-tipped wooden poles attached by string, measuring off straight lines as row markers for the next planting. The soil in the field was soft and easy to work, having just been plowed. At our location, several horse-drawn carts had already arrived, drivers dumping their loads of manure into small squares marked with string. As one cart followed another, the men quickly spread the fertilizer in one square, then moved 20 feet down the field and began again. Looking unsuccessfully for a shovel, I soon realized that spreading manure was not to be my task. Instead, I was asked to join a smaller group of older men clearing an adjacent field of pre-cut cornstalks—obviously an assignment the team leader felt I could do fairly well.

But life on the other side of the village was not so harmonious. I learned about it late that afternoon from Zhang Dashen, an older woman field worker and a neighbor of the Wang household. It seemed that Su Xiulan, the young women's work team leader, had been criticized by Jiang Lijiang for the slowness of her team's effort in harvesting a cornfield. Because the stalks were not promptly cleared after cutting, the young men's team had to remain idle for an hour before they could begin fertilizing. The Party secretary just happened to pass by at that moment. In his remarks to Su, Jiang referred to Cui Huifang's older women's team and how they had been able to clear the adjoining field, of comparable size, in a shorter time. "Why is it," he had apparently asked, "that an older group of women can accomplish more than a younger group?"

With that remark, Su exploded.

"I don't want to be a leader and take all this grief. I try to do my best. If you don't think I'm qualified to be a leader, I'll be glad to quit."

During this exchange, Su continued her work, bending over, cutting the corn stalks and then hurling them to the ground. In this manner, she kept from confronting Jiang directly. The other women too went on harvesting the corn, although they listened to every word. Soon, Cui Huifang came over from the adjoining field and, on learning the nature of the argument, turned to the Party secretary.

"Secretary Jiang, Su is a good team leader. She is working just as hard, if not harder than anyone else in the team. And furthermore, there are more women in my team than in hers. How could they finish before my group?"

According to Zhang Dashen, the woman telling the story, Jiang, Su, and Cui continued down the field during the argument, with Su cutting corn stalks and then throwing them down—"getting her anger out" was the way Zhang later described it. Then, Cui turned to Su and spoke very quietly: "Su, we're all here for the same purpose. Let's go back to work." Su didn't say anything at the moment, but soon went over to other members of her team and began helping them. Jiang and Cui also turned away, and the argument was considered over.

In summing up the event, Zhang Dashen said, "Everyone knows that Su is tired. She spends almost every evening with her family working on her new house. But she has energy for the daytime too. She's strong and the women like her. That's why she was elected to head up the work team. Actually, Ma Haimen was the one who gave out the quota assignment for two groups. He knew that the younger team had fewer workers and therefore needed more time to complete their share of the work. But he wasn't around when Jiang showed up."

Several important insights are contained in this brief portrayal of a simple village conflict. First, the peasant workers stayed apart from the argument between the leaders—even when it involved their own team representative. Instead of stopping work to observe the conflict, they kept right on cutting corn. Such a response is typical of Red Flag's peasants. It was not primarily due to Jiang's presence, although given the nature of his criticism of Su Xiulan, such a factor has to be taken into account. Rather, the heart of the response is cultural, reflecting an important separation between public and private spheres of activity. Arguments are considered private, even when they occur in public. Since they are private, the public response is to pretend they haven't happened. So too, Su refrained from confronting Jiang directly, preferring to continue working even though she was very angry. "That is the typical Chinese way," reflected Zhang Dashen in recounting the event.

Still, this cultural pattern is under attack by villagers imbued with the spirit of changing the world rather than adapting to it. Workers, especially, largely freed by new and secure factory jobs from traditional economic and social obligations that link family and village together, are the ones most likely to challenge these old customs. And such individuals are not necessarily young.

Ke Liming, an older worker in a nearby furniture factory, once became involved in a sharp argument with his team leader over the quality of wood to be used in building wardrobes. He noticed that the leader regularly used high-quality four-by-eight-foot sheets of veneer in the interior construction. While such use enabled him to work more quickly and easily, it was also highly expensive. From Ke's point of view, it was far better to use small leftover pieces of veneer for the unseen inner portions. One day he took up the issue with the team leader, telling him he thought it was wasteful and wrong. The leader angry, and perhaps a little defensive, said to him, "Don't be like a dog trying to catch mice" (that is, stay out of other people's business and mind your own). Ke shot back, "Cats catch mice, not dogs" (that is, it *is* my business).

At this moment, a young woman Youth League member came over to where they were standing and defended her friend, the team leader. Ke, his voice rising in anger, shouted back.

"How can you be a member of the Communist Youth League when you are so backward?"

Her response was, "Well, you're too old to join."

Following this remark, Ke and the team leader began pushing and punching at one another until they had to be pulled apart by other workers. Finally, the head of the whole workshop came over and asked what was happening. After learning about the argument, he had everyone sit down right on the factory floor and discuss it. Soon, Ke's fellow workers offered their support to him and, by implication, criticized the team leader and the CYL member. Ke's final remark about the episode was, "The team leader was wrong and so was the woman. But she was also selfish."

Selected cases of how particular individuals and small groups approach differences with their leaders help illustrate the nature of conflict and efforts at its resolution. But illustrations of larger scale help even more. One well-known historical example took place in 1958. At the beginning of the Great Leap Forward, differences arose over what strategy to take in developing the countryside. Red Flag Commune, located near the dominant seat of power in Beijing, soon became a testing ground for some of the more radical theories of several national Party leaders.

Specifically, the commune leadership was asked to eliminate as much private ownership as possible. Banners and slogans proclaiming "Public Ownership for Everyone" were put up. Peasants in Half Moon and nearby villages were urged to turn in their chickens, pigs, grain, vegetables, and other produce to a common pool from which any household could take what it needed. Dining halls were set up in several large villages and families encouraged to eat there rather than in their homes.

While receiving initial support from a few of the more romantically inclined, the communist dream of "one for all and all for one" quickly faded. Dining halls were immediately rejected by peasant families as unappealing and impractical. The idea of taking what was needed in the way of food, coal for fuel, and other goods had a certain appeal, but shortages appeared quickly. And finally, tensions began to develop between those who worked hard for the collective welfare and those who either worked hard for themselves or hardly worked at all. Within a few months, the experiment at Red Flag collapsed, those leaders backing the plan discredited, and the villagers angered at having been pressured to participate in such a foolish scheme. Old Li Haiping, the Half Moon peasant activist of the early 1950s put it succinctly: "In those days, we had no experience in dealing with the 'communist wind.' Now we know better."

A second historical example of conflict between the leaders and the people occurred with the collectivization of private plots. Individually farmed plots were first made available to peasant households in Red Flag in 1962, reflecting a shift away from the collective emphasis of the Great Leap. In Half Moon, the size of family plots was calculated at .15 *mu* per person. At that time, the village population was 360, so the total area set aside for these plots was 54 *mu*. This land was cultivated by individual families until the political storm of the mid-1960s swept over the country and villagers were pressured to collectivize their private plots. In 1969, when a new constitution was drafted, Mao insisted on preserving private plots, and they were decollectivized. But in 1972, they were again recollectivized.

From 1972 until the present, private plots in Half Moon Village have remained collectivized. Actually, given the government's present reemphasis on expanding private plots, Half Moon's decision to continue its local collectivization is perhaps somewhat surprising. But most significant is not the choice, but the fact that they made it. All previous steps at collectivization of private plots were taken with little active discussion by and participation of the villagers. During the Cultural Revolution particularly, peasants criticizing collectivization were labeled "capitalist-roaders" and threatened with sundry penalties, including economic sanctions and physical punishment. Now that the government is again supporting an expansion of private plots, it is noteworthy that villages like Half Moon that want to continue collectivizing them can do so—even though local Party cadres have made it clear publicly that such a decision does not have their active support.

Illustrations such as these provide valuable insights into the relations between local leaders and the people they represent. But the portrayals only cover a very small canvas. The larger picture is considerably more complex. One important point not always given sufficient attention is that most of these leaders have grown up in the immediate area where they presently live and therefore have close relations with other residents. Emotionally linked to the village through kin and friendship ties, and economically linked through the work point system, their perceptions and actions reflect at least in part the needs of those they are trying to serve. And it should be noted in conclusion that some leaders in Half Moon Village and Red Flag Commune are exemplary in this regard.

4/Growing up

BIRTH

Wang Zhenlan was going to have a baby. Once she found she was pregnant and told her husband, Yu Xiake, a heightened sense of expectation entered the household. She noticed it immediately.

"Are you feeling all right today, Zhenlan?" her mother-in-law frequently asked. Previously, such solicitous concern for her welfare had never been expressed either by her mother-in-law or any other member of the household. Xiao Yu, too, not only observed her behavior more closely, but assumed an active role in carrying out various household chores. Of course, Zhenlan continued her daily trek to the brigade fields with the other young women. However, as she grew larger, her work team leader began assigning her lighter tasks. Although she brushed off such special attention as unnecessary, her teammates regularly took on the heavier work. Some suggested that she remain at home until after the birth of her child, but she preferred to continue as long as possible. Many village women did.

Shortly after learning of her pregnancy, Wang Zhenlan checked in with the village clinic for a prenatal examination. The three barefoot doctors were hardly surprised, since she had not sought any advice about birth control during the first year of her marriage. Once, Ma Xinxian, the older of the two women "doctors," stopped by her house to inquire whether she might be interested in such information. Zhenlan declined, feeling a little embarrassed to even discuss such matters. Nor did Ma make any attempt to follow up on her original query. In the countryside, efforts to reduce population are being taken much more seriously now than in the past. But such endeavors commonly are made after the birth of the first child, not before. Concluding the examination, Ma gave her approval, saying that Zhenlan was healthy and that she foresaw no difficulties ahead.

"You should drop in on Dong Shufang sometime, just to let her know," added Ma as Zhenlan stepped out the clinic door.

"I will," responded the quickly receding figure.

Dong Shufang, a fifty-three-year-old widow, has been the brigade midwife for quite a while. She arrived in Half Moon Village 30 years previously from Jian County in Hebei Province, following an arranged marriage with a local resident. In 1966, at the beginning of the Cultural Revolution, the village women were asked by the Women's Federation to choose a new brigade midwife. Much to

Dong's surprise and pleasure, they selected her. Qualities that led to her selection included a willingness to help others, a warm personality, cleanliness, few family responsibilities at home, and a mature age—between forty and fifty. Following an all-too-brief three-week training internship at the nearby commune hospital, she began her new practice. She does, however, return to the hospital each year for additional upgrading of her skills.

Since that time, Dong Shufang has delivered almost all the babies in Half Moon. Mostly, she works in the fields with the other women. Nevertheless, she is on call 24 hours a day, and is even available to neighboring villages when needed. For her efforts she receives an income based on the brigade's collective work point system—in midwife Dong's case, a rating of eight points. Parents of a newborn child often give her a little present, such as a piece of cloth or some food. If she lived in the city, she might be offered a small amount of money, but in the village, any money received by the midwife would have to be turned over to the brigade accumulation fund. So at Half Moon, all gifts are nonmonetary in nature.

Young Zhenlan was not the only one preparing for the coming event. As she grew in size, her mother-in-law, the expectant grandmother, began making some clothes so small Zhenlan thought they would never fit her as yet unborn child. Her own mother, who lived in a nearby village, was also busily at work knitting a warm red cotton blanket. As the time for her child's birth came close, she noticed that her sister-in-law stopped taking the family's fresh eggs down to the brigade store for sale. Instead, they were stored in containers of rice in expectation of their future use by the household's new mother-to-be.

One matter of common discussion by both relatives and friends was the possible date of the child's birth. From such a date many in the village believe that the child's fortune can be predicted. If, for example, the child were to be born on the first or fifteenth day of a given month (according to the lunar calendar), it would have good fortune, whereas if it were born on the eighth day, bad fortune would result. Wang Zhenlan knew several women who had been born on "bad" days, and, indeed, for the most part, their lives were not to be envied.

Similar beliefs could be applied to one's *shuxiang* or horoscope. Zhenlan was born in the year of the rabbit, and that was good. However, her older sister was born in the year of the sheep, and that was not—especially since the birth had occurred in winter. Sheep without grass in winter face a difficult time. So might a child. She knew some villagers scoffed at making such associations between infants and animals, considering them old-fashioned and foolish. However, many did not. Actually, it was more often the young who laughed at such ideas. Older people tended to believe in them. She wasn't sure. Perhaps in the old days, when there was much hardship and uncertainty, belief in luck helped to explain one's fortune, good or bad. Today, the village was much better off, and people her age didn't need to worry so much about whether there would be enough food to last the winter. Still, in childbirth something could always happen, so she hoped her child would be born on a good-luck day—just in case.

Shortly thereafter, Wang Zhenlan felt the first contraction. Sitting quietly in the courtyard taking in the warm midday sun, she didn't say anything, waiting to see if it would repeat itself. It did. Following Ma Xinxian's instructions, she tried to estimate the length of time between the contractions. They weren't very uncomfortable and were quite far apart. Still, she thought the time had arrived. She waited a little longer to make sure and then called her mother-in-law, who was washing some corn prior to taking it to the grinding mill.

"The contractions have begun. Perhaps Dong Shufang should be told."

After a brief discussion, the eldest daughter was dispatched to the Dong home with the request. Within minutes the news spread. A few married women from neighboring households soon appeared outside the courtyard gate to offer help. One woman, a family friend, stepped inside. A simple shake of the head from the mother-in-law was enough to confirm that no assistance was needed. However, a child was dispatched to the neighboring village to tell Zhenlan's mother of the approaching birth.

Shortly thereafter, Dong Shufang arrived. Striding through the courtyard gate, worn dark-brown cloth bag in hand, she immediately went to the room where Zhenlan was now lying down. Satisfied with the answers to her brief questions, she set about the task before her. Taking instruments from her bag, she asked that water be boiled for their sterilization. She also requested a pail of hot water and brush. When it was brought in, she added a cup of disinfectant to the liquid. Once satisfied with the mixture, she set out to thoroughly clean the room. She then changed the linen on the *kang*, only minimally disturbing Zhenlan. Glancing round the room, she seemed pleased at its orderliness and neatness. In a covered pan on the dresser, her instruments lay in steaming water. She was ready. Now it was simply a question of waiting. No matter how long it took, she would not leave until the baby had been delivered. Zhenlan's mother-in-law and elder sister were nearby. And, hopefully, her own mother would arrive soon. But that was all. The household had been instructed earlier than no one else was to enter the room until after the birth of the child.

Zhenlan felt the increasing frequency of the contractions and a little pain. Perhaps, she thought, it would be better to deliver the child in a kneeling position rather than lying down. Some of the elderly women in the village had told her that the old way was much easier, even though it was no longer done. As the pain continued, she felt Dong Shufang's hand reach out to hers. She squeezed her hand back in response. And she waited.

Outside in the courtyard, Xiao Yu also waited. A message had been brought to the field where he was working that Zhenlan was in labor and he could return home if he wished. Later in the afternoon, he was joined by his father, and then by his younger brother. They talked about unimportant matters, their words occasionally interrupted by little cries from inside the house. Anesthesia is not used in the countryside in either clinic or home. Xiao Yu and his father spoke a little more animatedly in the hope that such effort might lessen the sound within. Unsuccessful, they chose to resolve the problem by walking over to the village plaza and then down to the irrigation ditch, where several dead trees had been set aside for firewood. Together, they hauled some of the larger branches back to the courtyard and began breaking them up for the kitchen stove. Activity in the house increased. Finally, a face appeared at the entryway door. It was Xiao Yu's mother, her face flushed with excitement.

"It's a girl. Everyone is fine." A few moments later, she walked toward the courtyard gate, a small strip of bright-red cloth in her hand.

Lao Yu looked at his eldest son and spoke.

"So, you are now a father and I am a grandfather. It is a good day—a day of double happiness. Look. Your mother is tacking up the cloth. Soon everyone will know you are a father."

Neighbors and other villagers are informed of any local birth when the family takes a strip of red cloth and places it just outside the courtyard gate. Red is a sign of happiness, and in this instance, it means a new family member has been added to the household. The cloth carries other messages as well. Its presence helps prevent evil spirits who might harm mother and child from entering the home, and it informs other villagers that visitors are not welcome. Such guests are discouraged in the belief that they might carry with them malevolent ethers or wind (*xieqi*) that could bring sickness or misfortune to the newborn and mother.

Seemingly far from the neighbors' excited discussions in response to the red ribbon proudly displayed on the courtyard gate, a much quieter scene was being enacted in an inner room of the Yu household. Dong Shufang had finished suturing several minor tears that had occurred during the birth and was putting away her instruments in her old cloth bag. Near the door, the elder sister-in-law waited for her to finish. On the *kang* lay Zhenlan, and next to her, wrapped in a tiny red cotton quilt, was her newborn child. Not long ago Zhenlan had thought that the birth would soon be over. Now, she reflected, it was just the beginning.

INFANCY

In Half Moon Village, as elsewhere in rural China, a peasant mother and infant are expected to spend much of the first month indoors. This custom, called *zuo yuezi*, (literally, "sitting month") is believed to protect the mother and baby from harmful agents—whether natural or supernatural. For the first few days, the mother remains close to bed, breastfeeding the baby and being taken care of by her own mother. If her mother has died or lives too far away, the woman and child will be assisted by the mother-in-law or sister-in-law. In a few days, relatives and friends begin dropping by the house to leave one or two *jin* of dark brown sugar and a small cloth-covered basket of eggs, or perhaps a small helping of chicken. Dark sugar, particularly, is thought to help the body stay warm (whereas white sugar is thought to cool the body down). However, these villagers bringing gifts seldom remain to visit, for fear that through their presence they might bring some negative ether that could result in harm to mother or child.

By the end of the first week, the mother has begun to eat regular food and assume minor tasks around the house. Conscious of possible unknown dangers, she is careful to keep her face out of the wind. Further protection is afforded by wearing a square-shaped scarf to cover her hair and forehead. In summer a scarf is commonly worn for at least two months; in winter, even longer. As for the child, the mother of a first-born is frequently reminded not to place her baby on its stomach. "Remember the baby's heart," "Be careful not to let it smother," or

"If the baby spends too much time on its stomach it will affect the shape of the head" are common admonitions that have been passed down from one generation to another for centuries.

From the moment of birth, the baby is the recipient of a considerable amount of attention. If it cries, it will very likely be picked up and held, coddled, and played with by the mother or other available member of the family. Milk from the breast is offered whenever the child desires it, although an effort is made to follow a regular schedule. At night the baby sleeps close to the mother's side. When it wakes, its needs will be quickly taken care of, whether it be for feeding, emotional support, or the changing of clothes. The usual dress for a young baby includes diapers made out of old clothing and an undershirt. The child is then wrapped in a small quilt or blanket tied together by a piece of cloth. In poorer days, when old cloth was valued for making shoes, some babies' diapers even consisted of a kind of sandbag. Instead of changing the diaper, mother, grandmother, or sibling would simply change the sand.

When the child is one month old, a large celebration called *man yue* (full month) is held. All nearby relatives and friends are invited to attend. In preparation for the festivities, tables are set for the guests and stocked with special foods such as cooked pork and eggs mixed with red coloring. Drinks usually include *baiganr* (a strong white liquor) or other high-spirited grain alcohol. After all have arrived, the new infant is brought out for everyone to see. Presents from relatives and friends are also admired. Gifts include items such as a simple baby suit, a cotton padded mattress, a swaddling blanket, and a small cap or pair of shoes and socks. It is at this time that the baby is given a name.

The naming of infants has undergone considerable change in Half Moon Village in recent years. Men and women over 40 years of age usually have three-word names, such as *Zhang Guilin* for a man, which literally means "Zhang precious forest," and *Lu Yulan* for a woman, which means "Lu jade orchid." Not infrequently, old naming practices of this sort called on astrological charts utilizing the Five Elements of water, fire, wood, metal, and earth (see Baker 1979). Men's and women's names are quite distinct, of course, the former commonly associated with money, culture, or something official, and the latter with flowers, chastity, and the like. Given the high infant mortality rate at that time, parents also gave their children informal nicknames such as "ugly boy," "iron egg," "stupid donkey," and "left over by dogs," so that evil spirits or devils would be less likely to take their child away.

Another common naming pattern is to assign the same character to part of the given name in such a way as to indicate one's generation in the family—that is, one's generation name. After moving in with the Wang family, I quickly learned the children's formal names. I soon found they all had one character in common: *Hu.* Old Wang's eldest son was Wang Hulan; second son was Wang Hubau; eldest daughter was Wang Huying; second daughter was Wang Hurong; and the youngest daughter, Wang Huzeng. Needless to say, such a naming pattern is quite helpful in distinguishing the Wang family members from other Wang households in the village. I commented on the fact to Lao Wang.

"Of course," he responded, his face masked in a slight frown.

"But why is it that many babies born today only have two-character names?"

And I rattled off several names from my census list of Half Moon—boys living nearby called Mei Jian (Mei Healthy), Liu Wei (Liu Greatness), and Wu Ming (Wu Bright); and a baby girl born recently just down the lane called Sun Fang (Sun Fragrant). I knew that such naming practices had become quite common among the more intellectual families of urban Beijing, but was surprised the custom was taking hold in more rural Half Moon.

He responded patiently.

"Because we like to give babies modern names. Do names for children not change in America?"

I acknowledged that they did, and for the same reason.

In addition to regular names, which are formally registered in the brigade records, children also have nicknames, as mentioned earlier. A very common nickname is simply the word *xiao*, meaning "little" or "young." Thus, a girl whose formal name is Wu Pingping (Wu Apple) may be called by her close circle of relatives Xiao Ping. When she is older and takes a job, her co-workers are likely to call her Xiao Wu, utilizing the Chinese word for "young" and the surname. (In comparable fashion, when addressing someone more senior, the last name is prefixed with *lao*, meaning "old" or "older," as with Lao Wang, my family host.)

In summary, while naming customs vary from place to place and family to family, some features are quite common in rural areas of China: Men (and far less frequently, women) often have a character indicating generation as part of their formal name. Everyone has an informal nickname, and formal names usually have no relationship to informal ones. It should also be noted that in the past, peasant women didn't even have formal names. Informal names were only infant names. When such women married, they were still without names of their own, being referred to only by combining the husbands' and fathers' surnames.

After the baby's first-month naming ceremony, the household returns to a more normal routine. In most instances, the mother will begin at least part-time work outside the home, particularly if a mother-in-law or "auntie" is available to care for the child. Women who work in the fields are given as much as an hour off to feed the baby in addition to their regular morning and afternoon breaks. They also have the opportunity of placing their babies in the brigade nursery. Relatively few women have positions in nearby sideline industries and small factories, but those who do use comparable day-care facilities. Actually, the birth of a first grandchild provides a most convenient reason for a 40-to-50-year-old mother-in-law to retire from the hard life of an agricultural field worker. Who wants to spend a long day bent over a hoe when one can take care of a first grandchild.

Whether the baby is taken care of mostly by mother or grandmother, its day is largely spent in a supportive environment. In addition to its mother's milk, the infant soon finds itself being offered cakes, wheat-flour porridge, and other kinds of soup, and perhaps some milk powder mixed with other liquid. Meat, prechewed by mother or grandmother, is also added to the diet, as is salt—the latter perceived as insuring the child's future strength. All this time, the young baby is encouraged to shake its head, clench its fist, clap its hands, smile before friends, and in other ways demonstrate to the family and relatives that it is healthy and happy. By the time the child is a year old, it has become used to being cared for by many relatives other than mother and grandmother. Older sisters and

Grannies pushing baby carriages down the main road of the village.

occasionally brothers will feed the child, as will the father. When the weather is fine, grannies take delight in strolling down the main street of the village, pushing a sturdy handmade pram and conversing animatedly with their counterparts who are pushing similar carriages along the same roadway.

Between the age of one and two, most children will be weaned, although those in ill health may be breastfed a little longer. The task is accomplished rather quickly. If the child complains, the mother may spread a little red pepper on her nipple while offering as a substitute some liquid from warm porridge, egg and rice cake, or similar nutritious food.

Toilet training, by contrast, is undertaken in a more leisurely manner. By the time an infant is a year old, it will begin wearing trousers and a shirt or jacket. The design of such clothing is the ultimate in preparation for relaxed toilet training —a slit between the trouser legs enabling the child to squat down whenever the need arises. When the mother or grandmother notices the child about to urinate or defecate, she will bend over and help support it. At the same time she is holding the child, she will make a soft whistling sound. Seldom, if ever, will the mother or other family member bother to take the child to the household or public village toilet. For children, the convenience of a courtyard or lane is seen as a perfectly adequate location for such activity. Nor is an infant's "night soil" considered as dirty as that of an adult. Once the task is complete, a quick call to a waiting dog or a shovel toss into the courtyard pigsty is all that is needed to clean the area. Obviously, the transition from this pattern to that of actual toilet training occurs very easily. Between the ages of one and two, the mother begins to anticipate the child's bodily functions and at the appropriate time again holds the child and whistles softly, waiting for the desired result. For most children, such education is successfully completed by the age of two.

In Half Moon, as in other Chinese villages, responsibility for the upbringing of the infant is not limited to the mother and grandmother, although they do provide much of the day-to-day supervision. In most households, this activity is seen as a mutual responsibility of the extended family and even the larger community. In this socializing group of parents, grandparents, older siblings, and numerous "aunties" and "uncles," only some of which are real kin, the young child has a considerable support network. Indeed, some parents, grandparents, and "pseudo-kin" are often accused of spoiling their children.

Actually, the situation is more complex than this. For example, Half Moon villagers do not in fact recognize fictive kin. All kin are real. Terms like "auntie" and "uncle," when applied to nonrelatives, are usually modified by the adding of a prefix *ta*, meaning "not ours." In this way, villagers easily recognize distinctions between kin and nonkin.

So too, the seemingly abundant expression of affection given to young infants is not so much a traditional socialization practice of the countryside as it is of the city. Not surprisingly, given this difference, city people may even slur their rural counterparts, sometimes going as far as to suggest that peasant parents "treat their children like their pigs and dogs." Rural villagers, on the other hand, feel that many urban parents and grandparents overindulge their children and grandchildren. The fact that infants in Half Moon Village are often coddled, actively indulged, and not infrequently "spoiled"—particularly by grandmothers—may well reflect some urban influence.

Seldom are village infants punished. If a baby cries incessantly, or engages in some similar frustrating behavior, a parent might possibly spank it, but even these slaps are more symbolic than real, since they are given so gently. Much more likely, the child will be handed a wooden rattle or other plaything to distract its attention from whatever was bothering it. Or an older sibling will go over to the *kang* and stroke, play, or gently rock it back and forth until it stops fussing. In good weather, the baby is taken outside to play or watch some courtyard activity.

If the problem is more persistent, such as developing a habit of throwing food on the floor when no longer hungry, the mother responds first by telling the infant to be sensible and eat properly. If it continues to be "naughty," the mother then speaks more firmly. If it still misbehaves, the mother may then give the infant a brief swat on the buttocks. However, such an effort to teach good behavior is often sidetracked by the ever-attentive mother-in-law, who, seeing the baby being reprimanded, comes over to the table or chair, sweeps the infant up in her arms, and proceeds to coddle it in complete disregard for the educational efforts of her daughter-in-law.

CHILDHOOD

Between the ages of three and six, children begin to explore more actively the world outside their courtyard. Some of this time is spent in play with other children in the village. Boys spend a considerable amount of time playing marbles, climbing trees, making kites out of cornstalks and newspapers, or finding old iron hoops to roll along the road with a stick. Outdoor activities for girls include a variety of simple games. Mother and daughter may make a shuttlecock out of cloth and feathers. Taking it outside, the daughter kicks it in the air seeing how many times she can keep it up without it touching the ground. Then she will try and find other girls who may pair up in teams to see who can keep the toy in the air the longest. Or a girl may obtain a rubber band and attach it to a paddle and cloth ball, and then see how many times she can hit the ball.

Very popular group activities among girls are skip-rope and kick-stone. In the former, the girl is expected to sing a song of eight or ten stanzas without tripping on the rope. In the latter game, somewhat like hopscotch, four adjacent squares are drawn in the earth. Then, with one foot off the ground, the child tries to kick a stone from one square to the next without losing balance. One's turn is lost when the second foot touches the ground or the stone remains in the original square.

Other games carried on throughout childhood involve use of a six-sided ball filled with sand. Two teams of boys or girls are formed, each trying to hit an opposite team member without their catching the ball. When it is caught, the other team gains possession of the ball and attempts a similar process. Another game involves the use of a multicolored pig or sheep's knuckle bone. The participant must throw the bone in the air, walk across a line drawn in the earth, and then catch it, making sure the surface color differs from toss to catch. Of the relatively few games participated in by both boys and girls, hide-and-seek and card playing are the most popular.

Children playing games on the village street.

While adults rarely participate in these games, they often serve as objects of interest and entertainment for the children. A stranger automatically fits this category, whether the individual is a seller of pottery or a buyer of eggs for the district store, a member of a traveling puppet troupe, or a visiting film projectionist from commune headquarters setting up a movie screen. An American anthropologist is always worth a little observation, especially since his physical features, mannerisms, and expressions are so different. Attention can even become entertainment when such an individual tries to keep a shuttlecock in the air for more than a few seconds.

A time when children and adults do come together for leisure-time activities is in the evening. In summer particularly, following the close of the meal and cleanup, many family members will take their young children and walk down to the village plaza to visit with friends and neighbors—or very likely, to watch a program on the brigade-owned television set. In an average summer evening, one hundred or more villagers are likely to spend at least a half hour or more standing, seated on stools, or squatting close to the ground, taking in the latest Beijing opera, drama, or comedy. Always in the front are the young children with their mothers or older siblings, behind them the teenagers, followed by other adults.

Given the newness of television to the village, the first T.V. set arriving in 1978, almost all programs are acceptable forms of entertainment. Some, of course, utilize more traditional art forms. In comedy, the famous "crosstalk" dialogue, in which two men (never women) share a fast-paced and often straight-faced, but humorous commentary on some particular theme, is very popular. One summer evening, I walked over to the village plaza to find more than fifty adults and quite a few teenagers loudly laughing over a particularly funny crosstalk. The butt of the humor was the well-known pattern of Chinese film heroes who "will not die." Many propaganda movies of the recent past portray a courageous leader who, on his deathbed, fatally wounded or ill, continues to expound in a most lengthy monologue a rather amazing number of self-effacing pronouncements such as self-criticism over not serving the people enough or pledging to give all his money on his death to the Party.[1] I was impressed at the government-run television's ability to poke fun at its own officialdom. But I was not prepared for the response of the villagers, who thought the crosstalk uproariously funny. Of course, I had not seen these propaganda films anywhere near as many times as they had. Only the young children missed the humor.

The lives of children are not just filled with play, however. After reaching the age of three, youngsters are given responsibilities ranging from sweeping the floor to gathering sticks for fuel, weeding or picking vegetables, and washing rice for cooking. The actual age at which the child is introduced to work varies from family to family, the intervening factor usually being the number of children already available to assist in completing household chores. In the 1950s, when nurseries were nonexistent and families tended to be larger, older children spent considerable time looking after their younger siblings. Girls, particularly, ran errands for parents, helped with the cooking, and cleaned the courtyard. Not infrequently at

---

[1] The humor focused on the length of the hero's monologue, not the political content.

this time, parents would postpone a daughter's going to primary school until after the age of seven because her work at home was seen as being more important.

Today, as families become smaller (averaging between two and three rather than three to four or more) and more day-care nurseries are established, there is a reduction in the amount of responsibility given to children, young as well as older. The increase in standard of living has also lessened the family workload. Higher income shared within a smaller family enables its members to purchase more goods and services, thereby reducing the household chores.

Young children are also taught to be thrifty. If a child drops a few pieces of grain or some vegetables on the table, the parents ask that the child pick it up and eat it. If a larger amount of food is dropped on the floor by the child, a request is made to wash it off before eating it. Not surprisingly, such thrift applies equally to clothing use. Without exception, youngsters wear the outgrown clothing of older siblings. In the early years, such sharing causes little problem, since dress seldom distinguishes between the sexes. However, as the child grows older, such distinctions gain in importance. By late childhood, a boy asked to wear his older sister's shirt will complain to his mother. "I don't want to wear this." To his mother's questioning response, he might add, "This is for girls. Look at the flower pattern. It's for girls. I'm not wearing this. I'm a boy!"

Parents hold different expectations for girls and boys. If the child is a girl, she is held responsible for herself at an earlier age—especially if she is the oldest, since she may soon have to assist in caring for a younger sibling. When younger brothers and sisters are born, she is asked to help feed them, take them outside, clean them up, and in other ways free the mother or grandmother for other house-work tasks like feeding the pigs and washing clothes—tasks considered too heavy for young girls. If, due to death or other cause, the particular household is without a grandmother, the young girl will be given even more responsibilities for the sewing of clothes, simple cooking, and managing the fire.

A boy is also expected to care for himself at an early age. By the time he reaches three or four, he will help his father collect firewood, bring home the tools from the family plot, or even work a little in the garden, weeding or picking vege-tables. However, with the trend toward smaller families, young boys find themselves increasingly told to assist in housework and in caring for other siblings, effec-tively reducing the earlier differential expectations between the sexes. Needless to say, if a family consists of three boys and one younger sister, the boys carry the major childhood tasks in the home. The girl will not only have considerably less to do, but may become somewhat spoiled. This could also be true for the oldest girl if she were the only one in a large family. So too, a single boy in a family of girls soon finds himself being given much more care and special attention than is the case in a more sexually balanced group of siblings. In Half Moon, such a child is always perceived as spoiled.

As children become older, punishments for wrongdoing become more frequent and harsher. A child may be punished for not listening to his or her parents, especially when they have told the child not to do something, like going down to the drainage ditch and becoming dirty. If the child goes by itself to a ditch or pond that is full of water, the parents may become angry because of the danger involved. Punishment for such an act will most likely be a spanking on the buttocks.

Another form of behavior likely to bring on harsh punishment is serious fighting among children. Such fighting can quickly disrupt the tight web of harmonious relations that are encouraged within the village, thereby causing considerable unease among parents. Thus, when children begin to fight, parents quickly step in. The immediate point at issue is not who is right or wrong, but that the fighting must stop.

If fighting between children of different families is considered a serious offense, fighting within the family is condemned even more. Such conflict can assume several different forms. For example, an older sibling may become angry at a younger one. Since anger is not supposed to be expressed directly, the older child may try to frighten the younger. This is most likely to occur when the parents and other adults are temporarily away. During one fall evening in Half Moon Village, Liu Wei, a young boy of seven, was told by his parents that they were going next door to visit briefly with a neighbor. Before leaving, Wei was asked to keep a close watch over his younger sister, Fang. When they returned fifteen minutes later, they found a worried Wei trying to comfort his little sister, while wiping large tears from her face.

"What happened?" asked his mother.

"Fang is crying."

"That's obvious," said Father Liu, a little suspicious of Wei's remark.

Somewhat defensively, the boy countered with the admission that he had made a tiger face and growled at Fang, who then burst out crying.

"That's a bad thing to do," Father Liu shouted angrily. Raising his hand, he slapped Wei on the face, at which point Wei joined his sister in tears. The mother stood by the table, looking firm and saying nothing. Eventually, both children settled down, as did the parents, and the incident was laid to rest. But it was not forgotten. Hitting a child on the face is a major form of punishment, reserved for serious offenses. The usual admonition is "When hitting someone, never use the face; when cursing someone, never expose the defect." That is, never strike someone's face and never speak in anger about someone else's weakness, particularly in front of others.

While such an admonition is not infrequently broken, the lesson for Wei was clear: An older brother must not scare his younger sister. He must care for her, take responsibility for her. When siblings fight, the responsibility rests with the older child. Younger brothers and sisters are less knowledgeable, less understanding, less experienced in how to behave. Also, when a younger brother or sister does misbehave, older siblings should report the event to the parents, rather than punishing the child themselves.

Differences in parental approaches to childhood discipline begin to appear fairly quickly. As the child grows up, the father's manner becomes more aloof, and his role in discipline more important. Children, in turn, are more afraid of their fathers. Such fear is not only due to the greater strictness and more severe administration of punishment—including caning as well as spanking. It is also grounded in the social distance that characterizes the father-child relationship. Today, fathers are more likely to joke or play with their children than in the past. But they are still firm. They say little and seldom lose their tempers. Having less interpersonal contact, of course, makes them more venerable. While this too is changing, the father is still the dominant authority figure.

Mothers, on the other hand, are more sympathetic. They may be equally angry over a child's transgression; they may also slap or curse a child. But most often, their anger will express itself in words: "There is no supper for you. You get enough from fighting," or, "You must be too full to stay idle; so you go out and fight with other children. Since you are so full, you won't have any supper tonight." However, the child knows these are often empty words. Mother is too kind to let her child go hungry, especially if it is a girl. Boys normally receive stricter punishment.

Children are also punished for damage they inflict upon themselves while playing. If a boy falls down and injures an arm or leg, or if a girl cuts herself with a knife, the parent will punish the child first and take care of the hurt second. The message is that children must be careful about their bodies, take care of them. If children hurt themselves, they may not be able to carry out their responsibilities in the household, and others will have to do more.

In summary, Half Moon Village provides a secure environment for its children. Dangers are few, and the social conditioning precise. Children growing up in the household know from an early age their responsibilities and their freedoms, their obligations and their leisure. While firmness is the rule from age three on, and punishment for wrongdoing can be swift and direct, the security provided by this family patterning is substantial. It is little wonder that the children of Half Moon Village, like children throughout China, so often appear to outsiders as shy but friendly in manner and exemplary in behavior. Such "presentation of self" to strangers is exactly what they have been taught by their families, and usually they do it well.[2]

However, such expression should not be seen as composing the norm of early childhood life. The picture is much more complex, as has been already illustrated. While there is emotional support as well as firmness, the links are stronger between mothers and sons, fathers remaining more in the background. Daughters too know that once they marry, they will have to leave their family for that of the groom, frequently in another village. The old adage that "a daughter who has married out is like spilled water that cannot be replaced" still lingers in the minds of some parents, who know that eventually they will have to replace their daughters with one or more daughters-in-law.

Half Moon has one additional institution with some responsibility for the care and upbringing of young children—the brigade day-care nursery. Located in a renovated house and courtyard near the brigade office, this facility regularly accepts preschool children of parents who work in the nearby fields. However, most families prefer looking after the young infant at home, at least until it can speak

---

[2] Urban Beijing newspapers, commenting on the success of the one-child family planning campaign, also receive a great many letters to the editor complaining about one serious side-effect of "having only one"—a large increase in spoiled children!

and assume some responsibility for itself. For them, the day-care nursery is viewed as a very poor substitute for the much more personal attention given by mother and grandmother. Therefore, the majority of infants, whose households include a grandmother or nonworking mother, will remain at home for a year or longer. Still, for a variety of reasons, including limited availability of family members, economic need, and other personal factors, babies can be enrolled as early as one to six months.

For much of the year, the nursery opens at 7:00 in the morning, just before the village work team members head out to the fields; it closes temporarily for the noon break around 11:30 and opens again for the afternoon work period from 2:00 to 4:30, or for however long the villagers spend in the fields. At harvest time, when all work a twelve- or fourteen-hour day, the nursery stays open for a correspondingly longer time.

The nursery itself has one large room providing space for the 25 or more children that usually attend each day. At one end, a large *kang* stretching from wall to wall enables infants to take regular naps. At the other end, a few chairs and a table are used by slightly older children, who may draw on slate boards or play games together. The oldest will occasionally be encouraged to use their boards to learn numbers and simple Chinese characters. Outside, courtyard facilities are equally spartan. Except for a sliding board and roundabout, large toys are non-existent. Children do have access to smaller items such as rubber balls, beanbags, skip ropes, and picture books.

The nursery school staff includes two or more older women, the actual number depending on how many children are present, and two younger women who carry out more specific educational responsibilities. Staff income is based on the brigade work point system, although sometimes older women may serve as volunteer assistants. All look after the children in a general way, organizing simple games, telling stories, and making sure occasional disagreements and fights are resolved with minimum difficulty. The younger women, who have received some training in childhood education, are expected to provide the older infants with a little practical knowledge, as well as lead them in the singing of group songs and the learning of simple dance steps.

In all these activities, there is considerable continuity between what is learned at home and in school. Young children are held often and are well cared for. But they and their older playmates are seldom played with. In the adult-centered world of Half Moon Village, parents and nursery school staff are expected to teach their children, not play with them. Nor is much attention given to reasoning before six or seven. That effort is generally reserved for a later period, when the child enters primary school.

5/Schooling

A VISIT FROM THE TEACHER

Su Shitou, 10 years old, attends third grade in a nearby primary school. Though bright and full of wit, he doesn't like to study. For him, working with figures and characters is boring, especially when he can spend time with his dad in the fields or collecting different kinds of insects by the irrigation ditch at the edge of the village.

In class, Su doesn't listen to his teachers either, preferring to talk with his nearby schoolmates. For this reason, his teacher recently reassigned him to share a desk with a girl in the hope that his classroom behavior might improve. Yet just the other day, Su got into trouble again. He put a broom on top of the half-open classroom door, expecting it to fall on a student walking into the room. Only this time it fell on the teacher. There were a few giggles from his friends, but that was all. Every set of eyes focused on the tall man standing, broom in hand, at the front of the room. In a calm but firm voice, Teacher Wang addressed the class.

"Students, who is responsible for this?" he asked, gently waving the broom before him.

The room was still. Then, as Su Shitou rose from behind his desk, the other students turned in his direction.

"I'm sorry, teacher. I did not expect the broom to fall on you. I was playing a joke."

"Su Shitou, you and I will have a little talk after school." With that remark, the teacher turned, walked toward a small platform at the front of the room, and sat down behind his desk. Reaching into a drawer, he pulled out a black notebook. As the students watched, he wrote a few comments on a back page under the name Su. Then, looking at Shitou once again, he closed the book, returned it to his desk, and addressed the class, informing them that it was time to begin the day's language lesson.

In midafternoon, at the close of school, Shitou stood before his teacher, waiting for the pronouncement.

"Xiao Su, I want you to inform your parents I am coming by the village this evening before dark to talk with them."

It was the answer Shitou expected. He had been forewarned the last time he got into trouble. There are two reasons why a teacher might come to a student's home. One is simply to inform the parents how the child is progressing and answer any questions they have about the school. The other is the more dreaded *gaozhuang*, in which a complaint is lodged about bad behavior. Unfortunately for Shitou, this definitely appeared to be a *gaozhuang* type of visit. Since teachers are highly respected in Half Moon, as in other villages of Red Flag Commune, a complaint expressed by them about a student is taken seriously. But that's not all. Such a criticism also casts shame on the whole family. As a result, Shitou knew that, at the very least, he would get a good dressing down. More likely, it would be a good beating.

That evening, shortly before sunset, Teacher Wang arrived at the Su courtyard gate.

"Hello. May I come in?"

"Oh yes, Teacher Wang," responded Mother Su. "Come in and have a seat. Have you had your dinner? Please, let me give you some here."

Father Su added, "You must be tired, I'm sure. Have a seat. Shitou, make some hot water for your teacher." As a solemn-looking Shitou turned toward the kitchen, his father admonished him: "Shitou, say hello first."

"Hello, Xiao Shitou," the teacher said. "I've already had my dinner, so just some water will be fine. I simply dropped by to visit a little with your parents."

"Thank you, Teacher Wang," responded Mother Su. "You are always so busy attending to the students. Sometimes they don't understand very well. And other times, they are naughty. How is our Shitou doing in school? Does he cause any trouble in class?"

"Oh, no. He is a good boy. He has made real progress recently."

"Around here, he likes to play and run around. Can't sit still even for five minutes. He must give you a lot of headaches, I suppose?" inquired the father.

"Boys get restless easily. Shitou used to talk with other students in class, but he doesn't do that anymore. Is he reading at home and doing schoolwork by himself?"

"He reads picture books quite a bit. Stories about various heroes. But he doesn't like homework. When we force him, he does it with friends."

During this whole exchange, Xiao Shitou was sitting quietly on a *kang* in the back of the room, observing everything and saying nothing.

"I see. He likes to read story books. Good. What we have to do now is show him that he can't just learn from pictures. He must do well in schoolwork too."

"You're right. Mother Su and I are sorry we don't pay enough attention to his schoolwork. It's important to learn things. Children don't know that. Whenever I get angry with Shitou, I give him a good slapping."

"That's no use. It's not the way to put him on the right track. Remember, he is still young. Teachers and parents need to cooperate to train the younger generation to be useful to the country."

While addressing the teacher, Father Su kept glancing at his son. "Teacher Wang, what you say is correct. Whenever Shitou does anything wrong in school, tell him I support whatever punishment you give him."

"Punishment is not the best way to educate students. We do reasoning. The result is better. That way he will understand. Actually, Shitou is making progress. That's all that counts. Of course, sometimes he forgets. It is best if he listens to the teacher. Children are like small trees. It takes careful nurturing for them to grow straight and tall."

"You are right again, Teacher Wang. We should do more with Shitou. We don't pay enough attention to his schoolwork."

"I should do more too. But he is making some headway. Don't worry about him too much. Well, it's getting late. I must be going. Thanks for the water."

"Good-bye, Teacher Wang. Thank you for coming, and for all the work you are doing with Shitou. We appreciate it."

This portrayal of Teacher Wang's visit to the Su family, described in detail by a perceptive key informant, illustrates both continuity and change in the education of village children like Su Shitou. Teacher Wang, aware of the impact that his high status has in the village, chooses to underplay his problems with Shitou. He knows that his presence in the Su household is indication enough that the son is in difficulty at school. Such a visit is usually followed by punishment handed out by the father: a slap or beating if the child is in primary school, and at least a severe verbal reprimand if the student is older. In this case, the father not only indicates that he supports that course of action, but goes even further, giving blanket approval to the teacher to impose any punishment he deems advisable while Shitou is at school. Today, this common parental response is more likely to be challenged by modern teachers like Wang. That is, the family is encouraged to become involved in the child's education, rather than simply treating the offending son (almost never a daughter) as an object bringing shame to the household.[1]

From the beginning of primary schools in the early 1950s until the early 1970s, enrollment in the area around Half Moon was fairly small, many peasants questioning the importance of all but the first few years of schooling. At that time, knowledge gained in the classroom was seen to have little bearing on knowing how to plant, weed, and harvest crops. For young girls having to care for younger brothers and sisters at home, there was even more reason to either delay entrance into primary school or drop out early. Boys, on the other hand, not only had fewer tasks to complete in the home, but were not expected to begin work in the fields until their early or mid-teens. Relatively free of daily work responsibilities, they were better able to take advantage of what school had to offer. Furthermore, peasant parents, many of whom were illiterate, at least wanted their sons to be able to read newspapers and perhaps even simple books. Today, over 90 percent of the children, girls and boys, complete their five-year primary school education—a substantial achievement in two decades. Exactly what does that education entail?

---

[1] This belief that the shame of an individual (and also the honor) is shared by the family and lineage has a long history in China. Under the emperors, a well-known principle in the penal system, called *lianzuo*, stated that the whole family was to be held collectively responsible for serious political crimes committed by any one member. Even close relatives of the given family, such as the wife's patrilineal kin, could be executed along with the criminal—all pointing to the fact that within the traditional Chinese cultural framework, individuals were not seen as independent beings, but as members of the larger kinship network. This relationship between the individual and the group is discussed more fully in a later chapter.

PRIMARY EDUCATION

Children begin their formal education at age seven. Half Moon doesn't have its own primary school. So, depending on the students' ages, they attend one of two schools shared between several nearby villages. The total population of the two institutions is 416, less than 3 percent of Red Flag Commune's overall primary school enrollment of 14,000. Each of the five grades contains approximately 40 students each. There are ten teachers, one for each classroom. Other members of the staff include a director and a physical education instructor, who share their time between the two facilities.

Although school begins at 7:30, children usually arrive 15 to 20 minutes early. Chatting in small groups on the playground, they wait until a bell informs them of the approaching class time. At its sound, they jog twice around the yard and then split up, heading for their own home rooms. At the second bell, the teachers enter and classes begin.

Classrooms are arranged quite simply. In some, each student has his or her own table or desk, while in others they are shared. The much larger flat-topped desk at the front of the room is reserved for the teacher. On the wall behind the teacher's desk hangs a large blackboard, and above that, eight large Chinese characters are painted in bold red colors: *tuanjie, jinzhang, yan su, huopo,* meaning "Be united, alert, earnest, and lively." For the class, it is a reminder that all students should work together as one, not be lazy, be serious in study, and be energetic. By looking carefully high on the wall between the two sets of characters, one can also see a large, relatively clean rectangular space—the one remaining physical legacy of an earlier time in school history, when a picture of Mao Zedong hung in every classroom.

At the back of each room are "study gardens" (bulletin boards) where students post their better compositions. Other spaces are reserved for the names of students who have been helpful cleaning up or assisting others. Still another location in the "garden" contains a list of all the students and their success in recent personal hygiene inspections, in which hands, front and back, neck, and ears are checked. Those who do well receive a small red flag beside their names. Those who do not receive nothing. For this age group, negative evaluations are not considered helpful, especially when they are made public. Advanced primary grades also have "paper-clip gardens" (wall newspapers), where brief articles on current issues or new information of interest to students is posted. These wall gardens are organized by teachers and student members of a home room class committee.

The primary school curriculum begins with a concentrated focus on Chinese language and arithmetic, followed by courses in music, physical education, drawing, and calligraphy. From grade three on, depending on the availability and skill level of the teachers, courses are offered in common knowledge (elementary science), geography, history, and painting. Most classes meet for forty minutes. Lunch break is from 11:30 to 2:00, followed by two more class periods. Though school is over at 3:30, students are encouraged to remain longer to complete their homework or receive additional help from a teacher. Physical education is also included in the daily curriculum. Following the early-morning jog around the school yard, students participate in regular exercises during ten-minute intervals between two class periods throughout the day.

What is sometimes called "moral education" is a vital part of learning in both primary and middle school. Although the subject is not formally taught, it pervades school activity both in and outside the classroom. In meetings with teachers, in summaries of the semester's work, and in various outdoor activities, actions of students are utilized to illustrate important moral precepts such as "being responsible to others." Common illustrations include children who, on finding an object like a pen or workbook on the school playground, return it to the teacher, or children who find pieces of scrap metal and turn them in at the local state-run recycling center. Praise for such action is not given immediately, but reserved for a class meeting, where other children can learn what is good and proper behavior.[2]

Training in social responsibility is further developed through student committees. In the lower primary grades, such committees rely heavily on the teacher's guidance, although even here, children elect a monitor to organize simple group tasks. Classes in advanced primary grades elect committees that assume responsibility for leading morning exercises, supervising study periods, collecting homework assignments, and preparing class performances for holiday occasions.

Similar moral education occurs outside the classroom. In harvest season, primary school children are taken out to the fields to watch their parents and neighbors working. Older brothers and sisters from middle school also help with the harvest, as do retired peasant men and women, the latter organized through the Women's Federation. While there, the children husk small ears of corn left behind by their parents; or, if brought to the threshing ground, they sweep up gleanings of wheat for later storage. Such activity not only instills in the student the value of work, it also emphasizes the importance of being thrifty with what one produces. In all these efforts, the child is reminded to cooperate with teachers, parents, and "grannies," to follow instructions, and to share what one has with others. The values conveyed in such an environment—respect for age, cooperation in work, and generosity—are obvious extensions of similar themes inculcated at home.

Of course, moral education is sometimes overdone, as the parents of one young student found to their chagrin. In the early 1970s, during the Cultural Revolution, one son learned at school about a selfless hero named Lei Feng, who spent his whole life helping others rather than concentrating on his own interests and those of his family. The eager pupil, deciding to follow the hero's example of "devoting his life to the collective effort," proceeded to take some manure set aside for his family's courtyard plot and spread it over the adjacent collectively owned brigade land. His family was not impressed.

For the most part, this kind of education is not only pervasive, but effective. Students continually learn proper behavior from teachers, parents, textbooks, radio, newspapers, and television. In all these instances, they are encouraged to help each other, care for each other, learn from each other, and "take each others' happiness

---

[2] In this instance, face is "given" rather than "lost" (Hu 1944:56; Stover and Stover 1976: 206).

as their own." In contrast, activities that cause embarrassment or remarks that emphasize a negative attribute are discouraged. Envision, for example, a Chinese child's participation in a game like "musical chairs." In an American school, such a game encourages children to be competitive and to look out for themselves. But to young Chinese, the negative aspect is much more noticeable. That is, losers become objects of attention due to their having lost their space—and therefore "face." In China, winning is fun too. But it should not be achieved at the expense of causing someone else embarrassment. In all kinds of daily activity, including study as well as games, Chinese children are regularly reminded that they must work hard and be sensitive to the needs of others, for only through such effort will their own lives become truly meaningful. Of course, Shitou's classroom behavior is a reminder of the distance that separates reality from the ideal.

Self-discipline encouraged through moral education is also applied to "the three Rs." For example, in a second grade classroom, a great deal of effort is spent learning to read Chinese. American children have only 26 letters to memorize and a system of phonetics to assist in recognizing new words. Chinese students have no comparable system to assist them in learning an immensely larger set of characters that are needed to transcribe the Chinese language. Memorization, and its application through intensive reading, is the only way to master the many hundreds of ideographs that children must know in order to read and write effectively. And that takes considerable self-control.

On a typical day, the teacher enters the classroom and puts on the blackboard four words written in *pinyin*, the romanized form of standard Chinese. In primary school, this system is used to help children learn how to pronounce characters, a practice similar to the way in which phonetic systems are used in the United States to assist in learning English pronunciation. Next to each word is placed the corresponding ideograph. The teacher points to the written word and the ideograph, pronouncing it each time. Then, the character is broken down into its sub-parts and interpretations made.

Finally, using a pointer, the teacher demonstrates the correct steps for writing the ideograph—the stroke order—naming each part at the appropriate moment. Following this demonstration, a volunteer is asked to repeat the process. After being selected, the child stands straight up beside his or her desk and responds by drawing the Chinese character in the air with a finger. Next, the teacher asks the whole class to go through the same procedure. If a volunteer makes an error in answering, the teacher usually does not comment negatively, since any possible embarrassment to the student is to be avoided. Instead, another volunteer is quickly selected. Finally, flash cards are brought out with *pinyin* on one side and the Chinese character on the other. In sequence, the teacher and a volunteer, followed by the rest of the class, all recite what is inscribed on the card held in the air. Blackboard and cards are then used to reinforce each other. The quick pace of the lesson easily holds the attention of most children as they repeat over and over again the drill necessary to retain the new words.

This type of rote learning, while most pronounced in language classes, is not limited to such subject matter. In early primary grades the child is regularly expected to follow the instructions of the teacher. The idea of the child developing

A primary school classroom near Half Moon Village.

individual initiative or creative expression on his or her own or in "free" classroom periods is not a part of the educational process. Art classes, for example, are common in primary school, but the usual tasks involve paper cutting or copying drawings made on the blackboard by the teacher. They do not tap possible artistic talent of the student. So too, in Chinese literature classes, students are expected to respond briefly to precise questions posed by the teacher or participate in group recitation of selected passages of text, rather than discuss or debate possible interpretations of the author's meaning in the selected passage. Again, this cultural patterning in the classroom is consistent with similar learning in the home. Teachers, parents, and other authority figures are knowledgeable. Students and children are not. Therefore, they must listen, study hard, and emulate their elders, so that they too will have that knowledge in the future.

Such an approach to education instills a feeling of group solidarity among students. However, it does little to develop in the child a sense of inquiry, creative challenge, or deductive reasoning. Wanting to explore more deeply the relationship between group-oriented, rote-focused learning so common in the primary school and the more individual-oriented, problem-focused approach characteristic of middle-class America, I asked the director of the school near Half Moon Village if I could attend a class and then meet with him afterwards. He expressed his pleasure at my interest and welcomed me to attend any class I wished.

A few minutes before 7:00 on a chilly morning in early December, I left my room and walked down to the end of the lane, where another member of the Wang lineage lived. Wang Yingying, a fifth grade student, had agreed somewhat hesitantly that I could accompany her and her friends to school on this day. Outside her courtyard gate, Jia, another student, was already waiting.

"Yingying, it's time to go to school. Are you ready?" little Jia called through the open gate.

"Almost. I'll be there in a minute," Yingying responded.

Joining Jia, I listened as Yingying's mother spoke.

"Take your younger brother down to Granny's room. I have to go to the fields."

"But Mum, Jia is waiting for me. I'll be late for school."

"O.K. Give the baby to me. You go ahead, but come back right after class. Don't fool around, do you hear?"

Yingying headed toward the door.

"And listen to the teacher. . . ."

"I know, I know," responded Yingying, rapidly approaching the gate. Seeing both of us, she smiled, and with a quick tilt of her head suggested that we head on down the lane toward the main road beyond.

Ten minutes later, we arrived at the low one-story adobe and brick buildings that housed the school. Young people from other villages stood around in small groups waiting for the bell to ring. Two primary students had already entered a nearby classroom; one was sweeping the floor and the other cleaning the blackboard. At the bell, the rest made their usual jog around the outer perimeter of the playground and then headed toward their home rooms.

The school director, who had been waiting for my arrival, greeted me warmly and then introduced the fourth grade teacher who was to be my host for the morning. Together, we entered his classroom, and I sat down in the back trying unsuccessfully to be inconspicuous. Still, after a few brief stares and whispers, the class began to settle down. The 42 students were about evenly divided between boys and girls. Remembering the story of Su Shitou, I wasn't surprised to see several couples sharing small desks and benches. Young girls, who rarely misbehave in school, were used to help the teacher keep order in this classroom too.

Of the 42 students in the room, 12 wore red scarves indicating their participation in the Young Pioneers, a loosely organized group of children (somewhat similar to the scout movement in the United States) whose activities include those of a helpful nature—cleaning streets, assisting the elderly, and aiding teachers. Since most children between eight or nine and fourteen belong, it was obvious many hadn't bothered to wear their scarves on that day. Only a few children defined as "bad" or "consistently naughty" are excluded from the organization.[3] Needless to say, such naughty children are urged to improve their ways so that they too can become Young Pioneers.

As the teacher began the lessons, first in math, then in language, I watched the children's response. It was difficult, of course, to determine the extent to which my being in the room influenced their behavior. Most were attentive, sitting straight and fairly still unless they were writing, drawing, holding a notebook, or reciting.

[3] Until 1980, children from landlord, rich peasant, or "class enemy" households could also be excluded.

As the morning progressed, and one set of lessons and exercises followed another, some children began using their pencils and paper for play. A few others simply stared out the window. All sat quietly, however, and only infrequently did anyone disturb the tenor of the class by whispering loudly or getting up and walking around. On such occasions, the teacher first looked sternly at the child and asked that the whispering stop. If that tactic was unsuccessful, he then walked down the aisle and firmly tapped his pencil on the student's desk, at which time all inappropriate activity at the desk quickly ceased.

By midmorning, the old pot-bellied coal stove was laboring rather unsuccessfully to heat the drafty and still cold classroom. Most students wore padded jackets, and a few, mittens or gloves, the latter only being removed when the student wrote in a notebook or on the blackboard. When the next bell rang, indicating an outdoor exercise break, all filed out the door quickly, seeking to throw off the chill brought on by sitting so long in the drafty room. After thanking the fourth grade teacher, I too walked briskly around the school yard, and then headed for the director's office at the end of the long building. I stepped into his considerably warmer room, and we chatted informally for a short while. Then he offered his view of the present educational system. It was one I had heard on several earlier occasions that year while interviewing officials from the Ministry of Education in Beijing.

"Education is improving now," commented the middle-aged director, speaking in a friendly but slightly bored manner.

"Before (meaning during the decade of the Cultural Revolution) . . . the children had no discipline. They didn't behave properly and couldn't learn anything. Now that is all changed. We have ten rules and regulations for behavior, and they have settled down. Now they are learning very well."

I remembered the large poster I had seen on the classroom wall showing several students happily reading their textbooks. Below the picture was a statement urging everyone to study hard, work diligently, and help the teacher and others when needed.

"What changes do you envision for the future?"

"We want to help the teachers improve their skills. This coming year the commune will hold special enrichment classes for fifth grade teachers under the direction of the Ministry of Education. Unfortunately, our level of teacher training is quite low. Even in communes like this one, close to the city, funds for advanced training of our staff are very limited."

I was reminded of an earlier discussion with the Deputy Vice Minister of Education for Beijing Municipality, who had emphasized that education could not be disconnected from the development of the region as a whole. Given the overall limitations of the country's economy, funds to upgrade educational quality had to be weighed against other modernizing efforts. Because rural students are still the vast majority of the total student population—over one hundred million—the costs are immense. To spend one more dollar per student, the government official reminded me, would cost an additional 100 million dollars!

My thoughts returned to the more manageable Half Moon Village. The primary school director continued:

"The Ministry of Education plans to improve rural education in two ways in the next two or three years. First, we must raise the level of training of those teachers presently in the classroom. This will be done by setting up training centers. Teachers who pass examinations after taking the new courses will be given a more senior status. Second, we want to establish more "spare-time schools," so that the new illiteracy that has reemerged over the past ten years can be eliminated. Finally, I hope we will be able to reinstate the six years of primary school education that we had before the Cultural Revolution. But, unfortunately, that will not be soon, given the cost involved."

Both primary and secondary education had expanded significantly throughout the commune by the early 1970s. Much of this activity, closely linked to the educational policies of the Cultural Revolution, emphasized the importance of utilizing local initiative. And indeed, many villages established new primary (and junior middle) schools by using local people and urban-trained "educated youth" to staff them. Wages for these new teachers were largely paid by the villagers themselves, through brigade-based work points. In order to obtain additional teachers for the new facilities, the earlier system of six-year primary schools was reduced to five—justification for the step being summed up in the slogan "less but better."

This dramatic educational effort put forward during the Cultural Revolution brought the benefits of expanded primary and secondary education to many commune youth, a real achievement, given the large increase in population between 1950 and the 1970s. Yet it did so at the expense of improving educational quality. The local primary school director was obviously identifying with the quality side of this equation. After obtaining some data on the history and size of the school, I expressed my appreciation for his efforts and took my leave. Walking home, I thought about how far the primary schools serving Half Moon and other nearby villages have come from their small beginnings in the early 1950s. Given that progress, it wasn't surprising that attention had now shifted to the junior and senior middle school, which still has considerably fewer graduates.

MIDDLE SCHOOL

Of Red Flag Commune's 22,200 students, approximately 8200 are in secondary or middle school. Of the latter, the large majority are enrolled in three-year junior middle schools, which are organized at the district level. The commune also has a few two-year senior middle schools, whose total enrollment is about 2000. However, only one, located near the commune headquarters, offers sufficiently high-level courses (including English) that it can even consider preparing its students to take the nationwide examinations for advanced technical school or university. Not surprisingly, most of these students are sons and daughters of middle-level commune officials or senior-level state workers who live nearby. The highest-level commune officials (whose income is received from the state sector) usually maintain their residence in Beijing City, thereby enabling their children to have an even better, urban education.

Today, about 80 percent of all primary school graduates in the commune begin middle school, although less than 30 percent finish. Of those who do, almost none enter higher education. In 1979, for example, of the senior secondary school students in the commune who chose to take the nationwide examination for entrance to a technical school or university, only eighteen passed.[4] A few went on to university, but the large majority were admitted to a less competitive lower-level technical school. Educational quality at even the best commune school is simply not adequate to meet the highly competitive standards now set by the Ministry of Education for entrance to higher education. This is true even though nonurban students can receive a lower passing score on the entrance examination than their city counterparts. As a result, the gap between educational opportunities for urban and rural (or in this case, suburban) students is still very much an issue.

Why do so many middle school students drop out before finishing? There are several reasons, most of which pertain in one way or another to economic problems. From the point of view of the commune, secondary education costs more to support and requires more highly trained instructors. Furthermore, such teachers usually live in urban areas and have little or no interest in moving to more rural locations. Second, education is not compulsory. Many families feel they cannot spare their sons' and daughters' potential income after age fourteen, fifteen, or sixteen. This is particularly true in the poorer villages of the commune. Third, middle schools, and especially the very few senior middle schools, are located quite some distance from those aspiring to attend. With poor roads and lack of bus transportation, some students are unable to attend the school on a daily basis and unable to pay the cost of having someone house them away from home.

Given the unlikelihood of receiving a passing examination grade for university or technical school entrance, most students and their parents see little reason to spend more than a year or two furthering their education. True, some say that fourteen may be a little early to begin work in field or factory. But if the children continue in school, their parents must pay for notebooks, clothing, and other related costs. Poorer peasant families find this difficult. Furthermore, such expenses are always weighed against the gains. Not uncommon is the question: why waste time in school if the training doesn't help in the future? Especially so when the time can be better spent bringing more income into the household. (As we will see shortly, this perception is most often applied to male students.) And finally, some young people do not have either the interest or the ability to complete five additional years of school. Today, students must receive a passing grade of at least 60 to enter both junior and senior middle school. Failures always occur, whether through lack of commitment or ability.

The junior middle school that Half Moon students attend is located near district headquarters, not far from the village. As a district middle school, it offers a large range of courses, including Chinese language and literature, algebra, chemistry, biology, physics, agricultural machinery, politics, and Chinese and Western history. In 1979, a young teacher from the school was sent to Beijing

---

[4] Unfortunately, the number of students taking the examination could not be obtained.

Normal College to learn English, and upon her return that subject was added to the curriculum.

The school has one other distinguishing feature: a two-story-high classroom, library, and office building—a feature that sets it apart from all other structures for miles around. The over 600 district young people who attend this school have use of the enlarged facility due to the efforts of earlier students and staff. In 1971, as part of the "self-reliance in education" phase of the Cultural Revolution, the district government, with the active assistance of students and their parents, built a small pharmaceutical factory and print shop, which was then partially integrated into the school. Throughout China at this time, all students were expected to "combine mental and manual labor," spending at least part of each school week in constructive work.

Once construction was completed, Half Moon and other village students from the district worked part-time in factory or print shop for the 42 weeks of the school year. Eventually, they, together with newly hired district workers, produced enough chemical products for sale to the state that the district was able to pay off its loan for building materials and purchase much-needed school equipment and supplies. By 1978 (the last year for which records are available), the annual profits of the factory, all of which are allocated to the school, had reached 100,000 *yuan*. The total income earned in this educational sideline industry since 1971 is a substantial 530,000 *yuan*.

For peasants in the area, their junior middle school is a source of real pride. Furthermore, they perceive the effort to provide a middle school education for all eligible students, rather than a selected few, as basically sound. As several parents put it: Fifteen years ago, who thought our children could attend middle school? Now, anyone can go. When local people were asked what positive gains were made in the commune during the Cultural Revolution, this middle school was often given as an illustration.

Today, with educational policy strongly emphasizing the latter side of the quantity-quality equation, one might assume that the earlier Cultural Revolution focus would be completely rejected. But such an assumption is not quite accurate. For example, in the academic year 1978–79, students in the district middle school were divided into two groups, rapid and slow learners, and then placed in different classrooms according to their designation. Within a short period of time, serious problems began to emerge, leading eventually to a discontinuation of the tracking scheme. What happened? Evaluating the change at the end of the year, the principal reported, "It didn't work. It undermined the students' spirit and stereotyped their behavior. Therefore, we have gone back to the earlier system of mixing fast and slow learners in the same classes. Now, the faster ones are given more work and the slower ones more help. The result appears to be much better for everyone."

Most of the revised policies are supported by middle school teachers. Those almost universally acclaimed are regulations for proper behavior, stricter academic standards, with corresponding emphasis on grades, and removal of "revolutionary" (that is, rhetorical) content from the subject matter. Student responses to these changes are also significant. Academic study is taken much more seriously than when I first visited middle schools in the area in 1972. At that time, political study and manual labor accounted for a much larger portion of the student's time. Academic study, as such, had less appeal.

In Half Moon Village today, the greater commitment to studying is seen everywhere. Younger siblings regularly ask older ones for help in solving basic mathematical problems, writing a short essay, or classifying plants. Students speak positively of their elderly literature teacher, who joyfully uses old Chinese classics as basic reading material—now that they are no longer branded as unacceptable due to a lack of revolutionary content. And they worry about their examinations. Gone is Mao's famous quotation, once used to challenge the educational bureaucracy: "To take an examination is to participate in one's own ambush!" For those seeking positions requiring educational knowledge, examinations are vital. For the rest, simply necessary.

Does education have much influence on one's later employment? The question is an important one in Red Flag Commune. Interestingly, in at least one instance, the answer appears to be negative for young men and affirmative for young women. Commune statistics for the year 1978 reveal that there were 3202 male junior middle school students and 3037 female. However, senior middle school only had 859 young men, while 1035 were young women. Given the approximately equal balance between the sexes in the commune and equal access to school facilities, what is the reason for the difference?

Unfortunately, data was unavailable from the commune for further study. However, in Half Moon, information from a village-level census showed that while there is a strong relationship between having at least some junior middle school education and occupation for young men, its effect on income is not a positive factor. Whereas, for young women, the correlation between education and income is pronounced. It seems, therefore, that young men can enter the work force early without financial penalty, while young women only benefit financially by remaining in school.

PORTRAIT OF AN EDUCATED YOUTH

Not all young people living in Half Moon and surrounding villages have been educated in local schools. A few received their middle school education in Beijing City and other urban locations, following which they were assigned to Red Flag Commune as "sent-down educated youth." This movement, most closely associated with the Cultural Revolution, actually has a longer history—beginning on a small scale in the mid-1950s, increasing gradually from 1962–66, and then expanding dramatically from 1968 to 1976, before finally being concluded in late 1979 (see Bernstein 1977). Although difficult to estimate, it is probable that between eighteen and twenty million urban middle school graduates were sent to the countryside from 1956 to 1979. In this time period, over 7000 were assigned to Red Flag Commune alone, most to work in the state sector.

The goal underlying this effort was threefold: one, to alleviate urban unemployment, which by 1957 had become a problem, particularly in the placement of recently graduated middle school students; second, to enable city youth to bring to the countryside their recently acquired modernizing skills, and in so doing to help reduce the gap between urban and rural populations; and finally, to enable urban youth to live with, contribute to, and learn from the peasants in such a manner as to become ideologically "remolded" in order to assume the role of China's revolutionary successors.

The first aim was largely accomplished. Large-scale unemployment of urban youth did not become a serious problem in China until the late 1970s. The other two aims were successful only in particular instances in which sent-down youth were able to integrate themselves economically and socially into the life of the countryside. For the most part, while the experience of living in villages deepened the urban youths' understanding of the economic poverty and social problems of rural life, it did little to help alleviate that condition for the villagers. At least, that latter point was the characteristic response of Half Moon villagers asked to comment on this massive experiment. In the peasant's view, urban youth lacked the experience, physical stamina, and commitment to be able to work effectively in the fields.

However, this appraisal hides an important fact. The young people of Red Flag Commune, living as they do near Beijing City, have many advantages over those more isolated rural youths located at a greater distance from China's urban centers. While commune young people are not comparable with urban youth in their level of education, sophistication, and life experience, neither are they comparable with those in much of North China's vast hinterland. As a result, when Beijing youths were assigned to Half Moon and other Red Flag villages, they were immediately placed in competition with local young people for the few semiskilled or skilled positions requiring at least a partial middle school education.

Not surprisingly, local youths usually received better placements, such as that of accountant, while youths from Beijing found themselves relegated to the life of a relatively unskilled field worker. The latter's limited success in this endeavor is reflected in their work point average: In 1978, the last full year in which sent-down educated youth were assigned to Half Moon Village, the average was a very low six points.[5] The one real financial contribution received by the village came not from the educated youth themselves, but from a block grant of several hundred *yuan* that the central government gave the village for settling-in costs of each arriving youth. In other words, Half Moon didn't really need city youth—though it could always use them as field hands, especially if the government helped support them.

In the state-controlled sector of the country, the situation was different. Indeed, many thousands of urban youths had been initially assigned to state farms throughout China's countryside, especially in its remote border areas. So too, various state-run enterprises of Red Flag Commune received large numbers of urban youths, who were immediately put to work in tractor stations, machinery repair shops,

---

[5] Most were women, and their rating is consistently lower than that of men. Still, six points is quite low.

dairy farms, experimental agricultural plots, and other locations where their knowledge and experience could be put to more constructive use.

Interested in the innovative nature of the movement to send urban youth "Up to the Mountains and Down to the Villages," while at the same time wanting to learn more of the problems that seriously weakened its effectiveness, I sought out several relocated youth who still lived in the commune. Of those interviewed, one individual stood out as having the special kind of maturity, objectivity, and sensitivity that an anthropological fieldworker always seeks in a key informant. In my case, that person was Zhang Yanzi, the local tractor driver.

Actually, most of her life as a sent-down youth was not spent in the commune. Rather, she had originally volunteered to go to a state farm in China's Northeast. However, the fact that she had discussed her Northeast experiences with Half Moon Village and other commune members is important, for only by such means are local residents able to deepen their knowledge of the sent-down youth movement elsewhere in China. Wanting to learn what other villagers already knew, I asked if she would be willing to share that part of her life history. After some initial hesitation, she agreed.

It wasn't until late October that she was able to arrange some time in her busy schedule for our get-together. We met at the home of some common friends, who, after offering us some hot water in the courtyard, excused themselves to clean up and prepare for the evening meal. Sitting on two straight-backed wooden chairs, facing the warm rays of the late afternoon sun, we chatted for a few minutes, sipping our water and commenting on Half Moon's efforts to obtain a new tractor. It wasn't easy for her, having to exchange her role as tractor driver for that of social historian and analyst. I watched carefully as she tried to relax, leaning forward in her chair and blowing gently into a metal teacup held in both hands. A smudge of grease on her strong angular face helped communicate her occupation as mechanical worker, just as her muscular body spoke of a decade of outdoor work in the countryside. Only one incongruous feature gave any evidence of her earlier life as an urban youth: the slightly waved set of her dark hair. I switched on the tape recorder and began the interview with a question.

"Zhang Yanzi, when did you decide to join the movement to the countryside?"

"I first heard about the 'Going to the Countryside and Settling Down with the Peasants' campaign when I was in middle school and decided to apply. After graduation, I was assigned to a state farm in the Northeast and left Beijing on December 5, 1967. Really, it was run as an army production unit, but it was no different than a state farm except for the army. When I arrived, there were only 200 students, but in the following year 3000 more arrived. They came from all over, including Beijing, Shanghai, and Hangzhou. Many educated youth went to the Northeast—in all, about 300,000. Some of the farms had as many as 70, or even 90 percent youths in each unit. Before we came, there were only a few older cadre and workers. Some had been reassigned in 1955–1956, after the Korean War, and others had come from Shandong province in 1958. They were the only older people in the area. Having been in the army, they had a good work history and tradition.

"When I arrived at the farm, my first job was as an agricultural worker. Then

I was a primary school teacher for a while. I was only 16 then, and some of my students were older than me. I didn't feel much like teaching them because my parents were intellectuals. During the Cultural Revolution, my father was badly treated by his students, so I didn't want to be a teacher in the school. I complained a lot and finally got transferred to a production unit. The conditions were pretty bad. I fed pigs for a while and then worked as a cook. Finally I became a tractor driver. Then, for health reasons, I went back to teaching in 1976, and was finally transferred here in 1977."

"Were you under any pressure to go to the Northeast?" I asked Zhang.

"In the beginning, no pressure was put on anyone to go. It was all on a volunteer basis. Each individual had to pass the 'Three O.K.s.' One was from the actual student, one from the family, and one from the school. If there was any disagreement, then the person wouldn't go. Even if you hesitated just before climbing on the train you could stay. But we didn't do that. We were all very enthusiastic.

"Only later was the policy changed. Then, instead of volunteering, every urban family with three educated children had to send two of them to the countryside. Only one could stay behind. If you didn't go, your parents would be organized into a study group. Before my brother went, they had my parents in a study group. When the parents agree that the children can leave, then they stop. Otherwise, they have to continue."

"Were other means also used?"

"If a family still didn't agree, neighborhood committees would come out to the street and beat big gongs, hang up 'big character posters,' and use other kinds of propaganda to persuade you to let your children go. They would just keep on coming back, trying to talk to you over and over again until you finally agreed.

"But in the beginning it wasn't like that. It was different. We went because we were filled with the spirit of conquering difficulties. We knew the countryside was backward and life would be hard. Actually, except for the weather, it wasn't as bad as we thought it was going to be. We had good preparation, and we wanted to make a contribution. But it was cold. We were told that if you went outside in winter without a hat your ears would fall off. Nobody lost their ears, but a few lost some fingers and toes.

"We all ate together in the public dining halls with some of the older workers. Even though conditions were hard, they took pretty good care of us, giving us easier jobs and better housing. There were a few peasants at the farm, and they too were helpful. But not long afterward, the political factionalism began. It started among some of the older workers and soon spread throughout the farm. We got involved, and the younger workers did too. Because we dared to speak up, we were sometimes used as a tool by one faction against another. And more and more students arrived. After a while, all you could see on the farm were educated youth. We were supposed to learn from the peasants, but the only ones around were the storekeeper and a few others. Pretty soon the young people began talking down to the peasants, saying they were dirty and uncultured. They called them 'countrymen.' It sounded good but it was really sarcastic, sort of like 'country bumpkin.' In units where there were few educated youth, the work was done better, but where they were the majority, the problems became severe."

"What were some examples?"

"There were all sorts of problems. One was not enough concern being given to our political development. Another was the factionalism. Some of our leaders were not very healthy in their minds either. A few senior cadres, even those wearing army uniforms, began abusing the educated youth, molesting them. These included a few pretty high officials. One, in particular, molested many young girls, raped them and made them afraid to talk to anyone else. If they spoke out, he asked their units to accuse them, criticize them, and put a lot of 'labels' on them. If they wanted to go home for a vacation, he wouldn't let them go. It was like house arrest. At other times he would try to soften them up by giving them a better job.

"After a while, these corrupt officials became a network of people molesting and covering up for their activity. Once, the parents of an educated youth who were working in a central government office in Beijing started an investigation through the Ministry of Agriculture. It took a long time for the investigators to find out anything, mostly because people were afraid to tell the truth. Then, the PLA headquarters in Beijing also began investigating. Eventually, they came to the unit leader and asked him to admit his crime and rectify his ways. But he refused to admit it. He was then arrested and later executed. That shocked a lot of people, especially because he was so well known. Afterwards, the situation got a little better."

"Looking back on the overall policy, what is your evaluation of it?"

"I think educated youth going to the countryside was sound. It enabled them to learn more about the good qualities of the peasants and also some production skills. The problem was in the method used during the Cultural Revolution. Some locations didn't really need any more workers. In those places, rather than help the local cadre to do their jobs better, it actually caused a lot of trouble. On the surface, people supported it because Chairman Mao said it was a good thing to do. People agreed publicly, but not privately. That was especially true in the army units. There were few organized plans to open up new areas for agriculture, light industry, or sideline production. In many areas, this lack of planning meant that more labor power had to be used to solve problems rather than mechanization. This is not really the way out for agriculture. It is very tiring and low in efficiency. After a while, a lot of young people began to feel discouraged.

"In all those years, no machines were brought in to improve mechanization or open up new lands. Everyone looked to industry because it was developing faster. Eventually, the educated young people felt that anything was better than working in agriculture. Lots of empty slogans but no increase in production. So they began to talk about returning home. They said, 'If so little can be done here, we should be allowed to return to the city.' I, too, thought about returning. It wasn't an easy decision, and after I came to it, I found it was very hard to accomplish."

"What made you to decide to go home?"

"I have two younger brothers. Both of my parents went to a May Seventh Cadre School early in the Cultural Revolution for political reeducation. One younger brother was still in primary school, and the other had just begun middle school. The whole city was pretty much in chaos, and no one was really able to care for them. My parents were quite concerned about having to leave the two children in the city by themselves, but there was nothing they could do about it except come back from the cadre school and visit them once a month.

"Soon my eleven-year-old brother began running around with some bad kids. He learned to smoke and pretty much stopped going to school. The neighbors tried to help, but he wouldn't listen. My father still calls him illiterate. He thinks London is the capital of the United States and Spartacus is French. He is always confused about these things. Now, he is supposed to be a middle school graduate, but he sure didn't learn much of anything in all those years of school. That's what they got in the way of education during the Cultural Revolution. Anyway, when my older brother graduated and went to the countryside, that left my younger one home alone. So my parents thought I should return. Also, my health wasn't very good. So I applied to go home."

"Was it approved?"

"Going through the 'front door' is very difficult.[6] There are many procedures at different levels of government. And no one cares about you. First, they tell you to wait. Then you have to have a physical examination at the local hospital, followed by a check-up at the higher hospital. They just keep on delaying. They delayed my request for a year and a half, and still nothing happened.

"Some had their requests for going back to the city approved really fast. That raised many questions with the others. How did they do it? What did they depend on? Well, they depended on the 'back door.' At that time, the only way to get anything done was through the back door. My parents were once opposed to going through the back door. They didn't like that style of work. They told me that before the Cultural Revolution, backdoorism wasn't so common. So they asked themselves, if the Cultural Revolution is so good, why are there so many back doors now?"

"What happened then?"

"They didn't understand the change. They tried all the approved ways to get me back to the city, and nothing worked. They finally realized that if they didn't use the back door, nothing would happen. That had become my decision too. Others had submitted requests to return later than me, but all were approved except for me. They said my method was no good, that what was needed were cigarettes and wine to send to the right places. 'Go through the back door or it won't work,' they told me.

"I was hesitant. In some ways I wanted to stay in the Northeast. I had already been there almost 10 years. I saw all the changes. On arriving, there were only 9 units. By the time I left, there were over 40. I was personally involved in the construction of several new units. It was just grassland before we started. We built a lot of houses, a storage barn, and a day-care center. We also reclaimed some land. There is a lot of my work and sweat in that place. So I really loved it.

"Most of the educated youth didn't think about how the peasants had to work that hard all their life. They didn't compare themselves with the peasants at all. They just thought that if they had a way to return to the city, why should they

---

[6] In China, a commonly heard expression is *zou houmen*, which means "going through the back door." The history of this custom is as old as China's bureaucracy. It enables leaders, civil servant cadres, and others to benefit themselves, their kin, and groups they represent through personal ties, contacts, and behind-the-scenes dealings, often to the detriment of the larger population of which they are a part. Going through the "front door" is to follow proper procedures.

suffer there? Finally, in our company, there were only two educated youth left. All the others had fathers who were able to get them out. Then I began to think, 'How come my parents can't get me back to Beijing? I must not have a good father or I would be back there now.' That was my thought at the time. But still, I hadn't really made up my mind. Other things finally helped me to decide."

"What were they?"

"There were two reasons actually. On four different occasions, I applied to go to a university, once to Beijing and three other times in other parts of the country. There were tests then, but it was just a formality. The results didn't make any difference. Who went to school was still based on political requirements and one's class background. Whether one was qualified academically didn't make any difference. When I applied, each time I was approved by my local leadership. On three occasions I was almost admitted, but it fell through because of the political department. I was not a Party member. Secondly, my parents were not workers or peasants or cadres. For these reasons, I was seen as politically inferior, and therefore never was admitted to college. I wanted to learn mechanization, machine building, things like that, or go to agricultural school. I did a lot of self-study, and I wanted a university education. But it wasn't going to happen. So I felt very pained, very disappointed.

"The other reason why I finally decided to leave was that the Party branch was trying to train me and educate me. I was hard-working, sincere, and very active. I never complained about the work or that it was difficult and tiring. Also, I felt free to express my ideas. Two times I filled out an application form for Party membership at the local Party branch. Each time, they discussed it with me and then reported to the higher leadership. Neither time did they get approval. The higher leaders told them I was not determined to stay in the countryside. My boyfriend had joined the PLA for five years. He was in radar. After his service, he went back home. Because he returned to Beijing, I was in trouble. If my boyfriend is there, people will think I'll want to return also. A person without the determination to remain in the countryside cannot join the Party.

"Then my boyfriend asked his unit if he could be transferred to the Northeast, but it wasn't approved. His family opposed it strongly. So did his friends. The reputation about Heilongjiang [province] was really pretty bad, especially among Beijing people. Since his family and friends were opposed to his coming, it made me think about why everyone hated the Northeast and the army production unit. Finally, I decided I didn't want to stay there any longer. It was not for me any more.

"It was under these circumstances that I wrote my parents. Before I first left Beijing, my father told me something that made a deep impression on me. In his heart he didn't want me to leave home, but because he was a teacher, a 'bourgeois' intellectual, he couldn't say anything. If he opposed my going, a bad label would be put on him for trying to stop the revolutionary action of youth. So he could only support it. What he said was, 'We are not afraid to have you go now, but we are afraid you won't come back later.' He meant, if I were to go he still wanted me to come back. I have remembered his words all these years.

"After receiving my letter asking if he could get me home, my father wrote back and criticized me, saying I shouldn't think in such terms. I should not go through the back door. I should believe the Party's policy would solve my problems. Of course, I knew these were empty phrases. So I waited. A little later, a close friend of my parents who worked in the Education Ministry visited their home and told them they shouldn't be so honest. 'It won't work,' he said. Then he went on, 'Listen to me. I won't ask you for money. I won't ask you for anything else, not for cigarettes or liquor. Just find a good teacher for my children so they can be well tutored. If you do that, I will make a recommendation for your daughter to be transferred to the countryside near Beijing in Hebei Province. From there it is not difficult to transfer to the city. You can even help me write the recommendation letter.' My parents finally agreed.

"For me, that was great news. In the past, my parents had always helped other people but never asked for help in return. Now they were going to help me. During Spring Festival, my father asked me to come home. He then told me the whole story. I could either be assigned to the countryside in nearby Hebei or I could come home and wait for an assignment there. But I did have to return to the Northeast until the formal transfer and teaching certificate had been approved. It wasn't very long before I was home.

"While at home, I met my uncle who lives in Shijiazhuang. He is also an intellectual, an engineer in the city fire department. Because of his educated background and being a leader in the city, he too was hit during the Cultural Revolution. He was beaten up, and one of his legs was broken. He had three children, just like our family. Two went to the countryside. They both married local people and never came back again. My uncle once praised my father, saying that as a result of the Cultural Revolution, he had become an 'enlightened' intellectual. His remark actually had several meanings. On the one hand, he was telling my father that he was smart to have learned these tricks. Of course, he also knew that it could be dangerous if an intellectual was caught using the back door. But mostly, he was criticizing the Cultural Revolution for corrupting people. My uncle had been a Party member in Shijiazhuang and had had his membership taken away from him. Now, of course, it has been restored. But all during the Cultural Revolution, he never did use the back or side door for his kids. His wife cursed him, saying he was dumb, that he was a stubborn intellectual while my father was the enlightened one. But he never changed. Now he is doing research at an institute in Hebei."

"And you?"

"As for me, after staying home for a while, I had an opportunity to come here, not as a teacher but a tractor driver. After two years I could have gone back to Beijing. Still, if I accepted a transfer then I could only receive eighteen *yuan* a month, whereas if I decided to remain I could get thirty *yuan* or more. So, I decided to stay. I like it here driving a tractor. It is a good life."

I looked up from my note-taking. Having been immersed in her story, I was not quite prepared for its abrupt conclusion. And yet, as the cold chill of the late afternoon air replaced the fading rays of the sun, I knew we should stop. So did our friends, who called from inside the house to their two young children who were playing on the other side of the courtyard. It was time for their dinner and that of the rest of the family. I expressed my appreciation to Zhang for her assistance, said goodbye to our hosts, and took my leave.

Walking down the long lane to the other side of the village, I thought about the interview and how illuminating it was. In one sense, it was simply Zhang Yanzi's story told in her own words. But in another, her life experience and the insights she brought to it had a larger proprietorship, due to the many who could learn from it.

Zhang had committed herself to the same political ideal that guided the self-reliant construction and funding of the middle school near Half Moon. But the material success of this effort was not equaled in the movement of sent-down youth to the Northeast. Poor planning, increasing political factionalism, and corrupt management eventually led her to question the implementation of the whole project, and, therefore, her contribution to it. Like many Chinese youth with similar experiences (see Siu and Stern 1983; Liang and Shapiro 1982), she became disillusioned. Deciding to return to Beijing, she finally accepted help through the back door earlier rejected. However, what struck me most in listening to the story was not the adversity she overcame or the clarity she brought to her analysis, though both were considerable. Rather, it was Zhang Yanzi's ability to cast her experience in the context of the society's larger goals that gave her commentary such quality—that, and her sense of humanity.

6 / Becoming an adult

RELATIONS BETWEEN THE SEXES

When is a person considered an adult in Half Moon Village? The answer: when one marries. A twenty-two-year-old married man or woman is considered more adult than an unwed twenty-five-year-old. And this is true regardless of the financial contribution the man or woman may make to the family income. This is quite a contrast to the United States, where age and economic independence are the key indicators of adult status.

An equally significant cultural difference between China and America is found in relations between the sexes. In both societies, teenage boys and girls become increasingly attentive to one another. But there the similarity ends. In Half Moon Village, relations between young men and women are far more constrained than in a typical rural American community. This is illustrated in patterns of courtship and engagement. In Half Moon, courtship usually begins after one's engagement, rather than before. Why not the other way around? Part of the answer is found in the manner in which members of the opposite sex relate to one another socially and sexually. More significant is the close relationship maintained within the adult-centered family. And as far as the older generation is concerned, the selection of a marriage partner is far too important to be left to the son or daughter. Let's look at each relationshp in turn.

After finishing school, most village youths are assigned by the brigade production committee to work in the fields. Middle school graduates, and those who show particular promise or have good family "connections" (*guanxi*), hope for factory placements. Still, wherever they are assigned, young people soon learn that their new status greatly expands their ability to develop friendships with members of the opposite sex. In contrast to household and classroom, where parental constraints discourage close relations between the sexes, the workplace offers a more open environment. In the fields, young men and women occasionally share tasks, particularly during planting and harvesting seasons. In the factory, they often work side by side, and in other ways find time to talk and visit freely. Being attracted to each other, late adolescent youths make use of such settings to explore common interests out of which affection can grow.

Still, in Half Moon Village, any expression of serious interest between two young people is hidden from outsiders as much as possible. Those who have grown

95

up in the West, where contact between the sexes is relatively free of constraints, often find it difficult to understand the degree of furtiveness that accompanies the emergence of romantic feelings between two young people. Indeed, the strictures and pressures are sufficiently strong that even commonplace activities, such as informal conversations between two people of the opposite sex, can lead others in the village to suspect that a "love relationship" is being established. In villages where the large majority of peasants belong to the same lineage, informal social ties between two related members of the opposite sex do not lead to such conclusions. But in Half Moon, with its larger number of nonrelated families, a couple talking in a "natural" way, or conversing regularly, can easily become an object of gossip.

In evenings after work, accessibilty of young people to members of the opposite sex is more limited. Sporting events, Communist Youth League meetings, or political study classes bring young people together. But, for the most part, unmarried women remain indoors helping their mothers make clothes for younger siblings, or perhaps sewing their own. If they have nothing else to do, they can always knit! The underlying theme is obvious: women always have work to do. Furthermore, unmarried women should not wander around the village at night. To do so arouses unfavorable comment. Decent, well-behaved girls stay home and work.

In contrast, young men rarely remain at home in the evening. They do not have the responsibility of a family. Life is boring at home, and if they stay, they may be asked to do some housework, repair a tool, or take on another task preferably left to a younger sibling. So, after dinner and cleanup, young men head out the courtyard door for the cooperative store, plaza corner, clinic office, or other center of social activity where they can talk with friends or join one of the seemingly endless card games that form an important part of adolescent leisure-time activity.

However, one recent village innovation has substantially altered this pattern of youthful socializing—the brigade-owned television set. On any summer evening at the plaza's edge, crowds of people of all ages watch the news, drama, and other programming from Beijing and elsewhere. Young people too are drawn to the evening television fare, though not just for electronic entertainment. If an adolescent male wants to invite a woman friend to watch the community T.V. after dinner, he does not go to her home and ask directly, for that will draw suspicious remarks from others. Rather, he gets his seven-or-eight-year-old brother to propose to the girl's younger sibling that the two of them watch T.V. together—knowing full well that the woman he admires will be asked by her parents to go along too, just to keep an eye on her younger sibling. In that way, the couple can be together without being too obvious.

Finally, various festivals and celebrations offer opportunities for young people to meet and get to know one another. Spring Festival (Chinese New Year), held in late winter, is a particularly important period. With little work to do in the fields, more time is available to spend visiting friends and relatives.

The Communist Youth League is also quite active at this time, organizing young people to popularize the Party's policies, such as "Equal Pay for Equal Work" or "Strive to Implement the Four Modernizations." Such popularization commonly

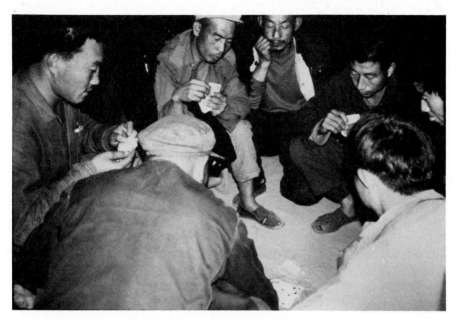

A young men's evening card game.

involves group performances, including singing, simple dancing, excerpts from traditional or local opera, and "crosstalks." Performances always involve a rehearsal or two, and sometimes even more. Thus, young people gain another opportunity to become better acquainted.

As these individuals approach their mid- to late teens, relations between the sexes can assume a more romantic flavor. I once asked several adolescent boys and girls what they looked for in a friend of the opposite sex. Most responded with embarrassed silence followed by nervous laughter. On further probing, they spoke of the importance of sharing common interests and "seeing things in a similar way." But my next question—"Might this individual be seen as a possible marriage partner?"—turned out to be my last. The topic was too uncomfortable for them to discuss with a foreigner in mixed company, or perhaps even separately. Still, older boys and girls are drawn to one another even though physical manifestations of this feeling are actively discouraged by elder guardians of village norms.

What about the sexual side of adolescent behavior? Is village life as puritan as it appears on the surface? Not really, although to a Westerner, the atmosphere appears strikingly asexual. Physical features are deemphasized by loose-fitting clothing. Sexually oriented advertising, whether direct or subliminal, is completely lacking. Touching between members of the opposite sex in public is rare. In this kind of environment, peasant youth simply do not have the problem so often faced by American youth of having to adapt to a multitude of sexual stimuli.

Discussion between youths and adults about human sexuality is also muted. Young girls, for example, receive little if any information about menstruation prior to its occurrence. Therefore, on the eventual day, a girl may have to ask her mother what is "wrong." Nor do mothers or grandmothers easily engage in discussions about sex with their unmarried daughters and granddaughters.[1] In contrast, training in modesty is emphasized over and over again. Girls are taught to sit with their legs close together and speak in a quiet voice. When resting in the fields, they must lie on their sides rather than face the sky. Today, natural science teachers or lecturers on family planning from the Women's Federation may refer to the biological aspects of sex, but that is all. For village girls, other knowledge of sexual matters comes from talks with older unmarried female youths or observation of local animals, and, occasionally, parents and resident married siblings.

Adolescent boys, on the other hand, are less constrained in discussions of sex. Peasant cursing, a popular pastime, is very detailed in its sexual descriptions. Boys commonly share sexually stimulating stories and songs, such as the tale "Great Auntie, Listen to Me," which describes a girl who travels to a local fair. On the way she meets a soldier, who grabs her and throws her down in a nearby field. The encounter that follows is highlighted with explicit sexual descriptions. Needless to say, the story also portrays the repressive side of male-female sexuality, with its accompanying dehumanization of women. Comparable sexually explicit stories deal with the rape of a bride on her wedding night, or songs about lovers who meet in secret.

Such an approach to this aspect of human relations has its obvious penalty. Expressions of warmth between individuals are viewed positively. Sex, other than for reproductive purposes, is viewed more ambiguously. Boys caught masturbating (literally translated, the word means "hand lewdness") are told that they will suffer from insomnia and impotence. Young unmarried men and women who express special friendliness toward one another are gossiped about. By the time a couple marries, social and psychological tensions about sexuality are fairly pronounced. Sex and procreation are largely synonymous, but sex and recreation are not.

Problems caused by this ambivalent attitude toward sexuality even have their ramifications in the political sphere. Walking by the plaza one day, I noticed several young men laughing over a newspaper cartoon that had recently been brought to the village by a worker from the city. Joining them, I asked what was so funny. They pointed to the cartoon and then looked at me, waiting for my response. The drawing was of a young man and woman talking with one another. However, the man was dressed to look much older, and he wore a fake long white beard, which was attached to the top of his head with a string. In his hand he held a wooden cane. From his lips came the words, "Comrade, the next meeting of the Communist Youth League will be held . . . ." The underlying message was that young men and women can have perfectly good reasons to meet together. One shouldn't have to pretend to be old in order to ward off gossip about being seen with a member of the opposite sex.

---

[1] Married women have few constraints in their discussions with one another. They joke about their husbands' sexual prowess or lack of it, comment on a rumored village adultery, and in other ways exhibit considerably greater freedom of expression than either unmarried peasant or urban women.

SELECTING A MATE

When a young man becomes nineteen or twenty, and a woman slightly younger, the parents—and particularly the mother—begin asking relatives in other villages, friends, and neighbors to look for a possible spouse for their son or daughter. If the parents have a specific person in mind, they ask a relative or friend to inquire of the other family whether they might be interested in such a marriage. The economic and social importance of this process is so significant that, historically, it often required the skills of a "go-between" or "matchmaker" to negotiate a fair exchange of goods between the families, taking into account the age, status, and wealth of the two groups. Today, except for receiving a small present, the introducer is not directly paid for her services. But she does exist in another form—as a friend who can assist in establishing a new link between two families. Usually, such an individual is a relative from a nearby village.

Regardless of who proposes the candidate, once a suitable prospect is found, parents discuss it with the son or daughter. Commonly, the mother is in charge of this activity; first she raises it with the father, and if he approves, then with the son or daughter. Throughout the whole process, the father remains in the background, acting more as a consultant than initiator. If both parents consider the potential match a good one, they actively encourage the son or daughter to accept the arrangement. If the son or daughter opposes it, the parents try to win the individual over. If these efforts are unsuccessful, the parents accept their child's decision, though not their judgment. If they did otherwise, they could be blamed for a mismatch, or even worse, a divorce.

What criteria do the parents draw upon in their selection of a spouse? Obviously, the individual should be able to make a good living. Beyond that, if their child is a daughter, the future husband should come from a family that doesn't have too many younger brothers and sisters; that is, it should not be too large. Second, the man should be honest, in good health, and have a good temper. Third, he should be capable. However, the daughter, taking a more romantic view, may well select appearance as the most important criterion, followed by personality, and finally, the size of the future groom's family. On the other hand, if the child is a son, the parents want a future wife who is strong and willing to work hard for the family. Second, she should be attractive in appearance and light-skinned in color. Light skin is a positive attribute reflecting a traditional North China peasant view that women should not have to spend as much time out-of-doors as men. But it is not limited to that. Light skin is also valued in its own right, as is softness of texture and quality of complexion. Peasant sons, too, usually esteem a woman's attractive features and personality more than her ability to work hard in the fields.

From the parents' point of view, and that of children as well, the relative status of the prospective in-laws is an important aspect of the selection process. The well-known Chinese phrase "matching doors and windows" (*men dang hu dui*) essentially means that social standing and economic and political background of the two families should be similar. During the Cultural Revolution, one's class background (poor or rich peasant, landlord, etc.) was also emphasized. Now this political criterion has been played down in favor of another emphasizing the individual's or family's overall worth. Indeed, so many families have been looking for future husbands and wives based on their wealth, or whether they have a TV set and good connections with powerful people, that the CYL and other Party-led organizations are actively campaigning against it. One amusing cartoon, prominently displayed on a bulletin board at the district headquarters near Half Moon, reflects this concern by showing a woman posing with a young man whose pockets are bulging with dollar bills and written contracts and whose face resembles a television set!

Following an initial exchange of views between the two families under the guidance of a relative or matchmaker, a preliminary meeting is arranged between the prospective spouses. This can take place at the home of the future groom or bride, or that of a friend or relative. In those Red Flag villages located near the market town, the gathering may even be held in a restaurant. Wherever the setting, the meeting is likely to involve a considerable element of tension. This is particularly true of situations in which the prospective spouses, living in different villages, have not previously met. One way to reduce this stress is to limit knowledge of the get-together to the families concerned, along with a few close relatives and friends.

For example, if the young man is a field worker, he may say nothing to his team members about the forthcoming meeting. So too, a girl is unlikely to mention it to others if she thinks the initial effort may not be successful. Most commonly, the event is planned around a noon meal. If the man comes to the woman's home, he lunches with the whole family, and in so doing has an opportunity to see what his potential wife looks like. But the prospective bride doesn't have to be present all the time. The main purpose of the visit is for the parents to get to know the young man, to learn more about his background and his thoughts of family and future. Nevertheless, while he is responding to questions raised by her family, she is sitting quietly, perhaps in a nearby room, listening most carefully to the conversation.

Obviously, this first meeting has an important bearing on the future. Shy young peasant men and women may say only a few words to each other, while more modern ones take an active role in the discussion. In either case, if the couple decides to go ahead with the arrangement, they inform their mothers, who tell the matchmaker, who in turn passes on the information to the members of the opposite family. At this point, the young man is free to go to the woman's village and visit her whenever he wishes. The girl is more restricted in her visits to his family home. If, on the other hand, either of the two are adamantly opposed to the proposed marriage, and so informs his or her parents, the matter will be quickly dropped, with little discussion occurring outside the immediate family.

What about the reverse situation, in which peasant youths choose to marry in defiance of their parents' wishes? This is very rare, even under conditions of modern courtship. Such a decision is invariably limited to well-educated youth, particularly cadres such as teachers, accountants, and specially trained workers. These young people, almost all of whom are middle school graduates, have greater exposure to the urban world of Beijing, where it is more acceptable for young people to make the major decision concerning a marriage partner.

This exposure, begun in the senior middle school, brings together students from a larger network of villages and from families with a higher social and political status. Out of this experience, new friendships are formed, expanding further the pool of possible spouses. Later on, when these young people are assigned work in the brigade and factory, they continue their association with one another in political meetings, social gatherings, sport competitions, and similar events. For them, the prospect of parents, relatives, or a matchmaker deciding who they should marry is old-fashioned and therefore no longer appropriate. Still, even in this circumstance, respect for one's elders leads young men to inform their parents of their interest in a particular girl, following which the mother, through a go-between, takes up the question with the woman's family.

These two different courtship patterns, one preceding and the other following the engagement, can occur within the same family. When I first moved to Half Moon Village, I soon learned that Hulan, Father Wang's eldest son, was a senior normal school graduate and a physical education teacher at one of the district middle schools. He had married Chao Liling, also a high school graduate and a very capable administrative cadre at a nearby factory. Both are Party members. Each became attracted to the other while they were student activists in the Cultural Revolution. Deciding to marry, they informed their parents. Hulan's mother then sought out an introducer, who went through the ritual of speaking with the bride-to-be's family, even though they were previously aware of their daughter's interest in Hulan. The couple had married several years prior to my arrival in the village.

In contrast, the Wang family's second son, Hubao, began the engagement process shortly after I moved into their house. Hubau was 24 years of age. He had had considerably less schooling than his elder brother, and was both awkward and shy in manner. Several days before the initial meeting between the prospective couple (who had not previously met), the whole family engaged in a massive house cleaning. Noticing the rather unusual collective output of energy, I asked Mother Wang the reason.

"Oh, it's nothing. Just a little cleaning up."

"Can I help too?" I asked, knowing full well that I had yet to bridge the gap between foreign guest and friend.

"No, no. Look, I'm all finished," she responded, putting away the straw broom with which she had been brushing leaves from the overhanging eaves of the roof. Obviously, my status as guest was still firmly entrenched.

Several days later, on a Saturday morning, an even greater flurry of household activity took place. Though unclear about what was happening, I was fascinated by the family's high state of excitement. Mother Wang first set to work making trays of vegetable-stuffed dumplings or *jiaozi*. Then she began cleaning and polishing everything in sight. Father Wang, who seldom worked hard around the house, saw fit to straighten the wooden chicken fence and rearrange the stove wood stacked against the courtyard wall. Even to my inexperienced eye, it became increasingly obvious that the family was preparing for an important visitor. And on Sunday morning, when the house was bright and spotless, Mother Wang finally informed me that several friends were arriving around noon and that the family would be quite busy for the remainder of the day—by which she meant, of course, that the gathering was strictly family.

It was not until some time later that I pieced the story together. Visually, it was clear that an important event had taken place. Everyone was carefully dressed in newly washed clothes. Hubao, extremely nervous, hardly talked to anyone, even though everyone else in the household was most attentive to his every movement. At noon, two guests arrived. One was a young, stocky, and quite poised woman of plain features. The other was considerably older. The two were immediately welcomed into the center parlor and offered tea and candy. Soon, a few close relatives dropped by, and their visit was followed by more tea and the serving of a large tray of delicately cooked *jiaozi*. During the whole visit, Hulan, the eldest son, remained with the visitors. However, as soon as the meal was concluded, second son Hubao and his two younger sisters withdrew to the courtyard. An hour or so later, as the invited guests prepared to leave, the family lined up on the dirt lane outside the arched brick gate to say goodbye. The brother of the young woman visitor, who had been seeing another friend in the village, briefly appeared, and shortly thereafter, all three departed.

What actually took place? On inquiring, I found that a few months previously, Mother Wang had let it be known to a few close relatives that her younger son was in need of a wife. She consulted as well with an old friend—"quite experienced in matters of this sort." After looking around, the old friend informed Mother Wang she had found an excellent prospective daughter-in-law, a strong and hard-working young woman of good family. Furthermore, she was a Party member. Wang Hubao's mother then informed her son of the matchmaker's efforts, and he agreed to the proposed meeting. However, following the luncheon, Hubao was far less certain about continuing the process. How much his hesitation was due to his own uncomfortableness about marrying and how much due to his initial evaluation of the young woman was difficult to determine. "She is not very pretty" was all he expressed of his feelings, and to that remark , his mother responded with her usual directness: "She's strong, she's capable, she's educated, and she has a good future. That should be enough!" The rest of the family agreed.

At that point, Hubao withdrew completely from the discussion, and there the matter rested for several weeks. I was unable to learn directly what further discussions had taken place within the family. Mother Wang did eventually inform me that, after thinking the matter over carefully, Hubao had decided to go ahead with the engagement. Very likely, the young couple would marry in a year or so. As for Hubao, he never said a word to me about it. Nor did I raise the issue with him. After all, it was strictly a family affair.

BEING ENGAGED

Once both families approve of a marriage, the engagement is formalized. However, the exact timing of the announcement varies from a few weeks to several months or longer after the decision has been made. In the interim, the couple gets together occasionally, particularly during traditional festival celebrations. At other times, such as harvest season or if the woman's family is building a new house, the young man may come over and help out. But rarely does the woman appear at the home of her future husband except for a serious crisis such as the death of a parent or close relative.

The formal engagement party usually takes place in the home of the future bride. Present on the occasion are both sets of parents and other family members, plus the matchmaker and the young couple. A large meal is provided, following which the parents of the groom-to-be give the young woman some new clothes. In addition, her parents receive a gift of cash, perhaps 50 to 100 *yuan* or more. Such a gift is called "engagement money" rather than bride price, since it is not seen as a payment to the family for their daughter, but rather as a contribution to be used for the purchase of additional clothes, furniture, and other items needed by the bride in setting up the household.

The time between the engagement party and the actual marriage also varies. Both the Party and the Women's Federation exert substantial pressure on families to postpone any planned marriage until the man is at least twenty-five and the woman twenty-three. If the couple becomes engaged at an earlier age, they are asked to wait until they have reached the approved age before marrying. Yet, with the exception of a few young villagers either in or close to the Party, most youths marry between the ages of nineteen and twenty-one. Why is this the case?

A major reason is that the groom's parents are anxious to obtain the additional labor of the new daughter-in-law, who will move into the household at marriage Another factor encouraging earlier marriages occurs when the groom must leave the village for an extended period of time, due perhaps to his being in the army or receiving a work assignment elsewhere. In such instances, the parents not only want to help the son obtain a wife, they also want to be sure they gain a daughter-in-law. Several years ago, a village boy entered the army. On his return home, the parents found that all girls of suitable age were either engaged or married. Unable to find a wife for their son through the usual channels, the family was left with having to select a divorced woman—a highly undesirable prospect only chosen as a last resort.

The few more highly educated engaged couples feel less bound to tradition in contacts with their future spouses. Not only do they meet regularly, but they socialize together as a couple. Still, whether they come from different villages, which is usually the case, or live in the same village, they try not to offend their more conservative older relatives by this behavior. In other words, the couple doesn't flaunt the relationship by walking down the road by themselves, talking, smiling, and holding hands. They may do this in private, but in Half Moon and surrounding villages, such privacy is not easy to find

Although financial considerations are an important part of the proposed marriage contract, they have changed dramatically from years past, when a poor family with three or more daughters dreaded the prospect of marriage due to their limited ability to provide a dowry to the groom's family. The amount of dowry contributed, including furniture, clothes, and daily necessities, as well as money, immediately established the bride's family's status within the village. If they gave very little, they could be ridiculed by both the neighbors and the groom's family. The groom's parents, and most particularly the mother, might even express displeasure directly to the family, causing them even more embarrassment. And needless to say, following the marriage, treatment of the new daughter-in-law was even more exploitative.

In these earlier times, one of the major reasons for the high incidence of female infanticide among Chinese peasants was the high cost of providing for the daughter's marriage. The prospect of having to go into debt or sell land to provide an adequate dowry at the time of marriage was so economically threatening to poor peasant families that they sometimes chose the alternate course of killing their newborn female child by drowning or strangulation.[2]

Today, dowries are still given, but parents are more reasonable in their expectations, acknowledging that some families may find it difficult to contribute very much. Furthermore, what is contributed, such as clothing and household utensils, is usually given to the bride and groom. It is not the dowry, but the continuing practice of the "bride price" that is now receiving critical attention. Excessively demanding parents are criticized for treating their daughters as "money-shaking trees," requiring a large amount of money from the family of a prospective groom as a form of payment for raising their daughter. Their argument is that, today, when a young woman leaves the household, it represents a substantial loss of family income, in contrast to earlier years when women were less active field workers. Since they now earn more at home, the "price" of wives should go up!

Obviously, such an argument receives little favor from the Women's Federation and other brigade leaders, who point out that such thinking is a carryover from the past, when daughters were "sold" rather than given away in marriage. But it does occur, particularly in villages that are poorer than Half Moon, where financial need is greater and conservative views more pronounced. Again, the fact that the issue is regularly addressed in local newspaper and magazine articles reflects a continuing need to chastise this type of thinking.

Still, marriage is a costly step for all concerned. The issue is magnified when the groom's family has three or four sons, for along with money and presents, the

---

[2] Today, Chinese newspapers are reporting a recent increase in female infanticide, though for quite different reasons. With family planning policies trying to limit births to one, married couples want to be sure that the "one" is a boy. The issue of family planning is discussed in Chapter 7.

family must carry the responsibility for providing furniture and housing, usually within the parents' household. This is why families with many sons encourage one or more of them to try and find work outside the village. In such circumstances, if the son finds a wife by himself, the family doesn't have to spend so much money on his behalf. Or, the parents may allow one son to marry into a family that has only daughters. A family without sons always wants to have a son-in-law in the house. This, in turn, relieves the family with many sons of having to assist all of them in establishing new homes.

One example of this reverse (uxorilocal) residence pattern occurred in Half Moon about two years previous to my arrival in the village. In this instance, the bride had four sisters and no brothers. It was, in the words of Father Wang, "a very poor family indeed." However, with the arrival of the groom in the household, the family fortune took a decided turn for the better. The young man was welcomed by his new relatives, though he commented that it took quite a while to feel comfortable in his new position as a male in a family of "maternal kin." Some time later, one of the two women barefoot doctors, an educated youth from Beijing known for being more outspoken than was customary in the village, commented on the marriage arrangement: "I'm not surprised he found it difficult. Now he knows what we go through all the time."[3]

A second example of a groom moving in with the wife's family had a different cause. It occurred during the height of the Cultural Revolution, when those with a "bad" class background were being attacked by young Red Guards and members of a local radical faction. The young man in question was the grandson of a well-off landlord family. Having been the focus of much verbal abuse and worse, he rather neatly tried to resolve the problem by moving into his wife's household and assuming her parents lineage, thus improving his political status.

Today, in Half Moon, questions involving courtship and choice of spouse are given little attention by the local Party committee. Only if a villager holds an important position in the Party or brigade leadership does the committee become involved in the selection process—seeing to it that the person finds a spouse who has a good family background and is politically progressive. If a village youth is crippled, disfigured in some way, or partially disabled due to an accident and therefore less desirable as a potential spouse, the local Party committee will also assist in finding a mate. If they are successful, the person who marries the disabled person is held up in the local commune newspaper as a model for others to follow.

THE MARRIAGE DAY

The most popular time to hold a wedding is during Spring Festival in either January or February, depending on the lunar calendar. Historically, this is the

---

[3] Margery Wolf, analyzing this uxorilocal marriage pattern in Taiwan, points out that the wife's relatives, fearful that the husband will take his family and leave the household, may create conflicts between him and his children, in the hope that if he does leave, the children will remain (Wolf 1970:59).

slack season for field work, giving peasants more free time for other activities. The old belief system has long supported this custom. If one works through the new year without taking several days off, bad luck will abound. So Spring Festival is a time for relaxation, visiting relatives and friends, cleaning house, and having a big feast. If a marriage is in the offing, what better time than Spring Festival, when villagers are relieved from work, able to travel, and in a holiday mood? Also, to wait a few months might place a burden on the stored food supply drained by a long winter.

Planning for the event can last anywhere from several days to a year or more. As far as the law is concerned, a wedding is easily accomplished. All the groom and bride have to do is bicycle over to the commune headquarters with relevant documents showing age, marital status, and occupation. After informing the couple of the legal implications, headquarters staff issues a certificate, and the marriage is completed. Party officials discourage villagers from having an elaborate wedding, since the considerable cost can easily drain the financial resources of the family. However, such a perspective is not shared by many peasants. Instead, they see the day as highly important, in that the marriage ceremony defines a new status for the couple—for, as noted earlier, it is not age that defines adulthood in Half Moon Village, but marriage. On such an occasion, a big celebration is called for, with liquor, sweet wine, and special foods. Appropriate rituals are taken seriously as well.

One day, a young and urbane college teacher from Beijing joined me for dinner at the Wang house. Also at the table was Huzeng, the Wang's eldest daughter. During our conversation, I commented on her recent engagement and asked her to describe her forthcoming marriage ceremony. With considerable shyness, Huzeng spoke first of the feast to be prepared by the groom's parents, and then, on the wedding day, her arrival at the groom's house and meeting his many relatives and friends. Village leaders would also attend. After a few speeches had been made and acknowledged, she and her husband-to-be would go to the front of the room. Once there, they would bow three times to a picture of Mao—and she turned and pointed to the wall behind our dining room table, on which was tacked a colored poster of the famous leader—three times to the family elders and assembled guests, and three times to each other. Then they would be considered married.

At this point, new and old China came together in a most vivid fashion. The young, sophisticated teacher burst out laughing, slapping his knee, and offering an unexpected but joking criticism of Huzeng for her "old-fashioned thinking"— particularly her expression of a feudal-like worship of Mao. Huzeng, red-faced and hurt, looked down at the food before her, embarrassed and angry at the urbanite teacher's response to her simple exposition of what she considered to be proper village behavior. I too was a little distressed at the young teacher's remark, for it was quite clear that it had caused Huzeng real discomfort. It also meant that there would be no further discussion that day of her forthcoming wedding. Still, even her brief description illustrated rather well how old village rituals associated with marriage still continue into the present. Of course, some content has changed, such as the shift in public veneration from heaven and earth and one's deceased ancestors to Mao. But traditional respect for living relatives remains very much intact.

As the time for the wedding approaches, family responsibilities increase considerably. New quarters for the bride and groom must be found, usually a room in the groom's family home. Once selected, it is thoroughly cleaned and the walls either whitewashed or covered with colorful paper. Preparations for the feast are made, including the killing of a pig by father or son; the pig is then sold to the district store in exchange for pork, special vegetables, cigarettes, candy, and cookies. Friends are asked to assume certain responsibilities, such as recording the arrival of guests and keeping a list of presents given. A careful accounting is important so that when the next marriage takes place, gifts of equal value can be contributed in return.

Early on the morning of the wedding day, last-minute arrangements are made. A married daughter returned home for the event dusts rooms. Younger siblings run errands. The mother supervises the cooking and similar activities while the groom and his father set up tables and chairs and in other ways make final plans for meeting the guests. Is the couple's new room prepared for their arrival? Are the bed, dresser, table, and chairs properly arranged? Are the presents placed on the table so the new couple will see them when they first enter the room? Such presents include items like a clock, a large thermos bottle, a teapot, and glasses. Tacked on the wall above the table are several carefully drawn banners wishing the couple a "Happy Marriage" and offering advice to "Work and Study Hard Together Until Your Hair is White." Clearly displayed at the bottom of each banner are the signatures of those who made it. And finally, on the other side of the room, lying on a *kang*, will probably be a new satin-covered quilted blanket, a gift of the groom's family.

Between nine and ten o'clock in the morning, the groom, dressed in his finest new clothes, together with four or five young friends, sets out for the bride's home. Often they go on new bicycles borrowed especially for the occasion. When they arrive at the bride's village, her father invites them to enter the house and have some tea. They, in turn, offer the father cigarettes or a similar gift.

Prior to the groom's arrival, mother and daughter will have spent some emotional moments together, tearfully reflecting on the bride's forthcoming departure from her family. The bride's close friends are there also, helping her dress and comb her hair. An older experienced woman may be asked to carefully remove the bride's facial hairs by the roots, thereby communicating to others the woman's new married status.

When the bride is ready to depart, the groom brings his new bicycle to the doorway. After saying a final goodbye to her parents (who do not attend the wedding), she climbs on the back of the bike. Several of her close friends, also on bicycles, accompany the group back to the groom's house, watching all the way to be sure the bride's feet don't touch the ground—a sign of bad luck ahead.

At the groom's home, they find the courtyard filled with relatives, friends, village leaders, and family elders. Passing through the gate, the groom receives the congratulations of those present and thanks them in return. The bride stays in the background, head tilted down, shyly greeting a few guests but saying little until her friends guide her into the house for a brief rest.

The formal ceremony begins shortly thereafter, the Party secretary, work team leader, or other village authority asking the assembled guests to take their proper places. As voices quiet down, the bride and groom come together either in the courtyard or main room of the house, depending on the weather. Behind them is a table, and above that, hanging on a wall, is a picture of Mao or another more current Party leader. Standing at one side of the table are the family elders, at the other, the village leaders. In front are relatives and friends.

The couple is then introduced. This is followed by a short speech in which the village leader in charge extols the importance of marriage and urges the couple to work hard to improve the economic life of the brigade. Concluding, he may remind them of the importance of carrying out the Four Modernizations and the government's program on birth control. The speech is followed by another of equal brevity and similar in tone, usually offered by a second local official or Communist Youth League member.

Following these remarks, the groom expresses his thanks to the people present for their support and assures them of his determination to meet their expectations. At that point, the groom and bride turn and bow to the picture on the wall, to their relatives, and to each other—in each instance, acknowledging respect for the appropriate political and family authorities and, importantly, for themselves. A few others may speak briefly about the value of the marriage for the future of the family and the village, at which time the ceremony is completed and the feast begins.

During the feast, men and women sit separately. The bride soon excuses herself and goes to her new living quarters, again accompanied by her friends. Sitting on a chair or the *kang*, she is served tea and special foods prepared for the occasion. The new husband remains in the main room or courtyard, eating and talking with the guests until everyone is finished. By midafternoon the guests leave, and the couple retire to their room for a period of rest.

At this time, some couples may use the moment to perform certain magical practices, such as placing under their bed various objects symbolizing good fortune and harmony within the family. Dates are one such item. The Chinese pronunciation is *zao*. The sound is the same as that of the word meaning "early." An association is made between the two that is understood as "get a son early." Another item is peanuts (*huasheng*). The meat is big and white. Hopefully the son will also be fat (meaning strong) and white (meaning handsome).

The last of the day's challenges for the bride and groom is the custom of "hazing the couple on the wedding night" (*nao dongfang*). Around eight in the evening, young men begin gathering outside the couple's room. The more popular or important the family, the larger the number of visitors. As the men enter, the bride offers them candies and tea. However, the formality of the greeting soon gives way to a teasing of the bride that steadily increases in its intensity. First, she may be asked to sing. She in turn declines, head down and eyes averted, feigning total shyness. The young men insist. The bride, knowing that as soon as one request is fulfilled another more difficult one will follow, tries every possible strategy to postpone the requested action. But she must use good judgment, for if she declines too often, the men may leave early, a serious affront to the family.

One common request asked of the bride (and also the groom) is to describe how they first met, what they thought of each other, and any secret meetings they might have had. To the delight of the guests, the couple often turn away in confusion, blushing and hanging their heads in embarrassment. For while modesty demands their restraint, hospitality requires a response. Bit by bit, the story is coaxed out of them, to the immense entertainment of the listeners.

Although sex is not alluded to directly, sexual undertones often pervade the evening's "entertainment." As already described, in the day-to-day lives of Half Moon's young people, touching, holding each other's bodies in an embrace, or kissing in public is definitely considered improper. With that thought in mind, the guests may tie a piece of candy or fruit to a string hung from the ceiling and then ask the couple to each take a bite at the same time, all the while keeping their hands behind their backs. Any attempt to accomplish the task immediately brings the young couple's faces into close contact—again, to the great amusement of the observers.

In another game, a long narrow board is placed on the floor, and the bride and groom are told to stand at each end. Both must then walk to the opposite end without falling off. Everyone knows that when the couple meet at the middle, they must hold on to one another to keep their balance. Or, guests may go further and ask the couple to hug or kiss each other on the lips.[4] To keep the teasing from getting out of hand, the family may invite married couples to join the group. On one such occasion, several married sisters were so successful in protecting their younger sibling from the hazing that she was only called on to hand out candy all evening. Of course, the men also went home early. What is most significant, however, is whether the bride feels secure from the humiliation and loss of face that too much teasing can bring. If she does not have that security, her wedding day will be full of anxiety.

When the party finally ends later in the evening, the guests thank the bride and groom for their hospitality and depart. However, the newly married couple must still remain alert to possible harrassment from young teenagers attempting to look through the window or listen through the wall to whatever may or may not be happening inside.

I once asked an urban educated Chinese woman who had spent several years in a North China village about the custom of *nao dongfang*. Her response was not unexpected.

"During the Cultural Revolution, I was sent down to the countryside like so many other young people. While there, I heard a little about it, but not very much. One evening during Spring Festival, after the wedding of a neighbor, several of my city-bred girlfriends and I decided to go to the groom's home to find out more. On the way, we met the Women's Federation leader, who asked us where we were going. We said, to the new married couple's house. She then laughed heartily and commented, 'I'm glad you saw me when you did. Don't go there.' Of

---

[4] A villager reported that in one instance in the past, male guests attempted to learn more of the bride's physical anatomy by telling her to bare a breast in order to show "whether her future children will have enough to eat." In such instances, what initially was a game of mild sensual teasing became a very real sexual humiliation of the woman.

course, we asked why. She said, 'Girls are not supposed to go.' Out of curiosity we asked again. Then she told us a few things that could happen. I learned about even worse things later on. Some of them are unspeakable."

Care must be taken in interpreting this young Chinese woman's remarks. To most Americans, the word "unspeakable" is likely to conjure up images of sexual acts ranging from the bizarre to the brutal. However, in her cultural context, where modesty is expected of all Chinese women and sex itself carries many negative connotations, the use of such a word may evoke far less dramatic imagery. The subject itself is so taboo that I felt it best not to inquire further as to what she meant by the phrase.

For the first few weeks after the wedding, the couple regularly visits nearby relatives on both sides of the family. Perhaps a month later, the bride may return to her own family for a stay of several weeks, after which she and her husband settle down to a normal household routine. However, if they marry during seasons other than winter, or if the groom is a factory worker, he will go back to work shortly after the marriage ceremony. Even in winter, if few relatives are around, the man returns to work quickly. To stay at home with one's wife during the day is not a customary practice.

The wife, on the other hand, knowing that she has to carry increased household responsibilities in her new home, more frequently postpones going back to work. A woman field worker might even wait until summer harvest or another busy season to return. Today, such "waste" of field labor is actively being criticized on local radio stations and in the press. Short articles tacked on the district office bulletin board urge peasant brides to go back to the fields soon after marriage—an effort that appears to be having some effect. Of course, two related factors influence that decision. First, since the bride has joined the groom's family, their income is increased by the wife's employment. And second, by working during the day, she can escape many of the household chores she would be expected to perform if she remained at home.

Shortly after the couple settles into their new quarters, the husband returns to his earlier practice of spending evenings out. If he spends many evenings at home, he soon finds himself the target of his friends' teasing: "Tell us, how is your new wife?" "What do you do together? You must like her a lot, you spend so much time with her," and similar remarks designed to maintain the male evening recreational pattern intact.

Within a year or two, the married couple begins thinking about having a home of their own. However, since few can afford one right away, they usually remain with the groom's family for another year or two. The eldest son is always expected to remain at home, and other married sons may stay for as long as there is space. Of course, as children grow up and find work or spouses elsewhere, new rooms become available for those who wish to stay on. Parents, of course, want their married sons to remain, since they bring significant income to the family and are an important form of old-age security. However, if the older generation has many children or a small house, most sons and spouses must find other quarters.

When a couple has saved enough money, or if they are fortunate enough to have the financial help of their parents, they may decide to build a home. This requires

A young couple building their own house.

applying to the appropriate village leadership for an available piece of land. Since land is collectively owned and cannot be bought or sold, it is simply "loaned" without charge. However, land used for housing is no longer available for culti- vation. Thus, initial approval must be sought from the brigade production com- mittee. Once granted, construction begins. Costs of building materials, ranging from 3000 to 4000 *yuan* for a three-room house, are borne by the couple and their par- ents. Small loans can usually be obtained from friends. Depending on the extent of financial outlay and available resources, the couple may hire a bricklayer or carpenter to help in putting up the shell. But even with such skilled help, the major work of building a house is carried on by the couple and their nearby relatives.

All married couples electing to remain with the groom's family face the task of establishing a new set of relations with the older generation based on their recently acquired adult status as husband and wife. Needless to say, such efforts are fraught with difficulty, especially when the conservative views of family elders clash with the modern ones of their children.

7/Family relations

KIN TIES

Throughout much of Chinese history, the lineage or clan has been note-worthy as one of the few institutions able to give assistance to individuals and their families in time of need. Unlike the case in Japan, help provided by the Chinese clan even cut across class lines. But that type of kinship system bore little resemblance to the one utilized by the future residents of Half Moon Village. For them, such extended units were largely an ideal rather than a reality, and the prospect of distant, more well-to-do relatives giving aid very unlikely. Even the simple "stem" or three-generational family was difficult to hold together under their economic conditions.

However, the patriarchal nature of the old Chinese kinship system remained. All family members were taught to observe their "proper place," an arrangement obviously allowing little opportunity for the development of any sense of individuality among children. Instead, they were expected to accept the decisions of their elders without question. If they had any doubts about parental directives, they soon learned to keep them to themselves.

It wasn't until the early 1950s that this kinship system came under strong attack. A Marriage Law was passed in 1950 giving women new rights, including that of divorce. With land reform and the collectivization movement, control over fields, animals, and tools shifted from the (stem) family to the cooperative work team and then the village brigade.

The impact of these events on the patriarchal household was considerable.[1] Daughters-in-law were understandably hesitant to leave a household they believed to be oppressive for an unknown future elsewhere, but at least that legal right became available to them. Decisions over land, though still under the control of the male-dominated extended family, were more collectively undertaken. At this same time, new village leaders like Li Haiping and Yu Futian, emerging out of the land reform movement, began challenging the older established patriarchy. Or, put more precisely, the opportunity to assume a leadership position became in-

[1] See Parish and Whyte (1978) for a thorough study of family and village life in a South China setting.

creasingly open to capable, revolutionary-minded peasants regardless of their age. Age was no longer automatically respected irrespective of capability. All these events dealt direct blows to the hierarchical status and privilege of the more senior male members of Half Moon Village. Later on, during the activist years of the Cultural Revolution, so-called "feudal backward patriarchal thinking" underwent even more criticism.

While such efforts to change village thinking should not be underestimated, neither should those social forces operating in support of the older family system. For example, despite the improved transportation and communication facilities at Half Moon, its peasant population is relatively immobile—due largely to the strict residency policy enacted in 1954, severely limiting migration to urban areas. So too, the city's concern to obtain an adequate supply of vegetables for urban dwellers insured a certain agricultural stability, which also had its social counterpart. That is, a peasantry working long hours in the fields under a steadily improving economy spent little time questioning traditional ways.

Furthermore, although productivity has increased in the village, there is always the fear that something might happen that can again bring serious economic hardship. In principle, the national government now assures any elderly or infirmed Chinese of the "five guarantees" (wubao) of food, clothing, medical care, housing, and burial expense. The assumption is that children or other relatives will usually provide such assistance. In situations in which no relatives are available, the question of who is to care for such an individual is less clear. In any case, actual requests for such help are rare. Over the past five years, only four elderly villagers sought any aid at all. All had been unable to work, had little income, and most important, had no nearby relatives. One additional partial recipient is mentally ill and barely able to care for herself. When queried, villagers will admit that some sense of shame is associated with the receiving of such assistance. But they emphasize that if relatives are unavailable, the brigade or commune should assume responsibility.

In other words, at Half Moon, kin are still seen as the most essential form of social security for the family. This is why many villagers still want three or more children, particularly male children, since they can be counted on to bring more income into the household, and later on, to care for their elderly parents. Obviously, such hopes go directly counter to the government's recently implemented family planning policy.

Finally, the traditional kinship system is supported by the custom of using backdoor connections. An important example found in Half Moon is when local leaders place their relatives in state factory jobs, a decision that generates great bitterness among those who either refuse to seek individual benefits through such means, or, more likely, who do not have relatives or friends in leadership positions.

It is against this historical backdrop that present-day family relations can best be understood. When a young married couple settles in with the groom's family, they are expected to adjust much of their lives to the needs of the parents and grandparents. This means, for example, that income received by the couple does not really belong to them. Rather, it becomes part of the family's overall earnings, and decisions as to how it should be spent rest largely with the elders. Family chores are also assigned by mother, and the daughter-in-law is expected to assume as much, if not more, responsibility than other children in getting them done.

Before the birth of the first child, relations between parents and the young married couple tend to be fairly prescribed, in that the latter follow the guidelines established by the former. However, with the arrival of a baby, new conflicts are likely to arise. The new mother may wish to give most of her attention to the child while the husband works. Such a decision will both reduce the family income and increase the grandmother's cooking responsibilities. The grandmother may not have complained when the daughter-in-law brought home extra income. But a loss of income and an increase in work load too can cause real friction to develop between the two generations of women. How food is distributed at the table can also promote family conflicts. Ordinarily, the best food will be served to the older generation. But following a birth, the needs of the nursing mother and baby are considered primary, in which case they will be given the most nutritious meals. In most instances, such a decision is supported by all. However, if resources are scarce due to a low winter supply of food, problems can emerge quite easily. Finally, as the young mother begins to see her child, herself, and her husband as a distinct family, she devotes less attention to his family, which further widens the gap between the two generations.

Eventually, the question arises whether the new family should set up a separate household. If the husband is the eldest son, or if there are no younger sons, or just a daughter, the two generations may continue to live and eat together. Since the parents know that at some time they will need the help of their sons and daughters-in-law, they may cope with the situation by simply playing down any difficulties that arise. However, if that strategy isn't successful, they may actively encourage their son and his wife to move elsewhere, especially when they are assured that at least one other son is available to care for them later on. Or, the younger couple may themselves come to the conclusion that it is time to leave.

Whatever the reason, after a decision is made to establish separate households (though often within the same compound), new problems emerge. Usually, relations between the son and his parents change only slightly. In all likelihood, the mother will continue to spoil her son in the hope that he will care for her adequately in her later years, all the while remarking that "marrying a wife makes a son forget his mother." Of course, such a saying is based on a long history of experience. Being involved with his own family does indeed reduce the amount of time a son will spend with his mother and father.

However, more serious conflicts occur between the young wife and her mother-in-law. Residing in the same household, or at least in the same living area, the two women often spend time together. Though one or both women may work outside the house during the day, they still carry major responsibilities for completing household chores. Naturally, the older woman will have certain established ways of fulfilling these tasks that easily conflict with those of her daughter-in-law. Or the daughter-in-law may wish to try out new ways of doing things that disturb the existing pattern. Or, quite possibly, the older woman, remembering earlier days when she was required to do most of the household work for her own mother-in-law, feels that she has the right to make similar demands on her new in-law. (Of course, the mother-in-law may try to win her daughter-in-law's support through generosity and kindness as well.)

Obviously, such conflicts are mediated by other factors that work to bring grandparents, parents, and their children closer together. Young couples, with little experience in raising a family, look to their older relatives for knowledge and advice. As they become older, grandparents need the assistance of the younger generation. And as the children grow up, they too have more responsibility, carrying water, chopping wood, and caring for the garden. Essentially, each generation has a vested interest in maintaining relatively harmonious relations with the other. In Half Moon Village, this benefit is still sufficiently pronounced that compromise becomes the dominant means of conflict resolution within the family.

Nor will the newly established married couple have to face many difficulties with the husband's younger siblings or grandparents. Younger children delight in having someone new around the house. Later on, the prospect of their becoming an aunt or uncle—a very important rise in family status—will be even more appealing. The kind of conflicts that do occur are caused by brothers and sisters having too high expectations of the sister-in-law, or she of them. Or the new bride may feel that she is receiving less than equal treatment from her husband's parents in comparison with her sisters- or brothers-in-law, who may have less to do around the house or receive more from their parents in the way of gifts, clothing, or other items. On the other hand, the unmarried sisters, noticing that their mother has additional cooking and housework, may criticize their brother's new wife for not contributing enough labor to the family. Younger brothers, being less involved in household chores, hardly ever find themselves in competition with the new sister-in-law and therefore have a more relaxed relationship with her, although, again, she is expected to assist them when the need arises. As for grandparents, they try to remain aloof from any direct involvement in serious family disputes. If forced to intercede, they will commonly do so in support of their grandson's position.

Most disagreements that occur between kin are half-buried in subtle nuances not always recognizable to those outside the family. However, within the family, the "message" is clear. For example, in one village home, a daughter-in-law who was often criticized for not carrying out her share of the family housework, wanted to go to a nearby movie with her husband. Furthermore, she wanted her mother-in-law to care for her child while she was gone.

"Mother, there is a film being shown tonight in Old Cyprus Village. People say it's very good. Do you want to go?"

"I don't have the time. What are you going to do with the baby?"

"I can take him with me, but if you don't mind . . . ."

"I have a lot of work to do tonight. Youngest son's shoes need repairing. Food needs preparing for tomorrow."

"Well, in that case, I think husband and I can take him with us."

"Isn't he too young to spend a cold evening outside? If he catches cold, you'll be in trouble."

"Mother, do you mean I had better not go?"

"Suit yourself."

In a somewhat similar incident, a village mother again chastises her daughter-in-law for not helping after the evening meal.

"Come help with the dishes."

"Mother, I can't do the dishes now because the brigade meeting is about to begin. Can I do them when I get back?"

"Well, I hate to see dirty dishes around. Let me do them myself. Next time, I hope you will finish the work first. Then do whatever you want."

These two examples, though somewhat lacking in subtlety for the sake of clarity, reflect the kind of criticism that is regularly shared between kin. Rarely is a negative comment presented directly to the offending individual, for such an act would cause the person to lose face. In the first instance, the woman alluded to her daughter-in-law that work needed to be done at home. In the second, when a direct request for assistance was denied, the mother did not confront the daughter-in-law with the demand that she remain, but she did make her thoughts on the matter clear.

Sometimes, of course, people become so angry that they are unable to control themselves. Yet, even here, face-saving mechanisms are usually respected. Early one Saturday evening, while sitting in the Wang courtyard talking with friends, I heard over the wall the loud shouts of an angry wife speaking to her husband.

"You only come home from the factory one day in seven. Today, I made a really special dinner for you, and you didn't even show up. Where have you been?"

"Now, take it easy. When I got to the village I met some friends in the plaza, and we got to talking about my new bicycle."

"You're always talking with your friends. You don't spend any time at home. The food's cold. Eat by yourself. I'm going out!" Just at the moment, a visitor walked into the courtyard. The woman immediately stopped shouting, welcomed the guest, and together the three of them went inside the house for a visit.

Of course, most neighbors in the lane heard the argument, but none spoke about it in front of others. Nor did the wife share her frustration with those outside her own family. Angry confrontations of this sort are common in a few families, but they are certainly not a usual occurrence in the village. However, when family problems multiply, the wife, or more commonly the husband, can become increasingly hostile toward the other spouse. If angry outbursts increase in intensity, or if the husband begins to physically abuse his wife, then the neighbors intervene, either by calling for the couple's son if one lives nearby, or by taking the woman to her own family home. In such situations, the son faces an obvious dilemma. While he may be embarrassed over his parents' behavior, and in all likelihood is supportive of his mother's position in the dispute, he should not openly criticize his parents in front of others. Usually he chooses to remain silent in the matter, displeasing both parents in the process, since each wants his support.

If a couple finds that they are totally incompatible, one or both may seek a divorce. But such a step is rare. In Half Moon, there have only been two divorces in over twenty years. Among the over 20,000 families in Red Flag Commune, there were less than 30 divorces in the year 1979. Why so few? Traditionally, divorce represented a break between two families as much as between two people.

It was seen as a failure in which both families lost face. Such an event might also carry financial penalties, not the least of which could involve the necessity of families having to exchange money orginally donated as dowry or bride price. At an individual level, the greatest problem was the penalty divorce brought to women. A divorced woman was considered so "stained" that she would be rejected as a possible spouse by all but the poorest of families.

Today, divorce is at least legally possible. Such a request will be given to the legal affairs office of the commune, which, in turn, will establish whether the local brigade leaders and Women's Federation have done everything they could to resolve the marital conflict. Reasons given in seeking a divorce have included ill-treatment by the husband; adultery, most frequently by the husband (although one husband complained that his wife continued to maintain ties with "an old boyfriend in her native village"); and inability of the wife to become pregnant after two years of marriage. However, in almost every instance, the pressure put on the husband and wife by both family and village leadership is so strong that the couple remains married, coping as best they can, even if that entails an almost complete refusal to communicate with one another except through others. But this is the exceptional case. In most families, conflicts are common, but so too is their resolution.[2]

In conclusion, the traditional Chinese kinship system placed great emphasis on male heirs—individuals who would care for the parents in their old age, inherit the family property, and most important, carry on the ancestral lineage. With the changing economic, social, and political conditions in the village, including a real increase in the standard of living, this old system has undergone substantial change. No longer is the kinship system an instrument of domination residing in the hands of the elder generation, most particularly the men. Still, due to the uneven economic development in the village, which enhances competition for the limited available resources, and the continuation of many traditional beliefs and household practices, a number of these older patterns endure. One of the most entrenched, and therefore most difficult to change, is the economic exploitation of women.

THE CHANGING STATUS OF WOMEN

Before coming to Half Moon Village, I had read much about rural Chinese women and how their existence from birth to death was largely devoted to serving the male side of the family. This custom, summed up in the famous phrase *san cong si de* ("three obediences and four virtues") required a woman to first follow the lead of her father, then her husband, and on his death, her son; and to be virtuous in morality, proper speech, modesty, and diligent work. Of course, through

---

[2] The fact that the divorce rate has been consistently low at Red Flag reflects the low intensity of political campaigns in the commune. Divorce has always been justified during these campaigns as a way of "drawing a line" between a given individual and an accused spouse. In urban Beijing, high divorce rates matched the most intense periods of political movements, such as the Anti-Rightist Campaign and the Cultural Revolution.

personal ties with husbands and sons, women could manipulate the situation so as to gain some measure of control over their own lives. But such efforts were limited to the informal sphere. Women had no legal rights.

Perhaps the most significant event reminding a woman of her powerlessness was the day she left her own home for that of her new husband. Wanting to learn more of these customs of the past, I asked several villagers who might be able to help. As it turned out, Guo Dasao, a hefty, 53-year-old peasant woman who had spent the last 40 years of her life in Half Moon, appeared to be the best candidate. She agreed to the interview as long as two of her friends could attend as well. A week later, following dinner, I went over to her house. In the courtyard, several chairs were arranged in a semicircle. As her friends and I sat down, we were offered the usual hot water and, as a special treat, a bowlful of peanuts. As we slowly sipped our water, Guo Dasao began her story.

"I guess you could say I was a child bride. Or perhaps an 'un-paid-for' daughter-in-law. Usually, the bride's family paid money to the groom's family for taking on the burden of feeding the child. But it my case there was no exchange. My mother felt badly about that, and many years later tried to make up for it by sending me money. Mother always told me that I had bad fortune and that it was in the stars that I would have a poor life. Of course, giving me away was a good example."

In response to my obvious question, she went on to describe life in her new home.

"I was poorly treated in my (future) husband's household. I never had enough to eat and was always being beaten."

Reaching behind her neck, she slightly lowered the back of her blouse. Then, turning around, she showed me several scars in verification of her remarks.

"As soon as I arrived here, my mother-in-law told me what to do. She never let up. For four years I did nothing but housework from morning till night . . . .

"My wedding day was a very sad one for me. I soon found that my relationship with my husband was not good. I wanted to run away but had no place to go. I lost contact with my parents, and my three sisters had also been given away because there was no money to feed them. I felt very bitter toward my parents, although I knew they had no choice. It was a difficult time."

Then, turning to her friend Zhou, who was busily eating peanuts out of the bowl, she concluded her commentary with the remark: "Your marriage was arranged when you were sixteen. But your mother-in-law had died earlier, so life wasn't so bad for you!"

From later discussions with Zhou and several other older peasant women about their early lives, I soon came to the conclusion that Guo Dasao's story was not unique. Actually, most older women willing to comment on the matter spoke not only of how they had become quite isolated from their own families after their marriages, but how they never really gained a new one. Since women were excluded from the father's descent group because of the patrilineal kinship system, and were often betrothed to another family at about the time they could have become economically valuable to their own households, it is hardly surprising that poorer peasant parents came to wonder about the usefulness of their female children. As mentioned earlier, it was not uncommon that such 'wonder' sometimes resulted in

A women's work team. Cabbages in the foreground will be used for pig food.

the death of the newborn child either by suffocation or drowning. Such was the intensity of the struggle for life among poorer peasant families. No names were mentioned, but it was clear that such events were not beyond the experience of a few of the older women of Half Moon Village.

If the marriage of a young peasant woman was the first step in achieving a lineage tie with her husband's family, the second was producing a son. Without such an event, the young woman could not become a part of the lineage genealogy, which effectively removed her from having any formal kinship status whatsoever. Her full acceptance into her husband's descent group was not achieved, however, until her death, when a family tablet was made in her honor—thereby permanently placing her in the ancestral registry!

Not surprisingly, old folk beliefs gave further support to this low status of women. Ghosts and evil spirits were thought to roam everywhere, often lying in wait for children, upon whom they could bring misfortune. To protect a child, the parents might slightly mutilate several fingers, thereby making it less attractive to nearby supernatural beings. But girls, having a status inferior to that of boys, were less likely to be sought by such spirits. Knowing this, parents might place a woman's earring on the head of their baby boy, thereby protecting him from some evil that could otherwise harm their precious male child.

Finally, as long as a woman had produced one or more sons by the time she reached old age, she had gained a significant measure of recognition. Yet, however much that improved status was enjoyed, it was nevertheless commonly marred by her exhibiting the same authoritarian control over younger women in the household that she had once so abhorred herself. This is not to suggest that women never enjoyed the affection of parents and happiness in their daily lives, or were unable to exert at least some influence on family relations. Indeed, many older studies of Chinese family life illustrate that the opposite was often the case (Wolf 1974). But in utilizing their varied skills to achieve goals large and small, they had to work through the existing kinship network and its spokesmen, sometimes the husband, more commonly the son (Pruitt 1979).

This hierarchical pattern was quite effective in enabling the family elders to maintain strict control over the decision-making process. As we know, daughters-in-law had little say in family affairs, and their husbands spent much of their waking hours in the fields. This left the older generation in a position to exert a major influence on the young, thereby reinforcing through the socialization process their own privileged position. However, it should be emphasized again that in the poorer areas of North China, from which most of the older inhabitants of Half Moon Village emigrated, even the three-generational family was not always able to maintain itself as an economically viable unit.

After 1949, the traditional kinship system could hardly serve as a solid base on which the build the socialist society envisioned by China's leaders. Significantly, however, it was not the extended family itself that came under attack, although that proposal had been offered in the early 1900s by Chinese liberal and radical intellectuals, who urged that such families be broken up since they were Confucian and therefore outdated. Rather, it was the issue of women's exploitation that became the focal point of criticism by the new government. In one sense, this new focus simply gave support to a struggle women had been carrying on for many years. Committing suicide was an active "choice" selected by more than a few women in opposition to the docile acceptance of their plight. Furthermore, for poor peasant families, the rallying cry of equality for women meant that they would no longer have to sell their daughters or give them away. Trying to address such problems, the new government passed the Marriage Law of 1950, which required free choice in marriage by both partners, guaranteed monogamy, and established the right of women to work and to obtain a divorce without necessarily losing their children.

This law, when combined with the land reform act, which gave women the right to own land in their own name, did much to challenge the most repressive features of the old family system. Still, much of the land that was redistributed eventually fell under the administrative control of the head of the male-dominated household, even though actual title to part of the land had been turned over to women. At the same time, peasant women, who were increasingly working in the fields, seeding, weeding, and bringing in the harvest, had yet to develop many agricultural skills. This too limited their ability to become involved in more complex economic transactions—to the detriment of their efforts at gaining greater economic equality.

Other difficulties arose over what to do with land treated as household property. When a woman moved to another village and joined her husband's lineage, the best she could do with her own land would be to "lease" it to a father or brother (Diamond 1975:377). Only in villages like Half Moon, where there were several lineages (in this case, the result of the immigration of squatters from Hebei and other nearby provinces) could women sometimes be able to marry within their own village—thereby maintaining their personal land holdings intact. Of course, this right to individual land ownership eventually disappeared with the collectivization process.

Finally, divorce, with its obvious threat to the stablity of the kinship network, was viewed negatively. Following implementation of the new Marriage Law in 1950, peasant women still found it difficult, if not impossible, to obtain one. Many didn't even try, as Guo Dasao makes clear in the conclusion of her story.

"After 1949, a new village government was set up in Half Moon. A little later I heard about the Marriage Law being passed. I thought quite a bit about getting a divorce, but finally decided against it. There were just too many pressures put on me not to. There's an old saying that 'if you marry a shoulder pole you have to carry it around. If you marry a chicken you have to follow it . . . ,' and so on. Instead of asking for a divorce, I tried to find my family again. This time I was successful, and shortly afterwards, I moved in with them and stayed two years.

"However, the Party not only began to discourage divorces, but also the breakup of the family. They kept coming to me and emphasizing that my husband and I should try and work it out. He and the others at Half Moon also wanted me to come back. So finally I did. I figured that things in the village were getting better, so maybe our marriage would improve too. At the time there were many meetings organized by the Party—a lot of talk about clearing our minds of old ideas. Slowly the situation got better for me, and I stayed."

Guo Dasao's reflections on the past offer important insights into the changing social relations of the time. In Half Moon, the Party leaders' efforts to reduce female-male disparities through the implementation of newly passed laws and the holding of nightly mass meetings was not simply based on a desire to bring greater equality to women, as important as that was. Very much on their minds was the question of how to increase the economic productivity of the land. One way to do both was to double the size of the work force by bringing village women fully into agricultural labor. The new Marriage Law of 1950, stressing the right of women to work, actively supported this economic effort. Furthermore, such action also had the support of the Marxist principle that only through participation in productive labor could women become fully liberated.

Still, public laws could not reach down into the private world of the household and legislate interactions between husband, wife, and mother-in-law. In addition, efforts to exercise these new rights in selecting a spouse or seeking a divorce often pitted men against women. If such conflicts became too severe, they could jeopardize the success of the land reform movement—a campaign considered by the Party leaders as its highest priority.

As a result of such deliberations, further actions to reduce the entrenched ideology of male domination, encased within the traditional kinship system, were postponed. Suggestions were made that perhaps after the new organized cooperatives had taken hold, leading, in turn, to a higher standard of living, political education could again be undertaken to raise the consciousness of the peasantry concerning the importance of equality between the sexes. To do otherwise now would jeopardize the precarious economic and political gains that had already been achieved. Furthermore, it would encourage more confrontation within the family, an institution that could not afford a high degree of instability, given its predominant responsibility for insuring the basic livelihood of the people.[3]

These were some of the reasons why the Party members in Half Moon saw fit to strongly discourage Guo Dasao from getting a divorce or even remaining separated from her husband. Obviously, the problem in this case is that such a course of action does little to challenge the self-interest of men, including the ideology of male supremacy found among many within the Party.

Several active campaigns relating to the furtherance of women's equality have been carried out since this time, particularly during the latter phase of the Cultural Revolution in the mid-1970s.[4] In Half Moon, one of the more successful of these was the effort to challenge the old custom of unequal pay for equal work. In 1975, the highest number of work points a woman could obtain was eight, while men received as many as ten. In several villages close to Half Moon, women even had their work points reduced after marriage, on the assumption that their responsibilities at home lessened their productivity in the fields.

A concerted attack on this inequality was orchestrated by the Women's Federation at the commune level. It began with wall posters going up in many villages protesting this reactionary thinking. They spoke especially about a highly capable and hard-working young woman who consistently finished her work more rapidly than her men co-workers doing the same task. Taking this woman as a model, political study classes, which all peasants and village workers were expected to attend, were asked to discuss her achievements, and then analyze the implicit Confucian assumption that men are superior to women.

As the campaign mounted, additional targets were selected for attention. Wife beating was one. In a village down the road from Half Moon, a man known for striking his wife was hauled before a mass meeting, criticized, arrested, and eventually sent off to a labor camp for reeducation. A much broader attack focused on the issue of housework. When the Women's Federation at Half Moon took up the question, they began by asking wives to report on what happened at the end of each work day. When experiences were shared, they bore out the expectation that on arriving home, most men would immediately head for the *kang* and light up their pipes while the wives prepared the evening meal. The obvious question was then posed: If men and women are both working, why should housework be left to the women?

By midwinter of 1975, the campaign reached a peak. During lunch break, daily reports on village loudspeakers praised one family after another for improving their backward "feudal" ways. Stories were told about how a man from a nearby village was given the nickname "Henpecked" Yang because he did whatever his wife asked him to do without complaint. Or how "Will-do-everything" Liu was teased because he too helped with the housework. Somewhat to their

---

[3] In other words, the Party opted for male peasant loyalty at the expense of women's rights (see Andors 1983; Croll 1981; Davin 1976; and Johnson 1980).

[4] Most specifically, the "Criticize Lin Biao and Confucius Campaign."

own surprise, these men were held up by commune leaders as models to be emulated rather than as individuals to be ridiculed.

Significantly, the campaign had a positive effect. By the spring of 1976, in over 70 percent of the commune villages, the most productive women had begun to receive ten work points. During the campaign, a few engaged men proposed to move to their wives' villages following marriage. Women were recommended by the brigade to receive special training at commune headquarters as tractor drivers and electricians. More women were recruited into leadership positions in brigade committees. And finally, Half Moon had its first woman Party secretary assigned to the village.

What has been the long-term result of this political campaign? It is possible that I asked the question improperly, but the answers I got were always elusive. Nevertheless, certain facts are available. Today in Half Moon Village, few local women are involved with the Women's Federation, quite possibly because the organization is devoting its full attention to issues of family planning—not a popular topic in village households. There are no women in the local Party branch. Li Guiying, the female Party secretary at Half Moon during the mid-1970s, is now working in a nearby factory. When asked why she moved away, she responded by saying that she had requested the transfer, that due to her lack of reading skills, she didn't feel able to handle the responsibilities associated with being the village Party leader. Nor is the effort to encourage new husbands to move to their brides' villages still mentioned. Most significant of all, the percentage of women engaged in unskilled field labor continues to grow, while men increasingly find placements in expanding sideline industries and nearby commune and state-run factories. And yet, all around me in the village, I regularly observed young men taking care of their children and assuming other tasks that had previously been the almost sole concern of women. Such sharing of family responsibilities is a real change from the past. Placing more women than men in the most menial forms of agricultural labor is not.

Today, China's new leaders are firmly opposed to the use of mass ideological campaigns such as those associated with the Great Leap Forward and the Cultural Revolution. Instead, the focus is on "following economic laws that upgrade productivity." With this shift in the Party's central task, the political issue of women's inequality has been largely set aside—not unlike an earlier decision following the land reform movement and the rise of collectivization (see Davin 1976). And, as in the past, social stability within the family is seen by most leaders as a necessary prerequisite to enhanced productivity. At the national level, such a decision may be seen as quite rational, although deeply held convictions of male superiority certainly continue to influence the leaders' actions. In Half Moon, the fact that fewer women are now involved in local-level decision making than a few short years ago suggests that traditional village patterns of male dominance are far from dormant; equally important, when the pressure for change is reduced, old ways easily reemerge.

However, there is one question of direct relevance to women that has received a great deal of attention in Half Moon and elsewhere: What is the optimum size of the family? An adequate answer to this question requires another: Optimum for whom? At the national level, the leaders state that China's expanding population is seriously limiting the country's economic development. Therefore, family size must be reduced (Chen 1979).

Indeed, family planning is a vital feature of any overall strategy for economic development, and in the abstract, Half Moon villagers accept the government's argument. But their own local experience leads them to a somewhat different final conclusion. That is, the economic resources of the village and commune are still not sufficiently developed to assure them of a standard of living during their working years sufficient to allow them to give up the patterns of the past. And when they are older, without a retirement pension and with limited social security (the "five guarantees"), who other than their nearby sons will assume responsibility for them? Perhaps four children are too many, older villagers say, but at least for now, one is not enough. The contradictions within this continuing conflict between national and local interests are complex, but their resolution is of great importance if China is to be successful in its modernization effort. Given this fact, what further insights can we gain from a more in-depth look at the problem in Half Moon Village?

FAMILY PLANNING

Ma Xixian, the older of the two female barefoot doctors, has the overall responsibility for providing birth control information and services to the village residents. In her clinic office, she keeps a record of the health condition of every woman in the brigade. For those of child-bearing age, this record includes the date of marriage, method of birth control utilized, and a listing of pregnancies and deliveries. At present, 80 married women in the village are defined in the child-bearing category.

Unmarried women are not included in this category, and, therefore, are ineligible to receive birth control devices. Of course, this practice presents the village with another problem: what to do with premarital pregnancies? Actually, such pregnancies are rather uncommon, and when they do occur, the couple is usually engaged. Such an event, though sharply criticized by local village authorities in general and Women's Federation leaders in particular, is resolved either by an immediate marriage or by an arranged abortion in a commune hospital some distance from the village.

The 80 Half Moon Village married women in the child-bearing category have selected a variety of methods for controlling births—all contraceptives being provided without charge. Condoms are available to men, but they are seldom used. As for the women, 26 have chosen the intrauterine device (IUD), a method strongly encouraged by Ma Xixian, who considers it the safest, easiest, and most reliable. Eighteen use the birth control pill. One prefers a monthly chemical injection. The diaphram is not looked on with favor by village women. Reasons given include inconvenience and problems of sanitation. Of the remaining 35 women, 17 have chosen sterilization after having had one or more children and 18 are not presently using any regular birth control methods, either because they do not

动员起来　把首都迫成奄齐涛洁的城市

*A Women's
Federation leader
from commune
headquarters
responsible for
family planning. The
poster is encouraging
the people in the
capital to improve
their sanitation.*

choose to control births by such means, or because "they haven't given the issue that much thought." The latter response, in the experience of Ma Xixian, is only characteristic of younger, newly married women.

The other alternative is abortion. This practice is considered less desirable than the preventive measures mentioned previously, but sometimes necessary given the particular circumstances. Ma's records indicated that no abortions were requested in the village during the first 10 months of 1979, although several women had obtained them at the nearby district hospital the previous year. Now that a new system of material incentives to reduce births is in effect, pregnant Half Moon peasant women can receive five *yuan* in cash and have several days off from work if they agree to abort their unborn child. Counseling women on such matters is the responsibility of the local Women's Federation. Technical medical questions (and related family planning lectures in the schools) are handled by barefoot doctors in consultation with the Federation. Counseling for men is undertaken either by the CYL, leaders of the individual's work team, or both. If the family already has three or more children, parents, and even grandparents, are sometimes contacted by a team leader or more senior village official. Obviously, such coordinated pressure on a given family can promote a substantial amount of conflict between household members and local authorities.

The decision to have a child is made jointly by the husband and wife, with other members of the husband's family, most often the mother, being consulted as well. However, if the couple remains childless for several years, the husband and wife will eventually find themselves pressured by family elders to produce a child, preferably male. Caught between the Women's Federation and the CYL, who strongly encourage that births be limited to one, and the older generation, who pressure the couple to have at least two (and if neither are boys, a third), some young married villagers have difficulty deciding what action to take. It is at this point that the government's economic (and ideological) incentive strategy comes into play.

In many urban areas and other affluent sectors of China, a fairly significant reward system has been put into effect to assist those couples promising to complete their family with a single birth. In Half Moon Village, such couples receive 200 *yuan*. If they later have a second child, the money must be returned. Usually, however, the mother is sterilized, in which case the issue is permanently resolved. Other innovative material incentives include guaranteeing the child's kindergarten enrollment, rather than placing it on the waiting list, and providing further reduction in already low health-care costs. Public praise for placing the interests of the country over that of the family is always given.

The negative sanctions applied by this new and controversial family planning policy place a financial burden on those families who produce a third child. In Half Moon, the Women's Federation tries to convince the couple to have an abortion. If they refuse, three repercussions follow: First, mothers will not receive any work points until 45 days after the baby is born.[5] Second, the parents must pay for all nursery school expenses. And third, the income of both parents is reduced by five percent until the child reaches the age of fourteen, this being the estimated amount that the state contributes to the upbringing of each child through various food and other related subsidies. When complaints are heard, the Women's Federation is told by the government to remind the family that, given the problems of trying to modernize a country of one billion people, the third child of any family should be the responsibility of that family alone.

In Half Moon, the response to the new policy is varied. A few people, cognizant of the national interest, are in basic support. These individuals hold the view that female and male children are of equal value. Party members, of course, are expected to support the policy, and most of them do. If they are in the Party but desire more than one child, they soon find themselves under maximum pressure to revise their opinion.

On the other hand, many villagers are opposed to it. They ask: "What if something happens to the child and the mother has been sterilized?" "What will hap-

---

[5] Other village mothers with one or two babies receive 45 days' leave with "pay," i.e., work points. Those few women working in the state sector receive 54 days' leave with pay.

pen to the family income?" "Who will take care of me in my old age?" "If the child is a girl, will her future husband move into our house?" Or they say, "One child is too lonely. There will be no one for it to play with." And a mother asks, "What will I do with my time if I have only one son or daughter?" If the family is opposed to the policy, they can take several measures to circumvent it. Some women try to hide the fact that they are pregnant until the latter part of the second trimester or beginning of the third in the hope that they can escape the pressure placed on them by the Women's Federation to abort. After a child is born, the family may "forget" to register it at the district records office, or enter a protest to local and commune officials offering various reasons why they should be exempted from the policy. Many feel that this campaign, like others before it, will eventually dissipate. For the moment, it is simply best to wait and be patient.

In nearby cities like Beijing, the new family planning policy is beginning to take hold. With a higher and more secure income, factory workers are in a better economic position to accept the one-child norm. But among the peasants of Half Moon, it will take both a continued improvement in the standard of living and a highly creative educational effort before the peasants see any advantage of a small family over a larger one. For most Half Moon residents today, neither criterion has as yet been met.

THE LATER YEARS

Growing old is never easy. But in Half Moon Village, the process is at least softened by the continuing opportunity to share in all aspects of daily life for as long as people choose and are able. When they can no longer work in the fields, the aging are cared for by their families. If there is no family, a rare occurrence in the village, the brigade and commune are expected to assume responsibility. The elderly are respected for their experience and knowledge, even when these attributes have limited applicability in the modern world. However, outside the home there is relatively little for them to do. Men often spend part of each day hanging around the plaza, the major nonfamily center for social activity. In early spring and late fall, a favorite meeting place is an adobe wall near the village clinic. Here, they can regularly catch the warmth of the sun's rays while chatting with friends and watching younger villagers working in the fields across the road. Older women, however, do not have such freedom of movement.

A few enterprising members of the older generation have offered to do some work for the village. It is quite striking to walk out to the junction of the main road and the plaza as the sun is coming up in the morning and see an old man sweeping the streets of the day's dust. Or one finds an aged woman offering to help take care of children at the nursery—particularly if none remain at home. Although they are not compensated for this activity, they do gain something else of considerable value—a recognition that they are still useful and wanted. In other words, respect for the elderly is not limited to the extended family, but carries into the larger community as well.

Still, for those villagers living out their later years in this supportive environment, memories of past hardships are not easily forgotten. Thus, grandparents are likely to remind their children and grandchildren not to take today's economic security for granted. The residents are quick to acknowledge that economic improvements have occurred since the "bitter years" prior to 1949. However, they also remember the early 1960s, following the Great Leap Forward campaign, when the combination of political and climatic disasters resulted in such poor harvests that hunger again became commonplace. A feeling of insecurity that arises from the possibility that similar misfortunes might occur in the future is always present.

Residents occasionally comment on the increased number of older people living in the village. This, of course, is due to the simultaneous increase in life expectancy and lowering of the birth rate. What implications does such a "demographic aging process" hold for Half Moon? Given the still limited economic development of the village, even the modest contribution of older people to the family income is quite helpful. Women stop working in the fields before men, usually when they reach their early fifties. As their physical strength declines, they receive fewer work points. At this time, it is more advantageous to the family for them to return home and take care of the young grandchildren. A daughter-in-law, younger, stronger, and able to command more work points, is thereby freed to return to the fields. Since private production, including such tasks as feeding and selling of pigs, is quite profitable in generating additional income (by as much as 15 to 20 percent), the mother can continue her contribution to the family welfare in a meaningful way.

Most peasant men, on the other hand, regularly work in the collective sphere of the brigade well into their sixties. To the extent that they are able to retain their strength longer than women, their work points are correspondingly reduced more slowly. The men of Half Moon Village also have more jobs in the state sector by a ratio of four to one. Since this is a far more economically rewarding form of employment, these workers continue on the job for thirty years, at which time they can receive a pension guaranteeing them 70 percent of their wages for the rest of their lives.

The fact that older parents are able to continue making economic contributions to the extended family helps greatly in strengthening kin ties between generations. Furthermore, since the parents own the house in which one or more sons reside, the latter feel an obligation in return. Daughters, on the other hand, once they marry and become part of their husbands' families, do not have a similar duty, although they often feel a personal responsibility irrespectve of social custom.

This same pattern carries into the matter of inheritance. Daughters do not inherit property. Upon the death of a father, the house will be passed on to one or more sons, including the eldest, who usually lives there. Savings are turned over to the widow. Her care is shared jointly by the sons, all of whom are expected to contribute a certain number of work points or amount of annual income for as long as she lives.

I once asked a young woman why it was that men received an inheritance and women in the village didn't. Her answer was insightful for several reasons, not the least of which was the way in which she framed it. She responded as if her older brother was speaking rather than she. Such a way of responding illustrates quite well the continuity of traditional values into the modern setting.

I asked, "Why is it that men receive inheritance and women do not?"

"A man says, 'We take care of the parents, we give them work points, while you are away from home. Maybe you come to visit the parents occasionally, but you don't have any responsibility. If the parents are ill and can't work, we will have to care for them.' "

"How do you feel about that?" I asked noncommittally.

"If women take responsibility for the parents, then they should be involved in the inheritance. But if they don't contribute, then . . . ." and her voice drifted off as she reflected on what she was saying. Then she continued.

"But some women do contribute. My mother did, and on her father's death in 1965, she said about the inheritance, 'I don't want it, I don't want it.' Now I am helping my mother because she went through so many hardships to bring me up. So I think it is my responsibility to do that."

I didn't ask whether she felt her efforts should result in the receiving of an inheritance. It seemed rather inappropriate at the time.

Upon the death of a villager, the family immediately prepares for the funeral. A relative or local carpenter is first asked to construct a simple coffin for the body. Then, the deceased, dressed in good clothes and placed on a blanket and pillow in the coffin, is taken to the center parlor of the house, where relatives and friends come and offer condolences. For those few who chose a "modern" funeral, this memorial service completes the process. The body is then removed and cremated.

However, years of lectures by local Party cadres on how the superstitious beliefs associated with old burial practices have harmed the villages—most notably by removing fertile land from use by the brigade—have not been well received by many older villagers. Neither has the idea of cremation, the alternative strongly urged by the commune leadership. In the minds of the elderly, such a practice lacks dignity and respect for the dead. Old people, especially, express their opposition with remarks such as, "My friend was poor most of his life, and now the family won't even give him a decent funeral." Another poignant remark came from an elderly peasant, who said softly, "It must hurt."

Since Half Moon is a relocated village, and the few ancestral plots in the area have long since been plowed up for agricultural use, the residents face a more difficult problem than do other nearby villages that still have their burial grounds. In Half Moon, the deceased are either cremated or the families make arrangements for the body to be sent to kin in other locations. But in nearby villages, old rituals often continue.

On the morning of the funeral, a day or so after the death, relatives gather outside the home of the deceased, wearing different clothes depending on their relationship to the departed. Close kin wear mourning robes of white. Women may also place a few white ribbons in their hair. Differing shapes of caps and shoes designate to outside observers the relationship of more distant kin to the deceased. Before the ceremony begins, the family members and relatives may talk and even laugh. But on hearing the sound of a bowl breaking as it is thrown to the ground—the signal for the ceremony to start—all talking stops. Straightening themselves up, the participants utter a unified wail as they line up for the procession to the grave site.

The eldest son, wearing white sack garments, carrying white-colored paper money, and holding a soul-calling flag, stands at the head, and a band playing mourning melodies brings up the rear. Others carry a paper horse (for a deceased man) or paper cow (for a woman) and more paper money, which are to be burned at the grave site for the deceased to use in the trip to the underworld.[6] As the procession passes through the village, several more bowls, jars, or mirrors are thrown against the ground and broken. Beyond the edge of the village lies the local burial ground, its location easily distinguished by mounds of raised earth scattered in a haphazard fashion—a puzzle to present-day observers unfamiliar with the ancient practice of geomancy, a custom that assures proper placement of the grave.

On arriving at the site, the coffin is lowered into the freshly dug grave. The villagers stand respectfully while the coffin is covered over, perhaps joining in with the family of the deceased as they softly repeat a common lament in a sing-song manner. After the grave is covered, offerings of eggs, cakes, and white paper money cut in an ancient shape are placed on top, and the money burned. The procession then returns to the village to participate in a large meal hosted by the family of the deceased. After partaking of elaborate dishes of dumplings, cakes, and other special foods, the mourners disband and return to their own homes. In April of each following year, at the time of the *qingming* festival, family members return to the grave site, add some new earth, weed or clean the area, and perhaps burn a little paper money and incense, thereby illustrating one more continuity in the life cycle of the village.

Given the extensive power once exercised by the elderly in the village, it would be possible to conclude that their status has diminished considerably. But such is not the case. This is due not only to the maintenance of traditional values and the continuation of the older generation's ability to contribute economically to the family welfare, but also to the collective nature of the socal system, which gives specific attention and care to those who in their later years are no longer able to work. Contrasting socialist China with the capitalist West, one well-educated commune member expressed his view on the matter rather directly when he looked at me and said, "We are not so rich that we can't afford to take care of our old people."

---

[6] In some areas of the country, modern-day mourners bring along paper television sets and stereos as well.

8/The changing political economy

AGRICULTURAL MODERNIZATION

Is there an inevitable conflict between the need for modern technology, and the skills required to utilize it, and the building of a socialist infrastructure designed to reduce major economic and social disparities among its people?

As part of the Four Modernizations campaign, China's government is committing itself to modernizing agriculture, thereby strengthening the economy and improving the people's livelihood. It has already removed the historic class-based relations that characterized landlord and poor peasant on the one hand and industrialist and worker on the other. Privately owned factories and farms are no more. Yet, throughout much of rural China, and even in suburban communes like Red Flag that lie close to large cities, major differences in the living standards of urban worker and peasant farmer still remain. How is the government trying to reduce these remaining differences? How successful is its effort?

One major plan to upgrade rural livelihood was announced in December 1978, when the Third Plenum of the Eleventh CCP Central Committee approved an increase in the state procurement price of grain by approximately 20 percent, with most of the profit from these sales being passed on to the peasant producers. Similar increases were allocated to other agricultural products, for example, the price of cotton going up 30 percent. But the overall cost of this effort to the state was so high (over a billion *yuan* a year just subsidizing grain supplies in urban areas) that it helped account for a significant state budget deficit in 1980 and 1981 (Oksenberg 1982). An additional factor encouraging the deficit was the wage increase given to state workers to offset the rise in food cost brought about by the higher price paid to the peasantry. In this classical illustration of an inflationary spiral, the initial goal—to improve the living standard of the peasantry—was partially offset by their having to pay more for those foods and other commodities purchased from the state. Nevertheless, the gain in peasant income was real.

A second strategy designed to increase both land productivity and peasant income has been to further mechanize agriculture. Many stationary operations such as pumping, chopping, grinding, crushing, and threshing are already mechanized. However, the mechanization of field work is much less developed. Even in technologically advanced vegetable-producing communes surrounding large cities, much

131

of the seeding, transplanting, and harvesting in the collective sector is still done by hand (Wiens 1980:319).

There are several reasons for this. One is the scarcity of capital. A second is the state's concern over how to utilize the released time of a peasant work force after mechanization without incurring serious underemployment. Negative unanticipated consequences can far outweigh a resolution of the initial problem. A third reason has to do with the history of China's technological development. On American farms, agricultural machines, from cutter bars to combines, were drawn by horses long before the invention of the tractor. When the tractor finally arrived, farmers had already developed the implements to attach to it. Therefore, the transition process was relatively easy.

China, on the other hand, has quite a different history of farm mechanization. As noted in an earlier chapter, most villages today have one or more two-wheel walking tractors. They are seen everywhere pulling wagons along roadways—mechanized transportation being a high-priority item for today's peasant farmers. But few are found in the fields, where they are also needed. Why? Because the design and extensive manufacture of appropriate farm implements to go with the tractor have not yet been adequately developed (Hinton 1978).

Nor is the problem simply one of importing or copying machines used elsewhere. In much of China, small terraced fields, surface irrigation, interplanting, and multiple cropping with transplanting create problems that require solutions drawn from the people's own conditions and experience (Hinton 1982:112–115). Only in relatively large expanses of semiflat land with limited population density can Western-designed tractors and seeding and harvesting equipment be effectively utilized. For most of China, a much simpler intermediate-level technology geared to the particular geographical conditions is more appropriate.

Although the government has given little consistent support to this type of agricultural mechanization, it has tried to stimulate production by lowering the state sale price of existing agricultural products such as farm machinery and fertilizer. However, this plan, first put into effect in late 1978, was soon withdrawn. The expected benefits in increased production and sale did not materialize rapidly enough to offset the high initial cost to the state, which by this time was facing a serious budgetary crisis.

This approach to economic planning, in which prices are manipulated by the government to stimulate rural development, is quite different from that utilized by the country's leaders from the 1960s to 1978, when brigades and communes were expected to rely on their own initiative—to practice "self-reliance"—rather than count on the government's financial strategies for stimulating economic growth. At that time, most state aid was allocated for large, collectively organized capital-investment projects such as the building of dams and diversion of waterways, which were seen as enhancing the productivity of whole counties as well as that of communes. Small loans to assist in the general development of brigades and communes were difficult to obtain.

If present-day efforts to modernize China's rural sector have required both readjustments and curtailments, what about those earlier policies based on the principle of local self-reliance? More specifically, how did the brigades within Red Flag Commune respond to this initiative?

We noted earlier that Half Moon, with many of its residents working either temporarily or permanently outside the village, has done little to develop the non-agricultural potential of the village. Today, it doesn't even have one sideline industry with full-time employees—neither the barrel-washing nor the chemical-mixing sideline enterprises having been able to obtain enough contracts with Beijing factories to keep its miniscule work force active. Nevertheless, other brigades within the commune have a different history—where the working population is not so scattered and where the people have established active local industries with little help from the outside. One such village is located within a ten-minute walk from Half Moon. It's called Little River.

DIFFERENCES BETWEEN VILLAGES

On arriving at Little River, one immediately notices its antiquated dwellings, well-worn pockmarked courtyard walls, the poorer dress of the inhabitants, and other attributes that suggest that it is considerably less prosperous than Half Moon. Initial exploration of the village also pointed up another difference. Painted on the adobe walls of narrow village lanes were faded but still visible slogans from the Cultural Revolution, such as "Learn from Dazhai," "Politics is the Life Line of All Work," "Heighten Vigilance, Defend the Motherland," and "Prepare for Wars and for Natural Disasters in the Interests of the People." It didn't take long to realize that Little River is quite a different kind of village than the cleaner and orderly affluent-looking community of Half Moon. And it seldom sees a foreign face.

Yet the village leaders, all of whom are a great deal younger than any I had met elsewhere, were nevertheless pleased to share their experience and knowledge with me. After several meetings with the Party secretary, the brigade head, a production vice chairman, and the woman brigade accountant, a fascinating portrayal of creative local-level planning began to unfold. I soon found that the leaders of Little River are far more ingenious than one might guess from a superficial inquiry.

The village is larger than Half Moon, with a little over 800 residents. More than 75 percent are brigade workers in either agriculture or sideline production. Also, the total amount of cultivated acreage available to the brigade is approximately 20 percent less than that at Half Moon. With less land and more people, the residents of Little River are limited in what they can extract from the soil. Therefore, it was without surprise that I learned that their income level was also lower than that of Half Moon. In Little River, the average value of a 10-point day was .77 yuan, a striking difference from Half Moon's 1.3 yuan.

However, on further investigation, it became clear that the initial comparison of differential collective income between the two villages was meaningless. For example, Little River's figure of .77 yuan is not based on the real level of productivity of the 10-point field worker, as first surmised. Rather, it is a purposely deflated

*Two leaders from
Little River.*

figure reflecting the decision of the village members in 1973 to cut their annual income in order to generate additional capital to develop new sideline industries. Realizing that they had less land than surrounding brigades, they decided to channel their surplus labor into a local sideline industry. Since the government's emphasis on self-reliance precluded any significant state support either by grants or loans, capital to start up the industry had to come from themselves. A decision was then made to reduce the 10-point day from the approximately one *yuan* the village had previously received to .77 *yuan*. With this newly generated capital, the brigade established its first sideline industry in 1973—a small jade-carving factory. Employing 33 people, it produced figurines for sale to the state in much the same manner as the larger district-level jade factory located nearby. This effort brought several thousand *yuan* profit a year to the village, but it wasn't enough. So the villagers continued to set aside part of their work point earnings for capital while their leaders looked for another opportunity.

Although it took several years, the brigade finally negotiated a contract with a Beijing factory in 1978 to make low-wattage fluorescent light bulbs of the kind commonly used in rural homes. The necessary machinery to produce such bulbs required an outlay of 60,000 *yuan*. By continuing their process of reducing in-dividual incomes through lowering the value of the work point, selling their brigade tractor, and bypassing the usual annual contribution to their community welfare fund, the village members amassed sufficient funds to purchase the needed machinery and start up their second sideline. For the moment, Little River peasants, working collectively in field and sideline, have a lower standard of living than their counterparts in Half Moon Village, but the potential for catching up and perhaps even surpassing their near neighbors is considerable. As the brigade leaders said proudly at our last meeting together, "And we didn't even have to ask for financial assistance from the commune."

Little River, at the lower end of the brigade income scale vis-a-vis Half Moon, may be compared with East Gate Village, at the higher end. East Gate, located 20 miles from Half Moon at the eastern border of the commune, is one of Red Flag's wealthiest villages. For the 873 residents living in 170 households (in 1979), the value of their 10-work-point day is 2.1 *yuan*, much higher than the 1.3 figure for Half Moon. Although East Gate has slightly more land per capita than Half Moon, that is not the major reason for the difference. Actually, before 1972, it was poorer than most other villages in the commune, including Half Moon. What brought greater wealth to East Gate in such a short number of years? The answer lies with the development of their sideline industries.

In 1972, the brigade only had 120 *yuan* in its welfare fund, and three needy families to support. It had sufficient problems in growing enough grain to feed its population that it was unable to contribute any income to its accumulation fund to be used for capital expenditures. Instead, over the years, the village had amassed a debt to the state of over 70,000 *yuan*. There was inadequate money to regularly ensure the purchase of electricity to run the pumps for irrigation and lighting for homes. The houses, made of mud and straw, were poor in quality.

That year, the commune loaned the village 18,000 *yuan* for the development of its sideline industries.[1] The brigade leaders then organized forty peasants into a construction team, which offered their services in building houses for surrounding villages. This activity brought in 3000 *yuan* the first year. Shortly thereafter, a contract was obtained to make cardboard. Eventually, they were able to clear their debt to the state and contribute more adequately to their welfare and accumula-tion funds. With this money, they purchased some agricultural machinery, which enabled them to become self-sufficient in grain production.

Finally, the enterprising leader of East Gate obtained from a Beijing factory an old wire-extruder machine, which reduced the thickness of copper wire to

[1] Throughout the 1970s, the policy at Red Flag Commune has been to utilize profits from its successful enterprises to assist in the economic development of its poorer brigades. The commune also has a bureau that assists these brigades in setting up and finding an outlet for small light-industry sidelines. Of course, brigades with "connections" (*guanxi*) can develop their own sideline industries as well.

Workers from a local factory.

various standard sizes. Through negotiation with the state, a contract was then arranged that enabled the sideline to significantly increase the collective worth of the village—so much so that the inhabitants now receive almost half of their income from a sideline industry that employs a very small percentage of its workers.

With this profit, East Gate Village has purchased more farm machinery, thereby freeing additional peasants from work in the fields. The brigade now has four large tractors of their own, eight walking tractors, three trucks, and a jeep. All rice planting is done by machine. As a result, out of the total of those villagers working in the collective sphere, a little less than a third (between 80 and 100) are still employed in agriculture, whereas the other two-thirds are setting up new sidelines and expanding their educational and social-service programs, including day-care, kindergarten, and primary school.[2] Indeed, the recent success of this brigade in raising its standard of living through sideline development is enough to raise a question in the minds of other nearby villagers: Why spend so much time and energy in agricultural field work?

Such questions send shock waves through government offices responsible for maintaining and expanding agricultural production. If sideline industries, a vital adjunct to agricultural production in raising the peasant standard of living, replaced food production as the primary economic activity, the resulting loss in available grain and other food staples could create a crisis of massive proportions. It is for this reason that the government set up a minimum production quota that

[2] In a recent study of the North China village Wugong, Mark Selden also shows how a successful combination of agricultural and sideline enterprise in the 1970s led to a substantial increase in accumulation and personal income (Selden 1982b).

all villages are expected to meet. And as discussed earlier, any sale of grain and vegetables to the state above that quota assures the villagers a large additional bonus.

In summary, even a brief comparison of these three villages in Red Flag Commune illustrates quite clearly the differing alternatives available to local leaders as they undertake to develop the economic potential of their brigades. It should also be obvious that such decisions can limit alternative strategies brigade leaders may wish to utilize in the future. That is, if many villagers are already employed in commune and state-level enterprises (as is the case in Half Moon), these peasants are no longer available to help in the development of local, collectively organized sideline industries. For Half Moon, the issue is not just that they have practically no sideline industry—a point of self-criticism among the leaders—but also that almost no one is available to develop this aspect of the village economy. At Little River and East Gate, a different situation prevails. Although Little River is poorer than Half Moon and East Gate is more prosperous, both have derived a greater amount of their annual income from collective sidelines organized by the local brigade.

Evaluation of the merits of these different approaches to raising the standard of living of China's rural villages is now being debated throughout the country.[3] Each tries to take into account the fact that different local conditions promote different solutions, and by implication, that no one strategy should be followed by everyone. This is a significant departure from the days of the Cultural Revolution, when the Dazhai Brigade served as the unitary model of rural development for all of China—emphasizing agricultural grain production over sideline industries and trade.[4] Now that China's approach to economic development has moved in a different direction, the Dazhai model has received considerable criticism (see Tsou, Blecher, and Meisner 1982). Nevertheless, in economically advanced Red Flag Commune, many leaders continue to advocate the collective approach as the key ingredient in the modernization process.

Having reviewed examples of alternative practices within the commune, let us now look at the political theory that underlies them.

PRODUCTIVITY, OWNERSHIP, AND DISTRIBUTION

The most basic premise of Marxist theory is that the material conditions of life shape one's social existence. More specifically, economic conditions, composed of available natural resources, tools, and the people who use them, are intimately influenced by, and in turn influence those who own or control these "means of

[3] Another alternative, the "responsibility system," will be discussed shortly.

[4] Dazhai Brigade, a small settlement in Shanxi Province, first became a national model in 1964 after it had, through immense effort, transformed the village's badly eroded loess soil of Tigerhead Mountain into highly productive terraced fields. It was also noted for emphasizing the placement of the collective interest over that of individual self-interest. Chen Yonggui, the brigade Party secretary, eventually rose to become a Vice Premier of the country and Politboro member of the Party before losing his position of importance following Mao's death and the change in leadership and political orientation.

production." Over the course of human history, these economic relations, and particularly, the relations shaped by divergent class interests, determine the overall character of a given society.

In the capitalist West, private ownership of the means of production prevails. In a socialist society, collective and state ownership become primary. For example, Liu Xing, a resident of Half Moon Village, works in the small barrel-washing sideline industry. When it is not operating, he works in the fields. Liu's wife, Meiying, is a full-time field worker. Since the sideline industry and agricultural field work are both organized under the collective ownership of the brigade, what Liu Xing and his wife Meiying receive for their collective labor is directly proportional to what they and the other brigade members contribute. There is no guarantee as to the amount of income received, no regular bonus, and no pension upon retirement. A small additional income is gained through the sale of privately owned pigs and chickens to the district store or peasant market.

On the other hand, Liu Xing's brother, also a resident of Half Moon Village, has a permanent position at the nearby state-owned chemical factory. As we already know, such workers receive a regular salary, a monthly bonus based on criteria determined by the workers themselves, and a generous retirement pension. Why the higher income and benefits? Because of the greater productivity.

According to some Marxist analysts of economic development theory, state ownership of the means of production, that is, ownership by the whole people, is a "more advanced" socialist form of economic organization than collective ownership.[5] This is because, under centralized planning, the state can invest its capital in the development of large industrial and state farm enterprises that can bring greater profits to the given unit, and in so doing, higher salaries and benefits to its workers. Certainly the state-controlled agricultural and industrial sectors of Red Flag Commune benefit greatly by their direct access to capital from the government, which enables them to invest in heavier agricultural and industrial machinery, increase their technological capability, and in other ways expand their productive capacity.[6]

Similarly, Half Moon villagers who work under the collective form of ownership can be considered "less advanced" in the sense that these peasants have to rely largely on their own efforts, with little assistance from the state. With minimum available capital, and having to use simpler agricultural and light-industrial machinery, they produce less, and therefore receive less. Put most simply: According to the pocketbooks and minds of Half Moon villagers, state workers make out much better economically than do the collectively based peasantry—hence, the almost universal comment by Half Moon youth that "it is better to be a worker than a peasant."

Further comparison can be made by contrasting differences between the collective economy of the village and that of the commune. Take, for example, our

[5] For example, Mao wrote in 1960, "Within a certain number of years our people's communes will have to carry through the transformation from ownership by the basic team to ownership by the basic commune, and then into ownership by the whole people" (Mao 1974:34).

[6] Unfortunately, the specific amount was not obtainable.

earlier discussion of how peasants should distribute their collective earnings. Should they divide them according to the amount of output of their small cooperative work group? Or should the accounting unit be the whole village production brigade— or even the commune itself, as the well-known radical "leftist" Chinese leader Chen Boda (one-time secretary to Mao Zedong) and his associates tried to do at Red Flag in the late 1950s. Quite clearly, the size of the work force is an important factor influencing such a decision—for several reasons.

Looked at organizationally, when dealing with a large commune like Red Flag, it is far easier for the Beijing municipal government authorities and higher-level commune administrators to negotiate grain and vegetable quotas with 116 village brigades than with many more hundreds of small work groups or production teams. So, from the point of view of bureaucratic efficiency, the production-brigade level of accounting in the distribution of income appears rather sensible.[7]

From a political perspective, the question of which accounting level to use becomes more complicated. For the past 2000 years, peasant households like those in the area of Red Flag could be called "basic accounting units." They still are today, in the sense that families have various household sidelines such as the raising of home-grown chickens and pigs and the raising of crops on private plots to be sold in the village, at the district store, and at a nearby free market.

Yet if we take the amount of productivity as our measure, the single-family accounting unit was first superseded in importance by the agricultural producers' cooperatives and production teams in the 1950s, and later (at places like Red Flag), by village-level brigades. Certainly, this latter collectivity is able to produce more, to organize itself to tackle village-wide projects such as building and repairing irrigation ditches, and in other ways to work toward a higher level of economic productivity for its members. Looking at rural economic development from a perspective that emphasizes the importance of collective endeavor, it would appear to many that the brigade, with its village-wide level of accounting, represents a substantial advance over the single-family unit.

However, to treat the whole village as the accounting unit can create serious problems in that this supposedly "higher" level can mask important differences between work teams with differing degrees of productivity. That is, under the brigade level of accounting, equal distribution of collective income is allocated to various production units even though their relative output may be unequal.

Let's take a specific example. In Half Moon, the young men's agricultural work team produces more collective income for the village than the women's work team. This differential productivity is recognized in the fact that members of the men's team generally receive more work points per day's labor than members of the women's team, although the reverse is occasionally found. Furthermore, the team members receive their work point classification according to their levels of

---

[7] G. William Skinner, in analyzing vegetable-farming communes in several suburban areas of China (including Beijing) in 1977, found a similar pattern: "Because of the preference on the part of state companies for dealing with a manageable number of production units, the brigade is given relatively more emphasis than the team in large municipalities; inevitably this eases the process of raising the level of accounting from the team to the brigade—a cardinal index of socialist progress" (Skinner 1978:792).

productivity as defined by the members of that specific work group—on the assumption that those who have daily contact with the person in the work setting are the best judge of his or her competence.

However, evaluations often vary between work teams, some groups ranking their members higher than others. Actually, conflicts between villagers arising from this method of distribution have become quite sharp, especially when the harvest is poor or when one work unit is known for giving itself a higher overall work point rating than their production output appears to deserve. Work team leaders, too, are sensitive to criticisms of their productivity—as was clearly illustrated in the argument at Half Moon between the women's team leader Su Xiulan and Party secretary Jiang Lijiang over the seemingly slow speed with which the young women's work team cleared a corn field.

Given these types of problems, the general principle followed within China until recently is that except for very small communities, the so-called "higher" brigade level of accounting should be reserved for those few villages that have a greater rate of productive output than is generally the case throughout the country. When more can be received by all, the unequal return based on human differences and abilities will become less important. But that time is far off in the future.[8]

In summary, through the 1970s, the general pattern in China has been to expand both the collective and state spheres of ownership. Thus, private production has of necessity been reduced. Yet, the actual amount of private economic activity during this time has varied considerably. Private plots, for example, were allowed up until the "communist wind" of the Great Leap Forward. During the early 1960s, they were again encouraged, and then in the Cultural Revolution they were often curtailed, as were the village markets. With the change in policies following the death of Mao, private plots and peasant markets are again expanding.

Furthermore, in the autumn of 1979, the government began allowing small work groups of three to five families to negotiate contracts with their local production units to produce specific amounts of grain, rice, vegetables, and other agricultural products. After fulfilling the agreed-upon quota (*baogan zhi*), the group could keep the rest for their own sale or use. However, if they didn't meet the quota, a fine was levied. One of several reasons for this significant change in policy was to stimulate the peasants to greater productivity by appealing to their direct economic self-interest—as opposed to the broader interest of the collective. A second was to reduce the stifling effect of the bureaucracy on the people's motivation. Needless to say, such an orientation to economic development stands in sharp contrast to the other model, which stresses the importance of the collectivity in promoting production, increasing the peasants' standard of living, and developing a socialist political consciousness.

---

[8] Today, this view is changing. While on a visit to the commune in October of 1979, a visiting horticultural scientist from Beijing utilized ongoing press criticism of Dazhai Brigade to offer a more blanket criticism of villages that had raised their accounting level to the brigade. He commented, "Dazhai's spirit of self-reliance and putting the collective first is fine. But Dazhai's distribution system is not suitable for China or for Dazhai. Distribution should be by work to release the peasant's enthusiasm. Dazhai drew on the prestige of the Party to win peasants to policies that outstripped the productive forces. This might be successful for a while, but in the long run it won't work."

Why has there been such a dramatic change in policy? There are many reasons, including one that has yet to be addressed—the problem of bureaucracy.

THE PROBLEM OF BUREAUCRACY

In discussing bureaucracy in Half Moon Village and Red Flag Commune, two issues should be kept in mind: one is the structure itself, the other, the way local officials relate to the people they serve—their "work style."

We already have some familiarity with the pyramid-like authority pattern of the bureaucratic system. At the core of political power is the Party. It generates policies like an executive. It establishes guidelines, which are equivalent to laws (for example, residency registration), like a legislature. It has various economic, social, and political divisions like an administration. And wrongdoings of officials and important criminals are handled by the Party like the judiciary. Over the past three and a half decades, some Chinese leaders (such as Mao) have advocated that the Party actively lead all activities within the country. Other leaders have encouraged greater separation between the political Party structure and the administrative government structure. But no one doubts that the Party is the ultimate decision-maker at either the national or local level.

As described earlier, at Red Flag, Party committees at the commune, district, and brigade levels determine policies, which are then carried out by various administrative committees and "mass organizations" (for example, the Women's Federation) involving both Party and non-Party members. At each organizational level, leading governing bodies expect their decisions to be followed by those under them. At the bottom of the pyramid are peasants and workers, who in most instances are relatively uninvolved in the decision-making process, but whose economic activities are substantially determined by those who lead.

Within this bureaucratic structure, leaders and followers relate to one another in various ways. Decisions may be undertaken in an elitist manner, with little involvement from below. Or they may be undertaken quite democratically, with extensive input by the participants. Half Moon villagers being told by the municipal Department of Agriculture in Beijing to undertake "triple cropping," even though they largely opposed it, provides a good example of a bureaucratic work style. In contrast, the establishment of a Worker's Congress at the new state factory near Half Moon, the members of which determine their own criteria for receiving bonuses, is an example of a democratic work style.

The bureaucratic structure and its accompanying methods has a very long history in China—dating back 2000 years ago when a rising gentry class trained some of its sons to become elite scholar-officials able to amass great power, privilege, and property. However, it was not so much control over property that conferred such long-lasting authority to this elite group as it was their indispensable role as managers—plus a multilevel educational system controlled by examinations at each level.

What was the ideological support for this powerful governing structure? Mencius, a well-known Confucian spokesman of the time, expressed it succinctly:

"Great men have their proper business and little men have their proper business. . . . Some labor with their minds and some with their strength. Those who labor with their minds govern others; those who labor with their strength are governed by others" (cited in Balazs 1964:154). Such was the social philosophy that legitimized the great bureaucracy that integrated a diverse population and supported China's many dynasties in the past. Today, few would argue that this same perspective is alive and well throughout all levels of the state and local government, and in the Party itself.[9]

Mencius' view on governance and the distinctions between mental and manual labor are firmly ensconced in Half Moon as well. We see it in Party secretary Jiang Lijiang's warning to the village field teams at the December village meeting. He knew the villagers wanted to finish digging their earthen courtyard cellars so that they could store their winter supply of brigade-grown cabbages. He was more concerned that they get the large piles of manure from the collective pig farm to the fields. But instead of raising both of these issues for discussion in a democratic manner, he summarily threatened his listeners with a loss in work point rating if they persisted in coming out late or going home early from the fields. In the day-to-day life of the village, he also tends to remain aloof from the people he is expected to serve. Ostentatiously busy, he is always on the move, chasing down a missing chicken, making sure the work teams get to work on time, or checking clinic records. But he never works side-by-side with the people he is expected to lead. Jiang Lijiang is not considered a bad leader, just one with a bureaucratic work style.

The first time I heard villagers comment on the subject was on a sunny fall afternoon while husking corn with the men's work team. We were sitting in a semicircle at the edge of a brigade field with our backs soaking up the warm rays of the sun. That we were barely working was obvious from the almost imperceptible growth of the pile of corn husks before us. The men, talking among themselves, disregarded the slight look of annoyance on the face of team leader Chen Defu until Chu Meiying, the lively woman village accountant, came up behind us. She had arrived to inform Chen of a meeting to be held shortly at the brigade office.

Seeing Chu, I began husking corn a little more diligently. The others continued talking with one another, paying little regard to Chen, Chu, or the task at hand. Finally, Chen told us we had better work a little harder. Looking up at the team leader from where he was sitting, one of the villagers responded in a semiserious tone of voice.

"Chen, why should we have to work when the people at the brigade office just sit around all day knocking heads together doing nothing?"

[9] In fact, one of the major reasons why Mao Zedong initiated the Cultural Revolution was because he perceived the reemergence of a bureaucratic elite as the major internal enemy of socialist development. Though the bureaucracy appeared quite able to survive and even grow under socialism, Mao feared that China's socialism couldn't survive the bureaucracy. Hence, the need for a cultural (i.e., ideological) revolution in which peasants and workers were to be exalted over bureaucrats and intellectuals.

Following that remark, others quickly joined in the teasing.

"That's right, Chen. Are you going to become one of those bureaucrats with a 'big mouth and lazy hands' (*dong kou bu dong shou*), only talking and not working, or are you going to stay with us and help get the work done?"

"Yes, Defu. Stick around. You're better off with us."

Chu, looking off toward the village, said nothing. But Chen Defu, disregarding the teasing, good-naturedly reminded the men of the need to finish the corn husking before the end of the day. Then, turning away, he and Chu both left for the brigade office.

Although team leaders like Chen Defu, Chu Huifang, and Su Xiulan occasionally meet with the brigade leaders, they are not regular village-level cadres. Their working day is spent in the fields, and except for carrying out requests in assigning work, they have little to do with making or implementing village policy. The colloquial expression "big mouth and lazy hands" reflects this historic division of labor between worker and manager quite well. The field worker who offered that remark was obviously reminding team leader Chen Defu where his loyalties should lie.

If team leaders are not part of the local bureaucracy, full-time brigade accountants like Chu Meiying definitely are. After finishing school, she spent four years in the fields with Su Xiulan's work team. Then, in 1978, she was chosen by the village leaders to be the accountant. In this position, she is responsible for keeping an accurate record of all financial transactions, as well as recording daily work points. The position is an important one, requiring both thoroughness and honesty. However, not being a Party member, her status in the decision-making hierarchy is still relatively low.

As described earlier, the key village leaders are members of the Party branch, followed by those in the brigade administrative committee, including both Party members and nonmembers. All the local CCP members are responsible to the district Party committee, which in turn is under the commune committee, and so on up the political ladder to the central leadership in Beijing. Of course, the brigade administrative committee is not bound by the decisions of the district body in the way that the Party committee is, since the principle of "democratic centralism" is not directly applicable here. But local administrative committees are expected to follow guidelines laid down by similar governing units at the district and commune levels, thereby insuring the continued maintenance of the bureaucratic structure.[10]

There is another feature of the governing process that enhances the bureaucratic structure at the expense of democratic input—the lack of a modern legal system. Until 1979, Half Moon villagers had almost no legal protections to call upon when they got into difficulty with the authorities. Given this lack, their only recourse was to appeal to higher official bodies or to mail statements of complaint to the

[10] In December 1982, the government reinstated the principle of township (*xiang*) governance, which in coming years will replace the commune as the major political institution concerned with bureaucratic responsibilities such as residency registration, taxation, and the maintenance of public security. This reemergence of the *xiang* or township form of government effectively removes from the commune its distinct political power base (see Postscript).

appropriate "Letters to the Editor" column of major newspapers like the *People's Daily*. Courts were available to handle serious crimes and civil disputes, but minor ones were either resolved by a local unit (*danwei*) or simply ignored.

Abuse of power by officials posed a more serious problem, since courts were never established to address this type of issue.[11] This fact was dramatically illustrated during my last week in the commune. Three Party officials at the district level—including one living in Half Moon—were removed from their positions due to their having used public funds for their own benefit. The whole matter was handled by the Party alone, an investigative committee deciding that the individuals concerned should not be prosecuted, though they must pay back the funds taken.

In 1979, China did draw up a formal criminal code offering new legal protection for its citizens. Though the code is still too undeveloped to be effectively used by Half Moon villagers today, a process has at least begun whereby individuals will be able to criticize a bureaucratic leader with less fear of being passed over for a factory job or having to wait endlessly for a permit to build a house. Furthermore, if the code is fully implemented, all groups, including the Party, are to be subject to the legal statutes, which are designed to protect both the individual and the state.

Of course, this lack of a formal civil code in the past does not mean the Chinese are without a sense of justice. Rather, the norms that define proper conduct continue to remain embedded in Confucian values closely linked to the family. Half Moon villagers, for example, have no concept of civil liberty or individual freedom like that found in the West. But they do have a strong sense of right and wrong. Uninvolved in a transcendental religion like Christianity, their concept of justice is rooted in an existing world that places greater emphasis on principles of reciprocity and proper interpersonal relations than is characteristic of societies where the value of individualism is primary.

While the centrifugal force of individualism presents its own problems in the West, in China, submissiveness to authority and subordination of the individual to the group provides fertile soil for the continuation of a bureaucratic work style. Other Chinese values, such as continuity and inclusiveness in family relations (Hsu 1979:262), have a similar impact. Under these circumstances, local cadres who feel that their position of authority gives them the right to make decisions with little regard for the views of the governed can quickly become abusive. If these abuses increase in severity, the anger of the villagers grows.

Nepotism and favoritism are the two most common targets of criticism. At first, I didn't appreciate the extent of nepotism in the village and the frustration it caused. Being an outsider largely excluded me from hearing this type of internal criticism. The need for maintaining face with a foreigner and fear of local criticism usually silenced such expressions. But as my presence was gradually accepted (and sometimes forgotten), I came to learn more of the villagers' disappointments, and on a few occasions, open anger.

While walking to the district store one day with a young field worker, I learned

---

[11] Needless to say, political campaigns did provide a convenient "solution" to such a dilemma.

for the first time of the bitterness felt by some villagers over the patronage system, which assured that many factory jobs went to kin and friends of leaders, and relatively few to other village families. The man who first told me of the problem came from a family that had yet to receive a factory assignment. A little later, I heard a similar remark from a local sent-down youth. The village household survey taken in the fall of 1979 illustrated the same pattern even more clearly. When the name of Chu Meiying, the local brigade accountant, appeared on the list drawn from the household sample, I went to see her for an interview. She had talked earlier about her forthcoming marriage to the male barefoot doctor, but never about her own life.

During the interview, she spoke of how hard she worked in the fields prior to becoming the brigade accountant and how the 9.4 work point rating she received was one of the highest held by any woman in the village. Then, last year, just before Jiang Lijiang became Party secretary, she was offered the brigade accounting position and accepted it. The new job entailed a great deal more responsibility than her work in the field. Yet her 9.4 work point income remained the same. Wondering how she felt about that, I decided to ask.

"Chu Meiying, do you like being an accountant?"

Her response was hardly what I had expected.

"Well, accounting is all right, but I'm really waiting for a factory job."

Having just completed the survey for her household, I knew that her three older sisters already had permanent positions in nearby factories. As I looked down at my notes to confirm the fact, she must have perceived my thoughts.

"I know that four members of one family having factory jobs is not very common. But you see, my father was head of the brigade for many years, and he was able to help. If people have the opportunity, they always use the back door. It's even getting worse. But what can be done? Nothing. I know it's not fair, but that's the way it is."

Several days later, while weeding with the young field worker who wanted a factory job, I asked whether he thought there was any possibility of his getting one.

"No. There is too much favoritism. If you don't have the right contacts you can do nothing. It's the fault of the leaders. But even they don't know how to change the situation."

The following month, I learned of still another local villager whose brother had found him a job in the state-run chemical factory. His brother had initially arranged it and then had gotten approval from the district leadership. That meant the family would have two members with state factory jobs. When other villagers without access to factory jobs heard about the arrangement, they complained bitterly to the brigade Party secretary. Apparently, they were successful, since when the new worker showed up at the factory gates for his first day on the job, he was told that "he had arrived too late" and that "someone else had been given the position." In this instance, the district leader had saved face, but the villagers had won the day.

Interested in the conflict, I searched through my kinship data, trying to develop a coherent picture of family relations and occupation. Chu Meiying's father's name was Li Yongshan. He was the Party secretary from 1970 until 1976. In that year, he was transferred to the commune electric power station. The leadership post was then briefly taken over by Li Guiying, the sister of another Li—Li Haiping, the retired Party member who was head of the local Poor Peasant's Association and the man I first interviewed about the early days of the village. Although Li Haiping never held a formal brigade office in Half Moon, his position in the Association obviously provided him with considerable influence in the village. Old Li, it turned out, also had ties with the Wang family with whom I was living.

Further study of the household survey showed that the Li family had done very well for itself. In addition to ex-brigade head Li Yongshan's three daughters who had factory jobs, all of Li Haiping's six children were factory workers, as were most of the children of Li Guiying, the woman Party secretary from 1976 to 1978. So too were half the members of the Wang family, in whose household I was living. Then, in 1979, Jiang Lijiang became the Party secretary of Half Moon, a man without any kinship ties to either the Li or Wang families. His name was not included on the household sample, and I never did obtain a record of his family's occupational status. But his wife's family was in the sample, and neither she nor any of her relatives living close by had factory jobs.

As far as the villagers were concerned, one back door had been definitely closed. However, it was not yet clear how wide other doors were to going to open. It was obvious, however, that though monopolizing access to scarce social or material resources by taking advantage of one's position might be moderated, this backdoorism would not disappear locally as long as similar practices occurred higher up in the bureaucratic structure.

Recognizing this, I decided it was a good time to take up the question with Yu Shanshan, a senior leader of Red Flag Commune. Forty-five years old, he looked far younger. More important, he had the kind of intelligence, openness, quiet energy, and relaxed manner that defined him as highly capable. From our first meeting, which took place while he was on an agricultural tour of the United States, I liked him immensely. The advice he gave me at the beginning of my study made me realize that anthropological field work has something in common with being a commune leader: "Talk to as many different people as you can. Cross-check what they tell you—and don't let them take you around in circles to avoid answering your questions!"

Now that I was deep into the research, I asked him for a meeting, to which he agreed. We talked of many things: the reemergence of peasant markets, the Party's summary views of Mao's role in the Cultural Revolution, the transition from peasant to worker, and finally, problems of bureaucracy. I laughingly reminded him of his remark about not letting anyone "take me around in circles," and he responded, face wrinkled in an amused smile, "You mean you have a tough question for me?"

"Yu Shanshan, how are new workers selected from the brigades for state factory jobs?"

"We usually hire new workers once a year. A factory submits its request to the commune, which then passes it on to each division (district) for an equal share of the quota. There is a lot of backdoorism. In any case, a number is given to each division, which then divides the number among the brigades. The brigades then select the individuals. In fact, the children of cadres often get the preference. There were a lot of complaints a few years ago, but the situation is getting better. Now we have introduced a policy that families without workers get the preference. Children of retired, dead, or injured workers also receive preferential treatment."

"Why should a retired worker's child inherit his or her father's job? Is that an example of backdoorism?"

"Many state enterprises practice this policy. It is not using the back door because it is policy. The main concern is to replace the 30 percent of the wage that the family loses when a worker retires. Hiring another family member will ease the financial burden. Especially when a worker is injured or killed in the factory, the family has a right to the job. Otherwise, people would become demoralized. This way, they remain satisfied."

"What about the criteria for selection?"

"Prospective workers must be junior or senior middle school graduates in good physical condition."

"In Half Moon, there appears to have been a good deal of behind-the-scenes maneuvering to place relatives in factory jobs."

"Backdoorism by brigade cadres cannot be solved just by supervision. It takes a great deal of cadre education. On the other hand, this village may have more people working outside than most because there is less land per capita. Also, the more people go out for jobs, the more contacts they have, and the easier it is for others in the village to find jobs there too."

Then, looking straight at me, his eyes firmly focused on mine and his voice full of feeling, he added, "Backdoorism is a general problem. The solution must start from the top. That's where the roots are. The manifestations are at the bottom."

I responded, "Perhaps the elimination of private plots, peasant markets, and the limited input of villagers into decisions like 'triple-cropping' has strengthened the centralized bureaucracy even more?"

"Perhaps. As for triple-cropping, we learned from the peasants on that one."

"And the problem of bureaucracy?"

With a grin, he concluded, "If there is only one flower blossoming, you get bureaucracy."

At the moment, I didn't really appreciate the depth of meaning contained in that last statement. Only in the weeks and months that followed did its significance become clear.

9/The face of the future

A TURNING POINT

"You know, it's all right to become rich."

The time was late September, 1979. The person making the remark was Xiao Cai, a young woman in charge of "foreign affairs" at Red Flag. For Cai, foreign affairs meant being responsible for the activities of all foreigners who came to the commune—including me. Mostly, she met visiting delegations of agricultural specialists, tourists, and political dignitaries, arranging tours of production facilities and planning meetings with commune leaders. She also came periodically to Half Moon Village to offer assistance in setting up interviews in neighboring villages or with leading personnel in some of the larger commune factories. On this day, I was helping her as well. For the past six months, she had been working hard to improve her spoken English by following language lessons on the local evening television broadcast. Today, I was her substitute teacher.

"What do you mean about becoming rich, Xiao Cai?" I thought perhaps the phrasing of her remark in English might carry a different meaning in her mind than in mine.

"I mean that individuals and families can work hard for their own benefit. If they make money at it, that's fine. They won't be criticized any more for being selfish."

Her comment was intriguing. In contrast to what Westerners might think about contemporary China, there is nothing unusual about expressing a desire to get rich. Of course, as the Chinese use the term, "rich" means achieving a comfortable and secure life rather than obtaining great wealth. Actually, the phrase "getting rich" became popular right after 1949, when it was used as a slogan for rural development.

Hao Ran, in his well-known novel *The Golden Road*, took up this theme in describing the effort of peasants in a North China village to overcome their poverty during the land reform movement. However, Hao's book, first published in 1972, was quite critical of individuals wanting to better themselves at the expense of the collective effort (see Hao 1981:115–128). So too were the results of a study of Wandong Village, a brigade located on the southeastern edge of Beijing. Written by local university students, the printed report included a section subtitled, "Getting Organized is the Only Way for Poor and Lower-Middle Peasants to All

148

Faces of the future.

Get Rich Together" (Beijing Foreign Languages Institute 1976). So getting rich was fine. The question was how?

Now Xiao Cai seemed to be saying that the collective orientation was less important. The fact that she was a Party member and therefore knowledgeable about current debates and strategies immediately crossed my mind. Without thinking, I broached the question directly.

"You mean there has been a change in policy?"

Her response was a simple, noncommittal smile. I let the matter drop, assuming that if she had any knowledge of the subject, she was not able to discuss it with me. To learn of policy changes before they appear in the Chinese press or news reports requires contact with spokespeople considerably more senior than Xiao Cai. So I had to wait—but not very long.

A few days later, the village loudspeaker system began broadcasting a series of taped radio reports about enterprising peasants who greatly increased their family income through private entrepreneurial activity. In one broadcast, the newscaster spoke of a young man who got up early every morning and tended his private bees before going to work in the collective fields. Significantly, the beekeeper made more money selling honey than he did working for the collective. But more revealing was what the commentator didn't say. Praising the initiative of the newly enriched peasant in earning additional money in his spare time, he bypassed the other question of how beekeeping might be collectivized so that this new source of wealth could benefit a larger number of people.

A little later, newspapers from the city, though seldom found outside the brigade office, began reporting similar events. One article on the front page of the *People's Daily* was prefaced by this headline: "The Policy of Allowing Peasants to Get Rich Greatly Liberates the Productive Forces." It went on to state, "To allow some peasants to get rich, to allow some areas, some brigades to get rich first, this is an important step in accelerating the Four Modernizations in our country. It is a step to improve the relations between our Party and the peasants." Xiao Cai had kept her thoughts to herself. But it looked like others were beginning to speak out.

A short while later, on the eve of the thirtieth anniversary of National Day, local radios carried a four-hour-long speech by Ye Jianying, an old and respected Party official, that offered the Party's summation of the Cultural Revolution—and, by implication, Mao Zedong's leadership of it. One or two local cadres listened to the speech. A few others caught the highlights. But no one, including the villagers, appeared surprised at the final summation, which stated, "The Cultural Revolution was an appalling disaster."

In the weeks that followed, the government emphasized in the press and on television that "collective effort must be linked to individual initiative." Under sound Party leadership, the reports went on to say, such initiative had been tapped. But generally, the political extremism of the Cultural Revolution, offering a simplistic notion of "capitalism" and unfairly labeling people as "capitalist roaders," had brought a large decrease in individual and household sideline activities, to the detriment of China's overall economic development. Furthermore, collectively organized units often had great difficulty setting up sideline industries due to the inertia or disinterest of government agencies responsible for approving such requests.

All these statements reinforced the view expressed in the *People's Daily* that it was necessary to rekindle the people's enthusiasm by allowing "some peasants, areas, and brigades to get rich first"—and by such means to improve the deteriorating relations between the Party and the people.

It was obvious to anyone following these pronouncements that a "new wind" was blowing out of the capital city. Politics in the mold of the Cultural Revolution were out. Loss of respect for the Party was pronounced. The future direction was uncertain. Recent government policy efforts to encourage agricultural growth through increasing procurement prices for food grains and other farm products was proving very costly. The weakened condition of the economy made it unfeasible to greatly reduce prices for agricultural equipment. At the local level, surplus earnings from brigade sidelines were often used for upgrading living standards rather than mechanizing agriculture. Problems of bureaucratic management continued. As a result of these problems, Party leaders in charge of agricultural policy were criticized (including Hua Guofeng, China's Premier at the time). Revised strategies were proposed, argued over, and compromised. When finally approved, they marked the beginning of a new turning point in China's development strategy.

Major changes didn't occur all at once; nor did they necessarily reflect the views of just one senior leadership group. Hua Guofeng, for example, reinitiated the policy of encouraging individual material incentives through the use of bonuses shortly after the removal of the "Gang of Four" from their position of importance. But most policy changes, many of them introduced after having been tested in different parts of the country, represented the views of Deng Xiaoping and his supporters. As Deng increasingly reestablished his influence within the Party (though often behind the scenes), the new direction began to take shape. One of the key steps in this process was the effort to reduce bureaucratic control over economic planning and distribution in favor of increased use of markets and floating prices. A second step reinforced the importance of individual bonuses as a form of economic incentive in the workplace. And finally, in some parts of the country, small "work groups" (*zuoye zu*) of three to five families were established that could assume responsibility for "contracting" from the brigade land, seed grains, and tools for cultivation—as long as they contributed the agreed-upon amount of production (*baogan zhi*) to the state through the appropriate accounting unit.[1]

This was the alternative Yu Shanshan was implicitly referring to when he spoke of a single blooming flower encouraging bureaucracy. To motivate the peasants to higher productivity—especially in poor or backward villages—the link between one's actual output and one's income should be strengthened, and the emphasis on the collective downgraded. By this means, China's rural villagers could free themselves from some of the stifling bureaucratic controls that had so limited agricultural productivity in the past.

THE INDIVIDUAL, THE COLLECTIVE, AND THE STATE

What was the response of Half Moon residents to these new ideas? Any suggestion that work groups be broken up into smaller units and land "contracted out" was not seen as applicable in their context. Since the village had already chosen to hold its private plots in common (in opposition to proposals of commune leaders) the idea of dividing up the larger brigade land and regular work teams wasn't even discussed.[2]

[1] This latter strategy was developed in the spring of 1978 and formalized in December—at the same Third Plenum CCP Central Committee meeting that had approved the higher state procurement price of grain to increase peasant income (Domes 1982:255–256).

[2] Actually, at this time, government efforts to strengthen individual initiative by reducing the collective input were primarily focused on poorer, more isolated villages and communes, and those whose local leadership was known to be weak. In affluent, more highly mechanized, well-developed suburban communes like Red Flag, the contract system was considered less necessary and, therefore, was less used (Lippit 1982:147).

However, maximizing individual incentives by means of bonuses and reestablishing peasant markets did stimulate considerable discussion. Local factory workers basically supported the idea of bonuses. But, like the issue of getting rich, implicit in the process was the question of how—in this case, how should bonuses be allocated?

The 300 workers at a large commune-run machine repair shop located near the administrative headquarters had a particularly difficult time deciding how to resolve the question. The shop, in addition to repairing tractors and other types of farm machinery, manufactured simple threshing machines and specially designed axles for sale to the state. When the shop leaders first introduced the principle of bonuses, the workers supported it. However, in discussing how to distribute the bonuses from the surplus income (profit) generated by the workers, they faced a dilemma.

Everyone knew it was much harder to derive a surplus from machine repairing than from manufacturing. But those in the manufacturing division represented less than one-third of the total work force. Should bonuses be limited to that smaller group? No, because if that happened, everyone would want to work in the manufacturing shop and no one in repair. After much further discussion, the factory members finally decided to divide the surplus income drawn from the manufacturing sector among all workers in the shop. Those in repair shouldn't be penalized because the nature of their responsibilities precluded them from generating surplus income.

Then the workers turned to the question of how to evaluate the productive value of each worker. Again, in the manufacturing sector, the evaluation was completed with little difficulty, since men and women worked closely together and each worker's productivity level was known to the other. In the repair shop, where the people were more isolated from one another and tasks more varied, the decision was made to establish for each form of work quotas from which bonuses could be determined. For example, a standard of 50 hours was decided upon for the overhaul of a tractor. If the individual regularly completed the overhaul in 45 hours or less (and the quality of performance was satisfactory), the savings in labor power represented a "profit" and therefore should be reflected in a higher bonus to that particular worker. Most repair workers, however, received the same bonus. Overall, it was an intriguing solution to a difficult problem—utilizing the strength of the bonus system in stimulating productivity while combining individual and collective incentives into one package.

I was also struck by the success of the government's individual incentive policy in much larger manufacturing centers, such as an automobile assembly plant in Beijing. One villager from Half Moon worked in such a factory—living in a worker's dormitory for most of the week and returning home on weekends or whenever he had time off. One day, I asked him whether bonuses were stimulating production at his plant.

"The new system really does some good. Before, when you went to the factory, nobody was too active at learning. One old worker told me that he always felt ashamed if he didn't know how to do something. But today, a lot of young people don't care. They say, 'If you don't know how to do something you won't have to do it.' Or, 'The more you know, the harder you have to work. The less you know, the less you have to work.' But in our factory, the work isn't even up to the capitalist standard."

"What do you mean?" I asked.

"I mean, here you get the same salary regardless of the amount of work you do. Until now, seniority has been the only real factor determining pay increase. The specific job you do hasn't counted. Some people like me, who try to learn as much as they can, end up working harder while others just sit on their tails doing nothing. And yet, we both get about the same income. Isn't that a form of exploitation? That's why I like the new system. Everyone has to take a test before receiving a raise and be evaluated before they get a bonus. That's the way it should be. So this bonus is doing some good. People are paying more attention and working harder. And everyone benefits."

Inquiring about the reemergence of peasant markets, I also found general support for this new policy. Today, the closest one to Half Moon is located just outside the commune border in the old market town, about a half hour away by bicycle. Markets have not been established within Red Flag's boundaries since there are few goods to exchange that local villagers don't already have. The market is most useful where local distribution is poor and where peasant-farmers can trade with town and urban residents. City workers with cash want to purchase fresh products from the countryside. Peasants not only need the money, but enjoy the respite from field work. However, in Red Flag, where most villagers earn over 1 *yuan* or more per day, some villagers oppose spending much time at the market.

Ma Haimen was one of these. "For many people, going to the market is really a waste of labor power. Say your hens lay 20 eggs and you want to sell them at the market. The city (state-controlled) price may be 10 *fen* (100 *fen* equals 1 *yuan*) per egg, and you can sell fresh ones for 15 *fen* per egg. That only brings you 5 *fen* per egg while you stand there all day. You aren't even going to earn the 1 *yuan* you would earn working in the fields or in a sideline. So, in this case, the market isn't going to do any good at all. Furthermore, there aren't enough goods to sell anyway."

Commune leader Yu Shanshan added another perspective on the reemergence of the market system at Red Flag: "Under current conditions, peasant markets play an important economic role in that brigade farmers are a bridge to the city. It is impossible for state-run commercial networks to satisfy all the people's needs. So local markets facilitate small production and compensate for the shortcomings of the state commercial network. Still, there is a need to strengthen supervision. State-owned stores should be able to influence market prices. If you don't have economic controls, the state sector will be in trouble. Sometimes prices in the peasant market are higher than in the state sector. Then the state stores raise their price, which can encourage an upward-spiraling competition. When that happens, the masses really curse somebody."

When viewed in combination with one another, recent changes (such as the proposed revision of the brigade's collective orientation, reemergence of the market, and the emphasis on individual material incentive) highlight another dimension of the new economic policy that sets it apart from the expressed goals of the recent past. This new dimension is a recognition that these steps will heighten rather than decrease economic inequalities presently existing between individuals, and between villages within the commune, and in the country at large.

With this recognition in mind, the government has mounted in the press, on television, and through various Party channels a major ideological campaign against "egalitarianism," emphasizing that under socialism, people should receive "according to their work." That is, the receiving of income should be proportional to one's contribution to the production process. Only in a communist society— that is, a classless society—in which major inequalities between its members have disappeared and the social wealth is fully developed, do the people "contribute according to their ability" and "receive according to their need" (Marx 1875:14).

Of course, this theory is hardly new, and in its utopian form can be traced back to political philosophers considerably before Marx. The overall goal involves not just a redistribution of wealth from private to collective and state ownership, but the political, economic, and social development of a society in which working people—peasant-farmers, workers, technicians, teachers, and others—gain an increasing role in the institutions that govern their lives.[3]

Is this process quite advanced in Red Flag? No, not really. Certainly, economic livelihood has improved greatly, particularly when compared with that of China's more isolated rural populace. But the development of political institutions that provide for increased democratic decision making is only just beginning.

Shortly before I left Half Moon, Ma Haimen, the vice brigade leader, spoke of a forthcoming election of the local administrative committee in which all candidates, both Party and non-Party, were to be placed on the same ballot. Those with the highest number of votes would become the new members. No longer, he said, were separate Party and non-Party slates to be presented. If these and similar political experiments continue, eventually resulting in the establishment of regularized voting procedures, the electoral aspect of the democratic process will certainly be strengthened. If, however, government bureaucracy at the national and local level becomes more pervasive, even this tentative, decentralized, Western-type "grass-roots" democracy will not develop, and other more direct forms of participation in decision making will not even be explored.

Over the past several decades, China's leadership has concerned itself with two major issues: One is to insure that the people become ideologically committed to the new social order. The other is to train scientists, technicians, and other intellectuals who can help to build a technologically developed, highly productive society that can substantially improve the living standard of its people.

During Mao's leadership, he emphasized that these two qualities should be nurtured within each individual, with "red-ness" guiding "expert-ness." Since, in his view, the existing society did not adequately provide this nurturance, he tried to change its structure so that it could. As we have seen, this effort took many forms, such as an attack on teaching methods, including temporarily doing away

---

[3] As noted in an earlier chapter, Mao Zedong and his supporters raised a further issue: At what point in the socialist transition process should distribution begin to take place according to need? Today, questions raised by Chinese Marxists focus more on the transition to socialism than to communism.

with examinations; an insistence that students and teachers should live with and learn from the working population; a challenge to authorities who saw the sole purpose of education as that of serving the state bureaucracy; and at the same time, a promotion of the skills and capabilities of peasants and workers (see Shirk 1982 and Unger 1982).

It was this same philosophy that both guided the self-reliant building of the middle school near Half Moon Village and frustrated the local principal and teachers, who were no longer able to follow their regular course of instruction. This same political ideal first led Zhang Yanzi to commit her life to helping build a socialist society in the Northeast, and later, to turn away in discouragement, accepting help through the back door that she had earlier rejected. Indeed, through the course of this period, the commitment to being "red" became mired in factionalism defined as purity, while the effort to develop "experts" deteriorated into a decrying of educational standards in general. And the youth, in whose name much of the struggle was fought, were left distrusting many of their leaders, and some, the cause of socialism itself.

Today, China is turning in a new direction, seeking a political approach to its rural development that links economic benefit more directly to the individual family and smaller work team, while still maintaining the collective form of ownership. What future implications do these recent changes hold for the 800 million peasant-farmers that live in China's villages? The answer to that question has yet to be determined.

On my last morning in Half Moon, I found it difficult to envision the future of the 543 people whom I had come to know and like. Rising early, I went down to the plaza for a final look around the village. Young students, clustered in small groups, had already begun their trek along the main road toward school. At the other end of the village, Jiang Lijiang stood at his usual location by the brigade office door, watching over the work teams out in the fields. Several team members, recognizing me and knowing that I was about to leave, waved a goodbye.

Turning back toward the Wang house to finish packing, I saw off in the distance Zhang Yanzi firmly seated on her red tractor. I stopped and watched as the machine moved slowly down a path toward a field beyond. Crossing the road, Zhang passed an elderly woman walking toward the district store. Tied around the old woman's head was a faded blue kerchief, and below that, a worn work jacket, baggy pants carefully patched, and tiny canvas shoes covering her deformed feet. In her fingers she held a small long-handled shovel. Every few feet she leaned forward and deftly scooped up from the roadway some animal manure, which was then expertly tossed into a shoulder basket strapped to her back. Once the basket was full, she would return home and enrich the soil of her family garden, in much the same way as her mother and grandmother had done before her. Standing quietly at the edge of the village, I thought about the scene before me, Zhang and the modern tractor in the field and the old woman on the road. China has changed immensely in 30 years. And yet, much remains to be done.

Postscript

Sweeping changes have continued throughout rural China well into the 1980s. Free markets continue to expand. Peasants from Red Flag and other communes are now taking their foodstuffs and wares directly into the city rather than remaining on the outskirts, as had been the previous pattern. In 1980, a new "responsibility system" (*zeren zhi*) was introduced whereby separate households, and even individuals, can contract with production teams and brigades to produce vegetables and other agricultural goods on specific plots of brigade land divided up for that purpose. New regulations allow private plots to range as high as 15 percent of the total land base of a given village. Not surprisingly, these events have changed the nature of commune organization.

Decentralization of production has reduced the number of cadres responsible for economic management. Political and administrative functions of the communes have decreased. In 1981, responsibilities for civil and social affairs such as residency registration, public security, schools, and health facilities still remained under commune jurisdiction (Domes 1982:262). But the newly approved Chinese constitution of 1982 clearly states that these administrative responsibilities are to be turned over to the township (*xiang*), the political unit of government below the county (*xian*) that was largely superseded by the communes in 1958 (Peng 1982:2).

As for the success of the responsibility system, official government figures for 1982 state that between 60 and 70 percent of the brigades in the county where Red Flag is located have broken up the land into smaller economic units in which more modest-sized work groups and households (including old lineages) negotiate contracts with production team or brigade. In some areas of the country, the level of collectivization is lower than that at the time of the advanced APCs (Domes 1982:262), though such a pattern is not pronounced in either Half Moon or Red Flag.

N.A.C.

May, 1983
North Hatley, Quebec

Glossary

baigang: A strong white liquor often used in celebrations.

baogan zhu: A "package-type" contract system in which land and tools are allotted to peasants on a long-term basis in return for the fulfilling of an agreed-upon quota of agricultural produce.

baojia: An administrative system of local population that originated in ancient China. The KMT government reintroduced it in the 1930s. In the KMT version, the *jia* was made up of 10 households and the *bao* was made up of 10 *jia.* The Japanese preserved this system during their occupation.

cadre: An official, representing an administrative institution, the government, and/or the Party.

danwei: A work unit to which an individual is assigned.

"dong kou bu dong shou": A phrase referring to cadres and others who spend their time talking but seldom use their hands, that is, "big mouth and lazy hands."

guanxi: "personal connections" that enable individuals to gain special benefits for themselves, their families, and their friends.

gaozhuang: A complaint lodged to the authorities for bad behavior.

huasheng: Peanut. Sometimes used as wedding food for good luck. *Hua* in Chinese also means "variety," and *sheng* means "birth." Hence the association "give birth to various sexes of children."

hukou: A residency status registered with the local government. A rural resident cannot legally move into the city without changing his or her residency status—a very difficult process to accomplish.

jiaozi: A popular kind of dumpling, often stuffed with vegetables or meat and eaten on special occasions, particularly during Spring Festival (Chinese New Year).

jin: 1 *jin* equals 0.5 kilogram, or 1.1 pounds.

jin jiaoqu: A municipal district lying just outside an urban center.

kang: A large raised platform made of earth or brick, which serves as a bed at night and a sitting area during the day and can be heated during the winter.

li: 0.5 kilometer, or 0.3107 of a mile.

lianzou: An old penal principle under which a whole family, clan, or neighborhood group could be held accountable for a serious crime committed by a given member.

man yue: A celebration of a newborn child's first month of life, attended by all nearby relatives and friends of the family.

"men dang hu dui": Literally, "matching doors and windows." The phrase means that families of young prospective marital candidates should be similar in personal, social, and economic background.

mu: 1 *mu* equals 0.0666 hectare, or 0.1647 acre.

nao dongfang: A traditional ritual on the wedding night that includes teasing the couple in various ways, some of which may carry sexual connotations.

pinyin (or *hanyu pinyin*):   The official (Han) Chinese system of spelling using the roman alphabet.

quingming: Annual day (April 5 or 6), during which people go and pay respect at the graves of deceased relatives. Such events often include a variety of ritual activities.

san cong si de: The "three obediences and four virtues," which required a woman to first follow the lead of her father, then her husband, and on his death, her sons, and to be virtuous in morality, proper speech, modesty, and diligent work.

shehui diaocha: A social investigation or field research study.

shuxiang: A horoscope utilized to determine one's fortune.

wubao: The "five guarantees," a form of social security provided by the collective for childless elderly and disabled people. The guarantees include housing, food, clothing, medical care, and burial expenses.

Shangshan Xiaxiang: The "Up to the Mountains and Down to the Countryside" campaign undertaken between 1956 and 1979, in which millions of urban middle school graduates were called upon to assist in developing China's rural areas. The movement also resolved problems of urban unemployment.

xian: A county.

xiang: A township, the administrative duties of which were largely taken over by China's communes in 1958. Today, townships are being reinstated as an important level of rural governmental organization.

xiao: Little or small. Often used as a nickname for someone younger than the speaker.

xiegi: A malevolent ether or wind that can bring sickness or misfortune.

yuan: A form of Chinese currency. 100 *fen* (cents) is equivalent to 1 *yuan*. In 1979, 1 *yuan* equaled approximately 0.58 cents (United States).

zao: A date (fruit). The sound is the same as that meaning "early." An association is sometimes made between the two that is understood to mean: "get a son early."

zeren zhi: The "responsibility system" introduced in 1980 whereby separate households (and individuals) can establish contracts with production teams and brigades to produce agricultural foods on brigade land divided up for that purpose.

zou houmen: The practice of obtaining exceptional, unfair, or illegal favors for one's self or others by resorting to personal contacts. Referred to as "going through the back door."

zuoye zu: A small working group or production unit.

zuo yuezi: Literally: "Sitting Month," a custom in which mother and child remain inside the house for the first month of the child's life so that they may be protected from harmful agents, natural or supernatural.

References cited and
recommended reading*

Andors, Phyllis, 1983, *The Unfinished Liberation of Chinese Women 1949–1980*. Bloomington: Indiana University Press.

*Baker, Hugh D. R., 1979, *Chinese Family and Kinship*. New York: Columbia University Press.

Balazs, Etienne, 1954, "Tradition and Revolution in China." In E. Balazs, *Chinese Civilization and Bureaucracy*. New Haven, Conn.: Yale University Press.

Baum, Richard, and F. C. Teiwes, 1968, *Ssu-Ching: the Socialist Education Movement in 1962–66*. Berkeley: University of California Press.

Beijing Foreign Language Institute, 1976, *The History of Wandong Village*. Beijing (mimeographed).

Bennett, Gordon, 1978, *Huadong: The Story of a Chinese People's Commune*. Boulder, Colo.: Westview Press.

Bernstein, Thomas P., 1977, *Up to the Mountains and Down to the Villages: The Transfer of Youth from Urban to Rural China*. New Haven, Conn.: Yale University Press.

*Bianco, Lucien, 1971, *The Origins of the Chinese Revolution*. Stanford, Calif.: Stanford University Press.

Chance, Norman A., 1973, "China's Socialist Development and the Dialectical Process," *Perspectives in Development and Social Change*, 8:1–12.

*Chen, Jack, 1973, *A Year In Upper Felicity*. New York: Macmillan.

Chen, Muhua, 1979, "To Realize the Four Modernizations, Is It Necessary to Control Population Increase in a Planned Way?" *People's Daily (Renmin Ribao)*, August 11, 1979.

*Chesneaux, Jean, 1973, *Peasant Revolts in China: 1840–1949*. London: Norton.

Croll, Elizabeth, 1981, *The Politics of Marriage in Contemporary China*. London: Oxford University Press.

Crook, Isabel, and David Crook, 1959, *Revolution in a Chinese Village: Ten Mile Inn*. London: Routledge and Kegan Paul.

———, 1966, *The First Years of Yangyi Commune*. London: Routledge and Kegan Paul.

*———, 1979, *Ten Mile Inn*. New York: Pantheon.

Davin, Delia, 1976, *Women-Work: Women and the Party in Revolutionary China*. London: Oxford University Press.

Diamond, Norma, 1969, *K'un Shen: A Taiwan Village*. New York: Holt, Rinehart and Winston.

———, 1975, "Collectivization, Kinship and the Status of Women in Rural China." In Rayna Reiter, ed., *Toward an Anthropology of Women*. New York: Monthly Review Press.

Domes, Jurgen, 1982, "New Policies in the Communes: Notes on Rural Societal Structures in China: 1976–1981," *Journal of Asian Studies*, 41(2):253–267.

* Recommended readings (marked with an asterisk) focus primarily on rural mainland China.

*Fei Hsiao-Tung (Fei Xiaodong), 1939, *Peasant Life in China.* London: Routledge and Kegan Paul.

Fei Xiaodong, 1980, "Toward a People's Anthropology," *Human Organization,* 39:115–119.

Fei Hsiao-Tung, Wu Wen-Chiao, and Lin Yueh-Hwa (Fei Xiaodong, Wu Wenzao, and Lin Yuehua), 1973, "Commentary," *Current Anthropology,* 14:482.

Fried, Morton H., 1953, *The Fabric of Chinese Society: A Study of Social Life in a Chinese County Seat.* New York: Praeger.

Frolic, B. Michael, 1978, "Reflections on the Chinese Model of Development," *Social Forces,* 57(2):384–418.

Gallin, Bernard, 1966, *Hsin Hsing, Taiwan: A Chinese Village.* Berkeley: University of California Press.

Gamble, Sidney, 1954, *Ting Hsien: A North China Rural Community.* New York: Institute of Pacific Relations.

Gurley, John G., 1971, "Capitalist and Maoist Economic Development." In E. Freedman and M. Selden, eds., *America's Asia: Dissenting Essays on Asian-American Relations.* New York: Vintage Books.

Hao, Ran (Liang Jinguang), 1981, *The Golden Road* (from the 1972 Chinese edition, Carma Hinton and Chris Gilmartin, trans.). Beijing: Foreign Languages Press.

*Hinton, William, 1966, *Fanshen: A Documentary of Revolutionary Change in a Chinese Village.* New York: Vintage Books.

———, 1970, *Iron Oxen: A Documentary of Revolution in Chinese Farming.* New York: Vintage Books.

———, 1978, "Shanxi Impressions: Agricultural Mechanization in China," *Moonson* (Hong Kong), June-July:22–29.

———, 1982, "Village in Transition." In Mark Selden and Victor Lippett, eds., *The Transition to Socialism in China.* Armonk: M. E. Sharpe.

*———, 1983, *Shenfan: Continuing Revolution in a Chinese Village.* New York: Random House.

Hsu, Francis L. K., 1979, "Traditional Culture in Contemporary China." In Godwin C. Chu and Francis L. K. Hsu, eds., *Moving a Mountain: Cultural Change in China.* Honolulu: University Press of Hawaii.

———, 1981, *Americans and Chinese: Passages to Difference* (3rd edition). Honolulu: University Press of Hawaii.

Hu, Hsien-Chin, 1944, "The Chinese Concept of Face," *American Anthropologist,* 46:45–64.

Johnson, Kay Ann, 1980, "Women in the People's Republic of China." In Sylvia A. Chipp and Justin J. Green, eds., *Asian Women.* University Park: Pennsylvania State University Press.

Leys, Simon, 1977, *Chinese Shadows.* New York: Viking.

Liang, Heng, and Judith Shapiro, 1982, *Son of the Revolution.* New York: Knopf.

*Lin, Yueh-Hua, 1947, *The Golden Wing: A Sociological Study of Chinese Familism.* New York: Oxford University Press.

*Lippit, Victor, 1982, "Socialist Development in China." In Mark Selden and Victor Lippit, eds., *The Transition to Socialism in China.* Armonk: M. E. Sharpe.

Mao Zedong, 1949, "Report to the Second Plenary Session of the Seventh Central Committee of the CCP." *Selected Works of Mao Tse-tung* (1969 ed.) IV: 361–375. Peking: Foreign Language Press.

———, 1955, "On the Question of Agricultural Cooperation." *Selected Readings of Mao Tse-tung* (1971 ed.). Peking: Foreign Language Press.

———, 1956, "On the Ten Great Relationships" (Speech to the Political Bureau of the Central Committee). Printed in *Peking Review,* January 1, 1977.

————, 1977, *A Critique of Soviet Economics* (Moss Roberts, trans.). New York: Monthly Review Press.

————, 1978, *Socialist Upsurge in the Countryside* (ed. from abridged edition, 1955). Peking: Foreign Language Press.

Marx, Karl, 1875, *Critique of the Gotha Programme* (1972 Chinese trans.). Peking: Foreign Language Press.

McGough, James P., 1979, *Fei Hsiao t'ung: Dilemma of a Chinese Intellectual*. Armonk: M. E. Sharpe.

Myers, Ramon H., 1970, *The Chinese Peasant Economy: Agricultural Development in Hopei and Shantung 1890–1949*. Cambridge, Mass.: Harvard University Press.

*Myrdal, Jan, 1963, *Report From a Chinese Village*. New York: Penguin.

Nee, Victor, and James Peck, eds., 1975, *China's Uninterrupted Revolution*. New York: Pantheon.

Oksenberg, Michel, 1982, "Economic Policy-Making in China: Summer 1981," *China Quarterly*, 9:165–194.

*Parish, William L., and Martin K. Whyte, 1978, *Village and Family in Contemporary China*. Chicago: University of Chicago Press.

Peng, Zhen, 1982, "Report on the Revised Draft of the Constitution of the People's Republic of China," *People's Daily (Renmin Ribao)*, December 6.

Priutt, Ida, 1979, *Old Madame Yin: A Memoir of Peking Life, 1926–1938*. Stanford, Calif.: Stanford University Press.

Schell, Orville, 1977, *In the People's Republic of China: An American's First-Hand View of Living and Working in China*. New York: Random House.

*Selden, Mark, 1982a, "Cooperation and Conflict: Cooperative and Collective Formation in China's Countryside." In Mark Selden and Victor Lippitt, eds., *The Transition to Socialism in China*. Armonk: M. E. Sharpe.

————, 1982b, "Accumulation, Diversification and China's Rural Development," *The Insurgent Sociologist*, 11(2):39–49.

Shirk, Susan L., 1982, *Competitive Comrades: Career Incentives and Student Strategies*. Berkeley: University of California Press.

*Siu, Helen, and Zelda Stern, 1983, *Mao's Harvest: Voices from China's New Generation*. New York: Oxford University Press.

Smith, Arthur, 1899, *Village in China*. (reprinted 1970). Boston: Little Brown.

*Shue, Vivienne, 1980, *Peasant China in Transition*. Berkeley: University of California Press.

Skinner, William G., 1978, "Vegetable Supply and Marketing in Chinese Cities," *China Quarterly*, 76:733–793.

Stavrianos, L. S., 1975, "The Mandarin View of China," *The Nation*, February 6.

Stover, Leon, and Takeko Stover, 1976, *China: An Anthropological Perspective*. Pacific Palisades: Goodyear.

Tsou tang, Marc Blecher, and Mitch Meisner, 1982, "National Agricultural Policy: The Dazhai Model and Local Change in the Post-Mao Era." In Mark Selden and Victor Lippitt, eds., *The Transition to Socialism in China*. Armonk: M. E. Sharpe.

Unger, Jonathan, 1982, *Education Under Mao: Class and Competition in Canton Schools, 1960–1980*. New York: Columbia University Press.

Whyte, Martin K., and Burton Pasternak, 1980, "Sociology and Anthropology." In A. Thurston and J. Parker, eds., *Humanistic and Social Science Research in China*. New York: Social Science Research Council.

Wolf, Margery, 1968, *The House of Lim*. New York: Appleton-Century-Crofts.

————, 1970, "Child Training and the Chinese Family," In Maurice Freedman, ed., *Family and Kinship in Chinese Society*. Stanford: Stanford University Press.

————, 1974, "Chinese Women: Old Skills in a New Context." In M. Zimbalist

Rosaldo and Louise Lamphere, eds., *Women, Culture and Society*. Stanford, Calif.: Stanford University Press.

Vermeer, E. B., 1982, "Income Differentials in Rural China," *China Quarterly*, 89:1–33.

Wiens, Thomas, 1981, "The Economics of Municipal Vegetable Supply in China." In Donald L. Plunkett and Halset L. Beemer, Jr., eds., *Vegetable Farming Systems in China*. Boulder, Colo.: Westview Press.

*Yang, C. K, 1959, *Chinese Communist Society: The Family and the Village*. Cambridge, Mass.: M.I.T. Press.

*Yang, Martin C., 1945, *A Chinese Village: Taitou, Shantung Province*. New York: Columbia University Press.

Index

Abortion, 125–126
Accounting System
  accumulation fund, 50, 61, 135
  contract system, 151 (*see also* Responsibility System)
  piecework method, 48–49
  workpoint system, 24–25, 37, 48–49, 61, 73, 83, 87, 122, 126, 133–135
  See also Economy
Agriculture
  animal husbandry, 45
  in competition with sideline industry, 136
  courtyard gardens, 19, 27, 45
  cycle of, 14–15, 23, 47, 110
  vegetable production, 139
Animals
  private and collective ownership of, 45–46, 50
  sharing of, 37

"Backdoor," 91–94, 113, 145–147, 155
  See also Corruption
Beijing, 26
  economic links to, 32, 50–52
  and "educated youth," 86
  impact on village life, 29–31, 96, 101, 106
Birth Control (*see* Family Planning)
Bonuses, for workers, 38, 53, 151–153
Bride Price, 103–104, 117
Bureaucracy, 141
  problems of, 52, 140–147, 151
  public administration, 7–8, 143n, 156
  values of, 7, 141–145

Ceremonies and Festivals, 13, 63–64, 96, 105–110, 130
Chen Boda, 139
Childbearing, 60–63
Children, desirability of male vs. female, 118–119
Chu, Meiying, 142–143, 145
Classes
  consciousness of, 34, 140
  significance of class background, 36–37, 81n, 92, 99, 105
  under-land reform, 36–37, 131
Communes
  rise of movement, 8, 39
  retreat from (1959–60), 58; (1978–) 11, 152, 156
  See also Red Flag Commune

Communication, forms of, 17–19, 21, 69, 105, 110, 113, 122, 144, 149–150
Communism, 154
Communist Party (of China)
  attitudes toward divorce, 121–122
  dealing with corruption in, 144
  history of, 3–4
  recruitment to and expulsion from, 92–93
  and village conflicts, 16, 43–44
  See also Half Moon Village
"Communist Wind," 59, 140
Communist Youth League, 41, 54, 58, 96, 98, 100, 108, 125–126
Conflict Resolution, 55–59
  See also Half Moon Village
Confucius, 10, 120, 122, 141, 144
Cooperatives
  degree of participation in, 5, 7, 37
  elementary and advanced stages of, 4–7, 37
  merged into commune, 38
  resistance to, 5, 7, 36–37
  support for, 5, 7, 37–38
  and women's equality, 121
  See also Mutual Aid Teams
Corruption
  bribery, 20–21, 93
  crime, 43, 143–144
  dealing within the Party, 144
  See also "Backdoor"
Courtship Patterns, 95–97, 99–103, 105
Cui Huifang, 17, 41, 56–57, 143
Cultural Revolution
  beginning of, 8, 20, 60
  and education, 78, 82–83, 90–91
  extremism of, 10, 59, 89, 93
  factionalism, 8, 89–90
  goals of, 8, 10, 41, 94
  impact on marriage and family, 99, 101
  positive gains made under, 85, 122–123
  significance of class background in, 81n, 92, 93
  and uxorilocal residence pattern, 105
  and women's equality, 113, 122–123

Dazhai Brigade, 133, 137, 140
Death, 103, 128, 130
Deng Xiaoping, 8, 151
Democratic Process, 6, 11, 53, 59, 141, 154
  and bureaucracy, 141–144
  and central planning, 6, 41
  vs. coercion, 7, 24–25, 37, 43–44, 89

Democratic Process (*cont.*)
  extent of in cooperatives, 5–7, 37–38
  in the family, 113
  limited development of, 154
  at local village level, 10–11, 154
  in selection of a spouse, 101, 103–104
  women's roles in, 117–118, 120, 122–124
Divorce, 99, 103, 112, 116–117, 121–122
Dong Shufang, 60–63

East Gate Village, 48, 135–137
Economy
  distribution of goods, 139–140
  inflation, 153
  ownership, private, collective and state,
    138–139
  peasant markets, 140, 147, 151–153, 156
  productivity under bonus system, 152–153
  See also Accounting System; Modernization
"Educated Youth," 20, 31, 83, 86–94, 109
  goals of movement, 86–87
  appraisal of, 87
Education
  classroom behavior, 74–77, 81–82
  higher education, 83–84, 92
  importance of, 76
  "moral education," 78–79 (*see also* Values)
  and punishment, 75–76
  and rote learning, 79–80
  and teacher training, 82–83
"Egalitarianism," criticism of, 154
Elderly, respect for, 127
  economic contribution of, 128
  retirement of, 15, 128

Factories
  commune and state owned, 39, 50, 52–54,
    134–136, 145–146, 152–153
  how workers selected, 52, 95, 146–147
  See also Bonuses
Family
  authority structure, 112–113
  conflicts in, 112, 114–117
  economic aspects of, 45–46
  father-child relations, 71–72
  mother-child relations, 72
  See also Marriage; Women
Family Planning, 11, 17, 41, 60, 72, 108,
  113, 123–127
"Five Guarantees," 113
Fortune and Misfortune, 61–63, 108, 118–
  119

Games, 68–69, 96, 109
"Gang of Four," 9, 41, 151
Gossip, 96, 98
Great Leap Forward, 7–8, 52, 58, 128, 140
Guo, Dasao, 118, 120–122

Half Moon Village
  as accounting unit, 47n, 139–140

agricultural production of, 26–27, 45–47
brigade organization, 16n
comparison with other villages, 133–137
conflicts within, 23–24, 43–44, 55–57, 126,
  140, 144–147
crime in, 43
description of, 26–33
"educated youth" in, 31–32
factory employment, 31, 50–55
history of, 33–39
housing, 13–14, 27, 33
income of, 24, 45–46, 47n, 48–55
leadership in, 15–17, 23, 40, 55–57, 60,
  123, 142–146
role of Party in, 6, 16–19, 35, 40–44, 103,
  105, 121, 126, 141–146
sideline industry, 29, 49–50, 133, 137
Hao Ran, 148
Hua Guofeng, 151
Humor, 24, 69, 74, 98, 109

Industry
  attitudes toward, 90
  collectively owned, 31, 39, 46–52, 133–140
  private enterprise, 45–46, 149–150, 151,
    156
  sideline, 29, 49–50, 134–137
  state-owned, 31, 52–55, 138
Infanticide, 104, 118–119
Inheritance, 117, 128–129

Jiang Lijiang, 14–25, 50, 55–57, 140, 142,
  145–146

Ke Kiming, 57–58
Kinship
  and ancestor worship, 117, 119
  and economic security, 113
  lineages, 16, 33, 96, 112, 117, 119, 121
  terms, 67
Kuomingtang Party (KMT), 3–4, 36

Land Reform, 4–6, 34–38, 112, 120–121,
  123
Li Guiying, 123, 146
Li Yongshan, 145–147
Liu Shaoqui, 8
Little River Village, 27, 133–135, 137

Ma Haimen, 17, 24, 40, 55–57, 153–154
Mao Zedong
  disagreements with, 90
  and education, 77, 86
  as policy maker, 4–5, 8–9, 142–143, 150,
    154
  on preserving private plots, 59
  veneration of, 74, 106, 108
Marriage
  age at, 103
  arranged, 60
  economic factors in, 103–105

"matchmaker," 99–100, 102–103
marriage law of 1950, 112, 120–121
wedding day, 107–110, 118
See also Divorce; Women
Marxist Theory, 121, 137–138, 154
May 7th Cadre Schools, 90
Medicine
    "barefoot doctors," 17, 31, 60–61, 105, 125
    and childbearing, 60–65
    cost of health care, 7
    sanitation, 45
    See also Family planning
Mechanization (*see* Modernization)
Mencius, 141–142
Militia, 8, 39, 42
Modernization
    and "contract system" (1978–79), 151
    and differing development strategies, 4–11,
        58, 131–137, 151–154, 156
    electrification, 32
    and "Four Modernizations," 41, 96, 108,
        131, 150
    goals of, 7–9
    and increased inequality, 154
    mechanization, 6–7, 38, 47–48, 90, 131–
        132
    politics of, 153–154
    and socialism, 7, 131, 154–155
Mutual Aid Teams, 6, 36

Naming Customs, 64–65, 67
Nursery, day-care, 69–70, 72–73

Peasantry
    attitudes toward, 8, 89–91
    "becoming rich," 148–150
    and farmers, 1–2
    restrictions in movement, 51, 54, 113
    and underemployment, 132
People's Liberation Army (PLA), 9, 42, 103
Private Plots, 45, 59, 140, 147, 151, 156

Rape, 90, 98
Red Flag Commune, 4, 26–28, 30–32
    description of, 39–40
    economy of, 45–50, 52–54, 132–133
    and "educated youth," 86–88
    modernization policy, 7, 135, 137
    recent changes in, 10, 132–133, 151–154,
        156

school enrollments in, 77, 83, 86
"Responsibility System," 11, 137, 156
Residency Permits, 51, 54, 113
    negative effect of, 51
    positive effect of, 51

Sexual Relations, 97–98, 109–110
Socialization, 67, 69–73, 75–76, 78–80
Su Shitou, 74–76, 79, 81
Su Xiulan, 56–57, 140, 143
Sun Yatsen, 3

Television, 21, 69, 78, 96, 100, 130, 148, 154
    (*see also* Communication)
Toilet Training, 64, 66–67
Transportation, 30, 32, 84, 113

Values
    of bureaucratic officials, 7, 141–145
    conflicts between, 19, 23–24, 82–83
    and conflict resolution, 55–59
    and education, 78–79, 82–83
    "face," concept of, 57, 71, 79, 90, 106,
        109, 117
    justice, concept of, 144
    and the role of the individual, 79–80, 112,
        144
    See also Democratic process; Education;
        Socialization

Wang Family, 14–15, 64, 101–103, 105–106,
        146
    courtyard of, 28
Weaning, 66
Women
    changing status of, 117–124
    and child care, 65–66
    humiliation of, 98, 109–110, 116, 122
    and proper behavior, 96, 98, 101, 117–118
    and suicide, 120
    See also Childbearing, Family, Marriage,
        Rape, Women's Federation
Women's Federation, 17, 39, 41, 60, 103–
        104, 109, 117, 122–123, 125–127
Worker's Congresses, 53
Workpoint System (*see* Accounting System)

Ye Jianying, 150
Young Pioneers, 81
Yu Futian, 34, 36–38, 112
Yu Shanshan, 146–147, 151, 153